Savage Frontier

Volume IV
1842–1845

Other Books by Stephen L. Moore

European Metal Detecting Guide: Techniques, Tips and Treasures. Garland, TX: RAM Books, 2010.

Last Stand of the Texas Cherokees: Chief Bowles and the 1839 Cherokee War in Texas. Garland, TX: RAM Books, 2009.

Presumed Lost: The Incredible Ordeal of America's Submarine Veteran POWs of World War II. Annapolis, MD: Naval Institute Press, 2009.

War of the Wolf: Texas' Memorial Submarine, World War II's Famous USS Seawolf. Dallas, TX: Atriad Press, 2008.

Savage Frontier: Rangers, Riflemen, and Indian Wars in Texas. Volume III: 1840–1841. Denton, TX: University of North Texas Press, 2007.

Savage Frontier: Rangers, Riflemen, and Indian Wars in Texas. Volume II: 1838–1839. Denton, TX: University of North Texas Press, 2006.

Spadefish: On Patrol With a Top-Scoring World War II Submarine. Dallas, TX: Atriad Press, 2006.

Eighteen Minutes: The Battle of San Jacinto and the Texas Independence Campaign. Plano, TX: Republic of Texas Press, 2004.

Savage Frontier: Rangers, Riflemen, and Indian Wars in Texas. Volume I: 1835–1837. Denton, TX: University of North Texas Press, 2002. Reprinted 2006.

Taming Texas: Captain William T. Sadler's Lone Star Service. Austin, TX: State House Press, 2000.

With William J. Shinneman and Robert W. Gruebel. *The Buzzard Brigade: Torpedo Squadron Ten at War.* Missoula, MT: Pictorial Histories Publishing, 1996.

For more information,visit www.stephenlmoore.com

Savage Frontier

Volume IV
1842–1845

Rangers, Riflemen, and Indian Wars in Texas

Stephen L. Moore

University of North Texas Press
Denton, Texas

10 9 8 7 6 5 4 3 2 1

Permissions
University of North Texas Press
PO Box 311336
Denton, TX 76203

The paper used in this book meets the minimum requirements of the American National Standard for Permanence of Paper for Printed Library Materials, Z39.48.1984.
∞

Library of Congress Cataloging-in-Publication Data

Moore, Stephen L.
Savage frontier IV: rangers, riflemen, and Indian wars in Texas/ Stephen L. Moore.
p. cm.
Includes bibliographical references and index.
ISBN-10: 1-57441-293-0 (cloth:alk. paper)
ISBN-13: 978-1-57441-293-2 (cloth: alk. paper)
ISBN-10: 1-57441-294-9 (pbk: alk. paper)
ISBN-13: 978-1-57441-294-9 (pbk. alk. paper)
1. Indians of North America—Wars—Texas. 2. Indians of North America—Texas—Government relations. 3. Texas Rangers—History. 4. Frontier and pioneer life—Texas—History. 5. Texas—Politics and government—1836–1846. I. Title
E78.T4 M675 2006
976.4—dc21
2002000480

Cover design based on Alan McCuller's Vol. I creation. Layout and typesetting by Stephen L. Moore.

Contents

Volume IV

Prologue

The completion of this final volume of the *Savage Frontier* series would not have been possible without the support of several key people. First and foremost, Donaly Brice of the Texas State Archives deserves great credit for his tireless efforts to support the research of this Texas Rangers series during the past ten years. For Volume IV, Donaly offered some of his personal time to pull muster rolls, copy relevant papers and do general research because he sincerely wanted to see this series reach its completion.

For the continuation of the *Savage Frontier* series, I thank Ron Chrisman and his staff at the University of North Texas Press for their confidence. Byron Johnson, Director of the Texas Ranger Hall of Fame and Museum in Waco, and archivist Christina Stopka granted permission for inclusion of the Walker Colt pistol for this volume. Texas Ranger historian Mike Cox kindly furnished a copy of his paper on the Paint Rock battle involving Jack Hays. The late Bobby Nieman, long-time editor of the Texas Ranger Dispatch electronic magazine, was always supportive of this series seeing its conclusion.

Professor Sam W. Haynes of the University of Texas, Arlington, and Dr. James Crisp of North Carolina State University both provided editorial suggestions and pointed toward new Native American studies which served to improve the content of this volume. Noted Texas artist Jack Terry kindly allowed the use of his painting, "Captain Hays and Company," which was provided by his wife. Edwin G. Pierson Jr. kindly furnished documents on the Mier Expedition that he has accumulated during research of his ancestor, Captain John G. W. Pierson.

This final volume on the early frontier fights of Texas covers the last years of the Republic of Texas era. The extermination policy of Texas President Mirabeau Lamar had changed the nature of Indian warfare in the Republic. Major expeditions by the Texas Militia had been carried out against the Native Americans during such engagements as the 1839 Cherokee War. By 1842, however, the encounters which occurred between Texas frontier forces and Indians generally constituted a company of Texas Rangers making a brief fight with a modest-sized band of Indians. The relationship between Tejanos and Anglo-Texans was put to the test during 1842 by Mexican Army offensives.

The nature of frontier warfare was evolving and one particular Indian fight of 1844 saw the most dramatic change. It was during the June 1844 Walker's Creek battle that Captain Jack Hays and 15 Texas Rangers successfully fought off Comanches who outnumbered them roughly five to one. The difference in this encounter was the Rangers' use of the Colt five-shooter repeating revolver, which enabled the Rangers to unload a deadly and continuous fire on their opponents without stopping to reload after each shot.

During the period of 1842–1845 covered in this study, Jack Hays had become the quintessential Texas Ranger. His company, in fact, was often the only company of Rangers in service for Texas during the majority of this time. They served almost continually during 1842 and fought with the volunteer forces which hastily assembled to repel two major Mexican Army thrusts: the Vasquez Invasion and the Woll Invasion.

Captain Hays' men also served as scouts for the ill-fated Somervell and Mier expeditions. They turned back for San Antonio shortly before the remaining men moved on to Mier and were subsequently captured and imprisoned in Mexico. In addition to engaging Mexican troops, Hays' rangers had numerous skirmishes with bandits who preyed upon traders within Texas.

Hays' company did have several notable encounters with Comanches during these years, including the Walker's Creek engagement and a lesser-known battle on the Guadalupe River. This latter battle has erroneously been claimed by some historians to have occurred at Bandera Pass in Bandera County. A closer study reveals that the historian who first related this battle simply gave the general area where a Ranger/Comanche battle took place.

Jack Hays commanded the only government-authorized Texas

Ranger company during 1843 and 1844. In late 1844, Henry Kinney took it upon himself to employ a ranging unit under Captain Henry Clay Davis to operate around the Corpus Christi area to protect his own trading efforts. As talks progressed in early 1845 concerning Texas joining the United States, the Texas Congress did authorize several smaller county ranging units in addition to Hays' Béxar County company and Davis' Corpus Christi rangers. Four smaller companies commanded by a lieutenant were authorized by the Texas Congress to operate in Travis County, Robertson County, Milam County, and Goliad and Refugio counties. An additional company under Lieutenant Jack McGarrah was formed in Fannin County in June 1845 and operated from the early frontier post known as Fort Buckner, which is now part of the present Dallas metroplex.

John Coffee Hays remained in command of his ranger company until September 28, 1845, on which date he was promoted to major commanding a four-company ranging battalion. Major Hays' battalion was mustered into federal service by General Zachary Taylor during the buildup to the impending war with Mexico which commenced in early 1846. The use of Texas Rangers in the Mexican War has been well documented so it seems appropriate to wrap up the *Savage Frontier* series with the end of the Republic of Texas era.

It should be noted that many of the storied ranger leaders of the Mexican War—Samuel Walker, Ben McCulloch, Henry McCulloch, Ad Gillespie, Shapley Ross and Mike Chevallie—had cut their teeth in Republic-era ranger service under the incomparable Jack Hays. The first governor of Texas, James Pinckney Henderson, turned over his office to his lieutenant governor and went into the field to lead the mounted men of Texas. The next two governors of Texas, George Wood and Peter Bell, had directly served as ranger commanders before assuming the highest office in their new state.

The Mexican War forced Mexico to recognize Texas as being part of the union of the United States and significant new territory was gained for the U.S. The Texas Rangers had provided a much-needed scouting and fighting ability to the U.S. regulars during this war. The seasoned frontiersmen comprising these companies were well versed on reconnoitering opposing forces and living off meager supplies.

The Texas Rangers continue in service today because of the trails that were blazed during the Republic years by frontiersmen who fought to keep a nation safe that they had defiantly claimed as their own in 1836. To them and their descendants this series is dedicated.

CHAPTER 1

The Vasquez Incursion

January–February 1842

In his first full year as a Texas Ranger captain, John Coffee Hays had gained the respect of the men he rode with and the men he rode against. His first combat had been under Captain Deaf Smith in 1837 and he had later helped defeat the Comanches in the battle of Plum Creek in August 1840. When not engaged in quelling frontier disturbances with hostile Indian bands, Jack Hays had run the northwestern boundary of Travis County and led numerous surveying expeditions to locate headright claims throughout 1840.

By the age of 29 in January 1841, Hays had been placed in command of his first official company of Texas Rangers. Operating out of San Antonio in Béxar County, Captain Hays' frontiersmen were alternately known as rangers, spies and the Béxar County Minutemen during 1841. His company had fought a battle with Mexican marauders led by Agatón Quiñones in April near Laredo. In the second half of the year, Hays' minutemen fought Comanches at Uvalde Canyon in June, killing ten Comanches and capturing two others at the cost of only one wounded ranger.

His next Comanche engagement occurred on July 24, 1841, at the Llano River. In this heated fight, one of his rangers was wounded and another was killed. Captain Hays was also shot in the finger but his company had killed an estimated ten Comanches. It was during this Llano fight that Hays' horse had galloped wildly through the midst of the Indian ranks. His trusted Lipan Apache ranger sidekick Flacco had spurred his own horse on to follow the daring Texan through the fire fight. Both men miraculously escaped, but Flacco was heard to comment that his captain was "bravo too much."

The most fabled story of John Hays involved his solitary stand against a band of Comanches atop Enchanted Rock in Llano County in the fall of 1841. Cut off from his men, he had been chased by Comanches to the granite mass, where Hays reportedly took cover and fought off his attackers single-handedly with his rifle and Colt repeating pistols until his companions could come to his aid.

Hays was believed by many of the Indians to be leading a charmed life. Some referred to him as "Devil Jack" (or "Devil Yack"), while the Tejanos who served under him commonly called him "Capitan Jack." One Indian chief visiting San Antonio for a treaty had remarked, "Captain Jack, great brave. No afraid go to hell by himself."

Such were the praises and the respect bestowed on the Texas Ranger captain who had commanded Béxar County's ranging forces throughout 1841. Newspaper editors credited him with breaking up the Comanche camps in the area during the year and praised him for creating a true sense of security for the citizens of the settlements around the San Antonio area.

Captain Hays' company had been disbanded before the end of the year and the start of 1842 had seen little action to necessitate the recall of his men to service. He had, in fact, returned to his mainstay of surveying during the early weeks of the year. Hays departed San Antonio in February 1842, with six men to locate another soldier's headright north of Béxar. During the course of running this property line, his surveyors were fired upon by a group of Indians. The Indians did not fully engage the surveyors but merely moved in close enough around the men to make things very uneasy. Undaunted, Hays fired periodic shots at the Indians to keep them at a safe distance while his men finished running their survey line.[1]

While Hays had been vigilant in the field fighting Indians during his surveying expeditions, events in early March 1842 would cause him to muster in his ranging unit again in force. This time his opponents were not Native Americans but instead

Mexican Army forces which were marching into Texas on the offensive.

★ ★ ★ ★ ★

A New Invasion of Texas

Sam Houston had reassumed his presidency of the Republic of Texas on December 13, 1841, and immediately prepared a series of recommendations which he hoped would rescue the country from financial collapse. He also recommended that the Cherokee lands now in public domain be pledged as a security for a foreign loan. Houston was the hero of San Jacinto but politics was one front in which his objectives were sharply different from his predecessor.[2]

With President Mirabeau Lamar—once his ally on the San Jacinto battlefield—out of office, Houston was free to set his own policies. Houston believed that Lamar's Indian extermination policy should be abandoned as a failure. The country should return to the ways he had tried to establish in his first administration. Mexico was no longer a serious threat, and he doubted that they would attempt another serious invasion of Texas. President Houston therefore believed that only a small force would be needed to counter the activities of the Texan and Mexican bandit gangs on the southwestern border and to defend the Indian frontier. Houston suggested that a number of small posts should be established at the western limit of settlement. Each should have a resident Indian trader to conduct all trade with the "savages" in the vicinity and a garrison of twenty-five or thirty men to protect the trader.[3]

President Houston did not favor rangers or minutemen to man these new trading outposts. He was not in favor of Lamar's county minuteman law, which did not authorize the executive to employ men for garrison duty. As originally created, the minuteman law was very limiting on the number of men to be employed and how many consecutive days they could remain in the field.

The regular army which Houston had only recently scoffed at a public dinner in late November 1841 would not be revived under Houston, either. Houston therefore sought Congress' approval to enroll ranging companies to operate under War Department orders. He felt that the organization of long-term ranger companies under the leadership of more capable men was the most sensible solution for the frontier defense problem.[4]

The Sixth Congress of the Republic of Texas did not pass Houston's recommendations without a broil. The Western, or Lamar, faction of Congress clashed with President Houston's proposal to move the seat of government from Austin to the east. The Congress did agree with Houston that government payment of public debt should be suspended and that the nearly worthless paper currency of the Republic should be replaced by a new paper issue, strictly limited in amount and maintained at par with gold and silver.[5]

Congress also proceeded to abolish a number of government positions, as recommended by Houston. Pay cuts were also instituted in all branches of Texas government. For current expenses during 1842, the War Department and the army received an appropriation of under $25,000. President Houston was additionally appropriated $20,000 to be used at his discretion "for the purposes of frontier protection." The Sixth Congress also allowed $2,000 "for redemption of captives from the Indians" and another $9,600 to pay off the county minutemen companies which had served during 1841.[6]

Just prior to passage of the February 3 General Appropriation Act, Congress had on January 29 authorized the President to raise a single company of mounted rangers for service in the Southwest. The resolution briefly authorized Sam Houston to employ "one company of mounted men, to act as rangers, on the southern frontier, on such terms as he may deem most beneficial to the public interest." This open approval gave Houston all the authority he needed to continue providing for the services of Jack Hays' rangers.[7]

Fortunately, a relative peace had settled on the Indian frontier during the winter of 1841–1842. Mexico was not believed to be interested in attacking Texas again and the Indians had remained relatively quiet for months. The sleeping giant south of the border, however, became restless during the early days of 1842. Rumors had always been present that a Mexican invasion was imminent but little heed had been paid to such talk as of late. The first serious hint of trouble came from General Mariano Arista, commander of the Mexican Army of the North, on January 9, 1842. Arista issued a proclamation to the residents of Texas. He said that Mexico had not consented to Texas' separation from the central government and did not recognize her independence. He said that only Mexico's own internal civil war problems had kept her from dealing with Texas for so long. If the Texans did not voluntarily return to their Mexican allegiance, the "persuasion of war" would be applied. Arista's proclamation was generally received with disbelief and given as much attention as ad interim Mexican President Carlos María Bustamante's previous hints of a Mexican invasion.[8]

President Houston, however, took Arista's threat a little more seriously. On February 15, he wrote to his friend and private secretary Washington D. Miller—a veteran of the 1840 battle of Plum Creek—that he believed Santa Anna "will if he can send a large force and station it upon the Rio Grande & from that line send out into our Territory parties of cavalry such as may annoy and injure us the most."[9]

Miller reported back to Houston that the Mexicans had become more active than usual in breaking up the forbidden trade between the Rio Grande and Texas settlements. This seemed to indicate more of an interest in Texas on the part of Mexico, but Texans in general seemed to show little concern.[10]

Juan Seguin, mayor of San Antonio, was one citizen who did show a growing concern about the rumors of Mexican invasion. Seguin had shown great loyalty to Texas during the revolution of 1836 and had commanded a Tejano company valiantly at the battle of San Jacinto. In the years thereafter he had commanded cavalry troops, participated in an expedition against Comanches, and he even resigned his seat in the Texas Congress to help support General Antonio Canales' Federalist troops in driving out the Centralists in 1840.

Seguin had returned to San Antonio, where he was elected mayor of the town in late 1840, in spite of rumors circulating from his enemies that he was secretly supporting Mexico's Centralist government. He wrote a letter in early 1842 to General Rafael Vasquez, commander of Mexican troops on the Rio Grande frontier, requesting a passport into Mexico to purchase sheep to pay off debts in Texas. Seguin would report that the tenor of Vasquez's reply letter made him believe that "an expedition was preparing against Texas, for the following month of March."[11]

Mayor Seguin thus called the San Antonio city councilmen

together to warn them that a Mexican invasion seemed imminent. He also wrote a letter of warning to President Houston on January 30 but Houston advised that he was unable to provide proper troops for defense due to the country's "impoverished condition." Further intelligence was received in San Antonio during the next two weeks which supported the Mexican invasion rumors. Seguin, already under suspicion of siding with Mexican forces, felt that it was impossible to properly defend his city and he declared that he would retire to his ranch and then to Seguin before his town could be taken.[12]

The remaining Anglo-Texan citizens of San Antonio met and elected frontier ranger leader Jack Hays to lead them and to declare martial law in the town. Among the prominent Béxar County citizens known to have assembled under Hays' direction were Duncan Campbell Ogden, French Strother Gray, Henry Clay Davis, John R. Cunningham, Hendrick Arnold, Cornelius Van Ness, Dr. Launcelot Smithers, John Twohig and James Ury, a former planter from Louisiana. These men were quickly joined by Benjamin McCulloch and Alsey S. Miller from Gonzales after they were specifically summoned by Captain Hays. The townspeople of San Antonio pledged money to help pay for his spies and other volunteers who would be needed. Others mounted the town's artillery pieces and began fortifying the city against a potential invasion from Mexican forces.[13]

The Béxar County Committee of Safety met on February 21 and sent two Tejanos to Mexican military posts near the Rio Grande to gather information. Just beyond the Nueces River, the two men were seized and briefly held captive by Agatón Quiñones, the noted Rio Grande robber who had long been the attention of Captain Hays' rangers. The two Tejanos, Damacio Galvan and Eusebio Farias, were told by Quiñones that his orders were to prevent all communications with the Rio Grande. They were ordered to return home and they reached San Antonio on the night of February 26.[14]

Captain Hays had no shortage of able men available to send out on scouting duties to monitor the approaching Mexican forces. Unfortunately, any muster roll which may have existed for Hays' unit for 1842 has not survived time but it is evident he had roughly two dozen men under his charge in San Antonio by the beginning of March.

Capt. Hays' Béxar County Rangers: March 1–Sept. 1, 1842

Captain:
John Coffee Hays
Privates:
Christopher Black Acklin [1]
Isaac Allen
Hendrick Arnold [1]
John Baker
Truman B. Beck
Peter Hansborough Bell [1]
Henry Bridger
John Henry Brown [2]
William Bugg [2]
Michael H. Chevallie
Antonio Coy
John R. Cunningham [1]
David Joseph (Joe) Davis
Henry Clay Davis [1]
James Dunn [1]
Cyrus Washburn Egery
Gustav Elley [3]
James "Keno" Ellison [1]
Archibald Fitzgerald
H. Stuart Foley [1]
Mason B. Foley
Thomas Galbreath [1]
French Strother Gray [1]
John A. Green
Beverly C. Greenwood
Hudson A. Greenwood
Nathaniel Harbert
John Hemphill
Benjamin Franklin Highsmith [1]
John W. Hinch
William Hudgeons
James Matthew Jett
Stephen Jett
William Glenn Jett [4]
John Richard (Jack) Johnson
John S. Johnson
John Lamon
John Himes Livergood
Nathaniel R. Mallon
Benjamin McCulloch [1]
Alsey Silvanus Miller [1]
Isaac N. Mitchell
Amos Moore
William Morrison [1]
Andrew Neill [1]
George Jefferson Neill [1]
James Wilson Nichols [1]
Samuel G. Norvell
Duncan Campbell Ogden [1]
Cicero Rufus Perry [2]
Marcus L. B. Rapier
William R. Rector [5]
Daniel Rice [6]
Shapley Prince Ross
Montrevell C. Roundtree
Launcelot Smithers [1]
William Smothers
Achilles Stapp
Guy S. Stokes [7]
Creed Taylor [1]
James Taylor [1]
Josiah Taylor [1]
Joshua Threadgill [1]
John Twohig [1]
James Ury [1]
Cornelius Van Ness [1]
Johann George Andreas Voss
Samuel Hamilton Walker [1]
William Alexander A. Wallace
Joseph Williams [1]
Jacob Woodward
John Young

1 Reported to have served; extant records unavailable to confirm dates. John Henry Brown's *History of Texas,* II: 211–13, 217 names some of Hays' early 1842 scouts.
2 Enrolled April 2, 1842.
3 Enrolled June 1, 1842.
4 Enrolled April 22, 1842.
5 Served May 1–June 9, 1842.
6 Enrolled April 1, 1842.
7 Enrolled April 3, 1842.

Source: Author's study of audited military claims of the Republic of Texas, including John H. Livergood PD, R 168, F 529–74. The men listed here served varying periods of time with Hays from March–September 1842.

Hays' men were well seasoned. Marcus Rapier had served in a post-revolutionary ranger company of the Colonel Coleman/ Major Smith battalion and had participated in Major Mark Lewis' spring 1841 expedition. Isaac Allen and Truman Beck had also made the Lewis expedition. The blue-eyed Jett brothers, 28-year-old Stephen and 30-year-old James Matthew Jett, had first joined the ranging service in November 1835 and they fought together at San Jacinto. James Dunn's ranger service dated back to January 1836 and he had commanded a company during the 1841 Lewis expedition. William "Bigfoot" Wallace, a 25-year-old former Virginian, had come to Texas to avenge the loss of a brother and cousin who were killed in the Goliad Massacre. The six-foot-two 240-pound frontiersman had since proven his able fighting skills at the battle of Plum Creek and during General Tarrant's 1841 Village Creek battle.

Mike Chevallie was well versed on frontier fighting. He had served in the 1840 Council House Fight, Major Howard's fall 1840 expedition, and had fought with Captain Hays in 1841. Cyrus Egery had twice ridden on expeditions against Comanches in 1839 with Hays and Henry Karnes. Antonio Coy, Nathaniel Harbert, Arch Fitzgerald and Matt Jett had been in Major Howard's fall 1840 Comanche expedition. Seven of Hays' March 1842 rangers had served with him in 1841—Matt Jett, Stephen Jett, John Young, Coy, Harbert, Fitzgerald and Chevallie.

On February 26 the citizens of Gonzales had sent a note from Andrew Neill to Cornelius Van Ness in San Antonio, offering their help to San Antonio in case of attack. Within two days, definite word of an impending invasion reached the Gonzales citizens. The word came from an officer in the Mexican army to a priest in San Antonio, who immediately spread the word to his parishioners. The alarm prompted Mexicans within San Antonio to move south and the Anglo-American settlers to move north and east of town. Word of the threatened attack was also spread to settlements on the Guadalupe River and to Austin.[15]

In response to the word from the two captured Tejanos, Captain Hays sent out other spies, including Mike Chevallie and James Dunn to make a scout toward the Rio Grande. A messenger was sent from Béxar to call on the people of Gonzales to provide 100 men to reinforce San Antonio. Chevallie and Dunn made it only as far as the Nueces River before they were also ambushed and captured by Colonel Calixto Bravo's Mexican troops. Chevallie cocked his pistol, pointed it at the Mexican general and made Bravo swear an oath that the rangers would be spared their lives for surrendering as prisoners of war.[16]

Hays next directed his Tejano servant Antonio Coy toward the Rio Frio to report on that vicinity. Coy was also captured by Mexican forces and was mistreated for his loyalty to the Texan cause. By March 2, the Gonzales volunteers under 1835 ranger Captain Daniel Boone Friar had reached San Antonio and Hays had heard nothing from his three scouts. That evening, he dispatched Benjamin McCulloch and Alsey S. Miller to gather information toward the Medina River. Miller and McCulloch proceeded to Hondo Creek, where they hid in the chaparral and counted the Mexican troops under Vasquez. The spies pushed on to the Nueces River, monitoring the Mexican forces in the area, before turning back for San Antonio by way of the hill country north of Béxar. They would rejoin Hays on March 6 opposite Seguin at the Flores Rancho.[17]

At 10:00 p.m. on March 4, Captain Hays sent a courier eastward with a warning message. "Two of our spies were shot at and run in from the Medina; again this evening, near the Leona, four spies were hailed and chased but they got in safe," he wrote. "Our two spies McCulloch and Miller are either cut off or are behind the enemy. Nothing further from Chevallie or Dunn, who have been out for ten days." Hays said that he was unable to give a good number of the invaders but sensed that the threat was real. "We are all in the dark, and have our spies out. Tell the Colorado men to hurry as fast as possible."[18]

By March 4, 40 local men and 80 more from the Guadalupe were entrenched at San Antonio and were expecting an attack. Captain Hays was in charge of them. He had obtained the appointment for the single government-authorized ranger company to operate in the Southwest. In addition to his San Antonio scouts and the small Cuero settlement company of Captain Friar, Hays was joined this day by a small company under the command of Captain James Hughes Callahan.

Thirty-year-old Callahan had been engaged in a labor detail in Victoria in March 1836, narrowly missing his own execution in the Goliad Massacre. In 1838, he had helped establish Seguin and most recently had commanded a minuteman company during 1841. As word spread from San Antonio during late February about the Vasquez incursion, James Callahan began gathering volunteers from Seguin and other settlements. His unit went into service on March 1 and served through April 2, 1842. According to company orderly sergeant John R. King, noted scout Benjamin McCulloch operated in conjunction with Callahan's company and acted as the unit's superior for some period of the Vasquez campaign. He was later paid as a major at the rate of $118 per month for a six-week period.[19]

His company had been organized on Cíbolo Creek on the Seguin and San Antonio road on March 1. Five young men from the Lavaca settlements joined him "in response to Hays' appeal" for help. They included 22-year-old John Henry Brown, another 1841 minuteman and veteran of the 1840 Plum Creek battle with the Comanches. According to Brown, Captain Callahan's company marched to San Antonio "and found Hays in chief command with Daniel B. Friar in command of a small company from the Cuero settlement."[20]

"Hays was recognized by all as chief in command," Brown wrote. In order to direct all scouting efforts, Hays placed Duncan Ogden in acting command of the San Antonio-area scouts. Twenty-nine-year-old Ogden, a former company commander of the First Regiment of Infantry from 1839–1841, had since settled in San Antonio, where he ran a mercantile business with George T. Howard. Jack Hays thus became acting colonel over the volunteers companies of captains Ogden, Callahan and Friar. "A call of the roll revealed the fact that the entire force at that time was 107 men," Brown recorded.[21]

San Antonio leader Andrew Neill wrote to the people on the Guadalupe from Colonel Hays' camp at San Antonio on March 4: "Do not break up the Guadalupe. Do not let a family remove. We can and will give you notice and that too in time." Neill and his companions obviously wanted to avoid touching off a second Runaway Scrape, which had caused all Texans to flee before Santa Anna in 1836.[22]

While the Texans awaited attack, the Mexican troops instead attacked Goliad on March 3. A 42-man detachment under Captain Miguel Aznar of Lieutenant Colonel Ramón Valera's command entered town to find the citizens barricaded in the old La Bahía mission. The citizens surrendered peacefully, were read a declaration from General Arista, and then the Mexican troops left in the direction of Victoria. Word was advanced to warn Victorians, but the Mexican troops successfully doubled back during the night and marched toward Refugio, 25 miles south of Goliad. Captain Aznar and 55 men struck Refugio at dawn on March 5. His men killed several Lipan Apaches, but the local citizens again surrendered peacefully.[23]

While the diversion in Refugio was taking place, General Rafael Vásquez arrived on the outskirts of San Antonio on the evening of March 5 with approximately 700 artillerymen, infantrymen, rancheros and Indian loyalists. Colonel Hays was well aware of the approach of Vásquez. He had sent out a special detail of scouts at dusk on March 4 to reconnoiter. This party consisted of veteran scout Hendrick Arnold, Isaac N. Mitchell, Stuart Foley, John Henry Brown, Joshua Threadgill, William Morrison and two other men. Brown later related their discovery.[24]

> Leaving at dark, in the chaparral four miles west of San Antonio, the party was fired upon from ambush, apprising them of the near approach of the Mexicans. Avoiding the road, the party moved on and soon discovered that the bluff on the west side of Leon Creek was illuminated by a hundred or more camp fires. Moving on to the west of the camp they estimated the force of the enemy at 1,400, which, subsequently, proved to be correct. Returning, they reached San Antonio, about eight miles distant, at daylight, and reported the facts to Col. Hays.

Jack Hays sent notice to Gonzales on March 5 of the impending danger. "The spies have just come in and report the enemy within six miles of town," he wrote. "Communicate with the committee on the Colorado. Tell them to raise all the forces they can, and we will endeavor to sustain ourselves until they can reinforce us."[25]

Just hours after his scouts had returned, Colonel Hays sent out the same nine riders with one additional ranger, James "Keno" Ellison, to watch the approach of the Mexicans. Scout John Henry Brown wrote that they "passed entirely round the Mexicans, exchanging occasional shots. On returning back to the road a white flag appeared at this point."[26]

Captain José María Carrasco, colonel by brevet in the Mexican regulars, had been sent toward town by Vásquez with a white flag to inform the Texans that they would be attacked if they did not surrender. Hendrick Arnold and Isaac Mitchell advanced to meet Carrasco, who stated the terms of General Vásquez. Scout Keno Ellison had the Mexican captain blindfolded and had him conducted back to the camp of Jack Hays. Carrasco informed the ranger commander that General Vásquez would extend surrender terms if the Texans would peacefully turn over possession of San Antonio. He said that the Mexican troops near town numbered 1,400 infantrymen, artillerymen and cavalrymen, and that thousands more would soon arrive as reinforcements. Carrasco also told the Texans that rangers Chevallie and Dunn were being held as prisoners in the Mexican camp.[27]

Colonel Hays told Carrasco that he would consider the terms of the Mexican forces and agreed to a truce until 2:00 p.m. Carrasco was re-escorted back to his command. Hays assembled the San Antonio leaders, his rangers and the Gonzales volunteers. Although the townspeople were in favor of defending the city, the Gonzales volunteers voted that the rangers and volunteers should retreat to the Guadalupe River. John Henry Brown later recorded the decision of this committee.[28]

> A council of war was then held, Hays presiding and Captains Ogden, Friar and Callahan, Lieut. James P. Kincannon and Messrs. Cornelius Van Ness, John D. Morris and other citizens participating. The question was, "Shall we retreat or fight?" On a parade of the men fifty-four voted to retreat, and fifty-three to stay and fight. Preparations were at once made to retreat.

While scouts went to deliver the surrender verdict to General Vasquez at 2:00 p.m. on March 5, the citizens of San Antonio began their retreat. Men wildly raced about destroying 327 kegs of powder, which were thrown in the San Antonio River with their heads knocked in. Knowing that the Mexican forces would loot the town, the citizens burned what they could not carry with them.[29]

The merchants and citizens drank all the liquor they could hold and smoked fine cigars as they went about destroying items.

The Alamo's artillery pieces were hauled toward Seguin by drunken men, some of whom had to be secured to the ox-drawn carriages to keep from being left behind. John Twohig, the 33-year-old Irish merchant who had often supplied Captain Hays' rangers during 1841, blew up his own warehouse to prevent looters from stealing his goods. In a pension claim he later filed, Twohig said that he "destroyed my house in San Antonio, when containing several thousand dollars worth of goods, blowing up the whole establishment with several kegs of powder, so as to keep the goods from falling into the hands of the enemy who were then marching on San Antonio under command of General Vasquez. I took up arms to defend this place against Vasquez's army and afterward joined the volunteer army at Seguin under Jack Hays.[30]

As the Texans marched from San Antonio, they noted Dr. Launcelot Smithers sitting upon the walls of the Alamo with two other local citizens, John McDonald and John Rhea. Smithers, a former 1836 Alamo courier, and his companions had no horses and thus declined to retreat. "Col. Hays and Capt. Ogden besought them to join us, but they refused," wrote Brown. All three men would survive their subsequent encounters with General Vasquez's troops. Their light regard for danger, however, would catch up with the three in 1842. Smithers, Rhea and McDonald would all be killed during the September Woll campaign.[31]

Colonel Hays' 100-odd remaining men marched toward Salado Creek on the Seguin road with their horse-drawn piece of artillery. A body of Mexican cavalrymen appeared that afternoon at the edge of some timber on Salado Creek and waved their hats in defiance at the retreating Texans. Infuriated, Duncan Ogden galloped down the line and called for 40 of the best mounted volunteers to attack the mocking Mexican horsemen. Among those who were instant to the charge were Andrew Neill, Isaac Mitchell, Christopher C. DeWitt, William Morrison, Calvin Turner, Henry Clay Davis and Stuart Foley. The cavalry fled without fighting although young Turner managed to shoot one Mexican from his horse and retrieve the mount. Ogden's volunteers returned unscathed save flesh ripped from the legs of Neill and others as they barreled through thorny brush in pursuit.[32]

As the Texans retreated toward Seguin with only the slight skirmish, the Vásquez force entered San Antonio on March 5

Reverend Zachariah Nehemiah Morrell (1803–1883) was a Baptist preacher and missionary who was born in South Carolina. Morrell fought the Comanches at Plum Creek in 1840 and volunteered against Mexican incursions in 1842, when his son Allen was captured by Mexican soldiers.
Early woodcut from Flowers and Fruits in the Wilderness by Z. N. Morrell.

without a fight. Vásquez had 500 soldiers, some Caddo scouts, and perhaps another 200 armed vaqueros. Finding the town largely deserted and stripped of goods, Vasquez's men raised their flag in town and proceeded to loot whatever could be found. By March 7, his men had taken all that was worthwhile and they started marching back south again toward Mexico. En route, Vasquez released the three rangers that had been taken prisoner—Coy, Chevallie and Dunn.[33]

Just like the Runaway Scrape during the Texas Revolution, rumor ran wild and panic spread during this time. One report said that 18,000 Mexican troops were scattered at various points from the Rio Grande north, with 3,000 at San Antonio. A new runaway flight ensued, as Guadalupe River settlers began to pack up and flee to the east with their wagons and carts.[34]

★ ★ ★ ★ ★

The courier sent from San Antonio on March 5 by Jack Hays reached Gonzales late Saturday evening. Reverend Zachariah Nehemiah Morrell had held a conference in his little Baptist church that day for the reception of new members. His 17-year-old son James Morrell was among the members scheduled to be baptized in the Guadalupe River at 10:00 a.m. the following Sunday morning. When the messenger reached Gonzales Saturday evening, however, Reverend Morrell noted that "everything of course was thrown into confusion."[35]

The 39-year-old preacher from South Carolina was not

opposed to fighting when the need was dire. He had helped secure the victory against Comanches at Plum Creek in 1840. During late 1841, he had spent three months traveling between churches between the Brazos and Colorado. Morrell was the only Baptist preacher west of the Colorado River by March 1842 and his Gonzales congregation met regularly. He was visited by Elder Daniel Carroll, a Methodist circuit rider who was travelling the Guadalupe valley to spread the gospel. Sporadic Indian attacks and horse thefts were the only acts of aggression his people had contended with during early 1842. The rider from San Antonio—with news of the Mexican forces seizing Béxar—brought an abrupt end to the relative peace.[36]

Instead of rising and preparing for his scheduled baptisms on Sunday morning, Reverend Morrell joined the Gonzales townspeople in preparing to ride to the assistance of the San Antonio citizens. "My little blacksmith shop was very soon surrounded with wagons, needing repairs for the journey," he wrote. "More wagon wheels were repaired on that Sunday than ever I witnessed at one little shop on any before or since."[37]

Wagons were loaded Sunday night and livestock were driven in from the fields on Monday morning. Families, flocks and herds moved east from Gonzales that morning. Reverend Morrell resumed his preaching for the next five months in the Colorado River valley settlement of Plum Grove until the Gonzales citizens felt secure enough to return to their homesteads around the first of September 1842.[38]

In the La Grange area, John Henry Moore organized volunteers and marched to Seguin to lead an attack on San Antonio. Republic Vice President Edward Burleson called for volunteers in Bastrop and marched to Austin to defend that town, where three volunteer militia companies were hastily organized which comprised about one hundred men. Artillery was spotted around President Houston's house and the fort at the capitol made ready for attack. Sam Houston was away in Galveston at the time and did not receive word of the invasion until March 8.[39]

Ever the politician, Houston remained calm for two days, assured that the Mexicans would do little unless provoked. The people of Galveston pressured him into releasing a carefully worded call to arms on March 10. He ordered militia commanders to hold their troops in readiness because rumors had reached him of a Mexican invasion. General Edwin Morehouse commanded the militia's Second Brigade. General Alexander Somervell of the First Militia Brigade was directed to take command of the troops already in the field. Houston also authorized Lieutenant John Wade of the Galveston Coast Guards to take a hundred volunteers and to cruise to Copano Bay in the steamer *Lafitte* to lend aid if needed there.[40]

As the buildup continued, Colonel Barry Gillespie estimated to President Houston on March 17 that about 700 Texans were encamped at San Antonio and probably several hundred more at a second camp at Victoria. General Somervell reached San Antonio on March 18 to take command of the volunteers. The men, however, refused to accept Somervell as their leader, insisting that they had the right to chose their own general. They elected Ned Burleson, who ignored Somervell's arguments. Somervell therefore left the army.[41]

General Burleson appointed Peter Hansborough Bell as adjutant, Robert Simpson Neighbors as quartermaster, and Greenberry Horras Harrison and Thomas Jefferson Green as his aides. He also sent out Jack Hays, William Patton, John Caldwell and James R. Cook to the south on scouting patrols to obtain information, forage and horses.[42]

Captain James H. Gillespie commanded a 71-man ranger-type unit which also joined the volunteers in San Antonio. Gillespie's company was organized in Bastrop and operated for six weeks under the direction of Ed Burleson. One of his volunteers was John Holland Jenkins, who recalled that the news of Vasquez's invasion "created a great deal of excitement among us. The little signal cannon called us together at Bastrop." San Jacinto captain veteran James Gillespie was elected captain, William H. Garrett became the company's first lieutenant and former ranger Samuel Haynie served as orderly sergeant. Pay records show that the unit operated for one month and 12 days. Gillespie's company reached San Antonio, which Jenkins found to be "in sackcloth and ashes."[43]

Burleson's forces found San Antonio to be a deserted town, where they had to take property and kill pigs just to sustain themselves. John Jenkins was disturbed to learn that Juan Seguin, the San Jacinto hero and former lieutenant colonel of the Texas Cavalry, was believed to have switched his allegiance back

Capt. Gillespie's Bastrop Volunteers: March 10-April 22, 1842

Captain:
James H. Gillespie
First Lieutenant:
William H. Garrett
Second Lieutenant:
Mark M. Rogers
Orderly Sergeant:
Samuel A. J. Haynie

Privates:
George Allen
George Alley
Franklin Anderson
John Avant
Marshall Bartlett
Everett Blakey
John N. Boyce
John M. Brite
David F. Brown
Nicholas Burk
Jonathan Burleson
William J. S. Carter
Nathan Clements
Josiah Clifton
Elkin G. Coffman
S. B. Conlee
N. W. Coulter
William C. Dalrymple
Jonathan Davis
William Dunbar
Lemuel Fentress
Wiley D. Fort
Shirley Gage
Thomas Glascock
William Glascock
William Gammell
Lewis S. Hancock
Cornelius M. Hemphill
John Herron
Samuel Highsmith
Abraham W. Hill
W. P. Hill
Marcus B. Huling
John Holland Jenkins
Edward H. Jobe
James L. Jobe
Addison Leftwick
Samuel Luther
Logan Maloney
John McDaniel
Marly M. Milion
Aaron Murchison
Lewis Nichols
Robert Owen
William E. Owen
James M. Patton
Cicero Rufus Perry
Cornelius Phillips
Henry Phillips
J. W. Reed
Robert Reed
Jonathan Rogers
Samuel Satterthwait
James Simpson
Bartlett Sims
James Smith
E. C. Smithson
John Stone
C. W. Strickland
C. Strothers
Larkin P. Sullivan
Willis Tatum
Benjamin F. Warnock
Joseph Weeks
J. W. Whitaker
Hamilton White
W. H. Woods
Francis Yoast

Source: Author's study of audited military claims of the Republic of Texas. Key source George Alley PD, R 132, F 226–30.

to Mexico. For this reason, the Texas troops in San Antonio "destroyed many of his hogs and property."[44]

Mayor Seguin was branded a traitor in the wake of the Vasquez invasion and his reputation was damaged. This was in spite of the fact that he and other San Antonio Tejanos—including Captain Manuel Flores, Lieutenant Ambrosio Rodríquez, Matías Curbier—joined Jack Hays in trailing Vasquez's departing forces in March. General Burleson issued orders to Captain Hays to secure mounts for the balance of his spy company in order to keep a strict vigilance. "The safety of the country depends on good spies," Burleson directed. "You will send two or three of your best spies mounted on good horses as far west upon the preceding road and also the Laredo road at least to the Nueces and farther, if in your judgement they would not be captured."[45]

Hays' rangers had camped on the bank of Cíbolo Creek on the night of March 6. He sent a courier to the government in Austin and moved his scouts to a new camp opposite from Seguin on the Guadalupe River the next night. Alsey Miller and Ben McCulloch rejoined Hays at the Flores Rancho on the Guadalupe, bringing with them the news that Vasquez had already retreated from San Antonio. Spies soon confirmed that Vasquez had crossed the Rio Grande back into Mexico apparently content that his threat had seriously alarmed Texan citizens.[46]

Juan Seguin returned to San Antonio with the scouts to find Ed Burleson in charge of the volunteers who had gathered in his city. Burleson refused to hold a court of inquiry regarding the treason charges against the Tejano mayor, who found the hostility against him so strong that he opted to retire back to his pillaged ranch. Burleson gave Seguin the duty of foraging supplies for the Texas Army from the lower ranches on the San Antonio River but he was forced to go into hiding to escape armed Texan parties who hoped to bring him to justice. The troubled hero of the Texas Revolution would thus elect on April 18 to resign as the mayor of San Antonio and make his way toward Mexico for his own safety. There, Seguin claims to have been given the ultimatum of choosing prison or military service against Texas.[47]

Captain Elijah Sterling Clack Robertson arrived in San Antonio on March 16 with a company of about 40 volunteers he had organized in Gonzales. News of the Mexican incursion made the citizens yearn for revenge, as Robertson noted in his diary. "The most of the men were, while drunk, anxious to storm Matamoros with fifty men. In fact they were [the] bravest men I ever saw in my life." When it came time to form his company, however, Robertson had new challenges. "Every man thought and acted for himself. We were volunteers, thrown together from different parts of the country by the impulse of the moment."[48]

Captain Robertson's company found General Burleson camped below town at the Mission Concepción with 150 men. "We remained several days, without knowing much of what was to be done," he wrote. The lack of action was frustrating to many and young Robertson was further distressed when he soon learned that his father—Texas colonizer and former Texas Ranger captain Sterling Clack Robertson—had passed away during his absence. He departed San Antonio feeling "lonely indeed. The last link is broken almost between men and the world."[49]

During mid-March, President Houston sent out a series of communications in which he indicated a desire to take on an aggressive campaign against Mexico. Houston was discouraged by the Texas Congress' inability to enact constructive legislation for frontier defense during its previous session. He therefore began executing his own plans for raising and equipping an army without calling Congress into a special session. The president confided to William H. Daingerfield that he simply did "not trust their wisdom in our present attitude." Houston cautioned Brigadier General Somervell to wait before advancing until he was certain that Mexico had mounted another invasion. He also instructed Somervell to enlist 200 rangers and spies to range the country from San Antonio to Corpus Christi and westward. These men should be "well prepared to pass the summer in service to range the frontier." Houston added that if this number could not be raised, then Somervell should organize two spy companies of 56 men for duty along the southern frontier, with Jack Hays to command this corps. While Somervell organized his invading force, Hays' rangers were to provide intelligence during those months.[50]

Little evidence exists that new ranging companies were organized during March besides that of Captain Hays. Captain Gillespie's Bastrop Mounted Volunteers stayed in service through mid-April, beyond the service time of many of Burleson's men. The abandoned town of San Antonio and lack of action compelled many of the volunteers to return home in short order. John Twohig and several San Antonio residents returned to town but many of the citizens stayed away, in fear of Vasquez's troops returning.

CHAPTER 2

Spring and Summer Ranger Actions

April–July 1842

The buildup of volunteer troops in Texas as a result of the Vasquez incursion lasted only for a month. In Goliad, citizen soldiers from Victoria, Jackson, Matagorda and Brazoria counties had remained on station for two weeks under the direction of commander Clark L. Owen before disbanding. The militiamen under Brigadier General Somervell and volunteers under Ned Burleson who gathered in San Antonio awaited orders from President Houston through March. Scouts brought in intelligence that the Mexican raiders had recrossed the Rio Grande and Burleson—still lacking orders to pursue them—decided to disband the San Antonio volunteers on April 2, 1842.[1]

Captain Jack Hays was thereby left with the only organized military force in San Antonio once again. Some of his volunteer rangers headed for home once the Vasquez crisis passed. Others who had assembled under Burleson opted to ride with Hays after their companies were disbanded. Among the men who joined Hays' rangers during April were Cicero Rufus Perry from Captain Gillespie's company, John Henry Brown from Captain Callahan's company, William Glenn Jett, William Bugg, Daniel Rice, Sam Norvell and Guy Stokes.

Hays' rangers were assisted in the San Antonio area during April and May by a 40-man company of mounted men raised on March 4 in Washington County by Captain Samuel Bogart. He was also assisted by a 52-man company of Lipan Apaches under

Capt. Bogart's Mounted Company: March 11–May 4, 1842

Captain:
Samuel Bogart
First Lieutenant:
N. Chambliss
Second Lieutenant:
Elisha D. Little
First Sergeant:
Thomas Niman
Second Sergeant:
Henry Day
Third Sergeant:
Rufus Charles

Privates:
John Ashmore
Francis Hall Ayers
Thomas Bailey
Samuel Bennett
C. H. Bogart
Jackson Browning
Hugh H. Calvert
George Chappell
Nimrod J. Chappell
William B. Dean
George H. DeMoss
Trimmier Dobson
Newton J. Edney
William Edney
John Ferrell
James W. Foster
Thomas Gilliland
George W. Harber
William Hardeman
William Hargrove
James W. McDade
John McDade
Joseph Marshall
Donald Meadows
John Michel
Thomas J. Middleton
B. F. Ravill
H. A. Reynolds
John M. Stevens
Thomas Stevens
James H. Stribling
John Trimmier
Thomas Trimmier

Source: Samuel Bogart PD, R 138, F 206–207; Nance, *Attack and Counterattack*, 587.

two chiefs, Flacco and Colonel John. The Lipan scouts operated at times under the direction of Hays and also under orders from the War Department of Texas.[2]

The Hays rangers remained in the field west of San Antonio throughout the spring and summer of 1842. No more than fifteen American families had returned to San Antonio following the withdrawal of Vasquez's troops and Mexican sympathizers felt that another Mexican invasion was imminent. Many Mexican families had fled the area for the Guadalupe or to join Mexican forces, leaving only a few businessmen and the rangers to occupy Béxar. The city council declared on May 23 that the new mayor, John W. Smith, should send out a ten-man patrol to work up and down the San Antonio River, making regular reports of activities.[3]

Capt. Stiff's Fannin County Minutemen: April 22–May 19, 1842

Captain:	John F. Hunter
Jesse Stiff	William Hunter
	Alonzo Larkins
Privates:	William Martin
Montgomery B. Birch	Jefferson C. Parish
William C. Caruthers	Source: Jesse Stiff PD, R 188, F 548–73.

Citizens in other settlements of Texas opted to provide for themselves with several similar small ranging companies. In Fannin County, a spy company was formed under the command of Captain Jesse Stiff. His "Fannin County Minutemen" or "Fannin County Guards" were mustered into service by order of the county's chief justice, James O'Neal, on April 22. Jesse Stiff had first served as a Fannin County Ranger under Captain James R. O'Neal in the spring of 1838. Later that fall, Stiff was captain of his own company of Fannin County Mounted Gunmen during Lieutenant Colonel Daniel Montague's Indian campaign. He had again seen action as a ranger in July 1841, when he served as a private in Captain Joseph Sowell's Fannin County Minutemen company.

The Fannin County Minutemen were originally enrolled to serve a one-year-period and they stationed themselves 35 miles from the settlements on the northwestern frontier. The eight-man ranging unit only served through May 19, 1842, before the lack of action compelled county leaders to disband the little unit.[4]

Sam Houston continued writing letters in the weeks following the brief seizure of San Antonio. His desire to build up a two-company ranging corps under Jack Hays did come to fruition. The second ranging company organized was that of Captain Ephraim Walton McLean in Corpus Christi. Born in Christian County, Kentucky, in 1816, McLean had arrived in Texas after the battle of San Jacinto. He had participated in Colonel Henry Karnes' October–November 1839 Comanche expedition as a member of the Galveston Mounted Gunmen and had been elected captain of the company by the end of the expedition.

Captain McLean went into service for Corpus Christi on April 9 and on the following day enrolled his first nine men. In time, McLean was able to round up only 20 men under his

Capt. McLean's Corpus Rangers: April 9 - August 15, 1842

Captain:
Ephraim Walton McLean
First Lieutenant:
George E. Hunter [1]
Orderly Sergeant:
James E. Haviland [2]

Privates:
John P. Davie [3]
William Dunbar [4]
William Dunlap [4]
Jesse Hammett [4]
Alfred B. LaForge [4]
J. S. LeClere [4]
W. S. Morton [5]
Y. Peters [4]
John Pollock [4]
Frederic Pomeray [3]
John Randon [4]
____ Reaves [3]
William R. Rector [5]
____ Rooter [3]
Peter Royal [6]
Riviero Ruocindo [7]
William Rupley [3]
William Thompson [8]
Isaac Tousey [3]

1 Served through June 9, 1842.
2 Served April 24–August 15, 1842.
3 Served April 24–June 9, 1842.
4 Served April 10–August 15, 1842.
5 Served May 4–June 9, 1842.
6 Served May 6–9, 1842.
7 Served April 25–August 10, 1842.
8 Served May 25–August 10, 1842.

Source: Ephraim McLean PD, R 199, F 444.

direction, even though he had been authorized to muster in 56 or more men. From the Executive Department in Houston, private secretary Washington Miller sent orders to Captain McLean on April 20 from Sam Houston.[5]

> Sir, before it will be possible for a campaign to open against the enemy, it is important that two companies should range upon the frontier as a corps of observation. Having great confidence in you, I hope that you will succeed in raising a company of fifty-six men or over that number. Congress places no means at my disposal to accomplish my wishes in relation to frontier defenses.
>
> For the salvation of Texas, I do hope that as many of the young men as can (under one hundred) will volunteer under you for six months. Previous to the end of that period, they may look for very important action.

Brigadier General Somervell of the Texas Militia sent out numerous appeals to various leaders during April, inviting them to join him in San Antonio for an invasion of Mexico. Captain Eli Chandler was the first to successfully enroll a company of volunteers in April to join Somervell. Sam Houston sent out his own invitations for volunteer companies to join the effort during the next two months. The small numbers of men who did turn out were often not fit for military service and by June 15, President Houston could see that his grand plan was not developing. Some of those who did volunteer from the United States lacked the proper discipline.[6]

In the interim, the ranging companies under captains Jack Hays and Ephraim McLean were the only two that saw any service. McLean's unit would remain in service through August 15 before disbanding. His company was officially labeled as being part of the "Corps of Observation," and McLean's muster roll states that his company was operating under orders from the War Department dated April 9, 1842. After forming in Galveston during April, his company went "ranging west of Corpus Christi." Lieutenant Hunter and nine other rangers left the company on June 9, but McLean and a dozen other rangers remained in service into early August.

Sam Houston attempted to add a third ranging company on June 18, when he wrote to Ben McCulloch to authorize him to raise an additional 56-man company. He was to maintain strict control of his men. During the Vasquez campaign, Major McCulloch had directed the actions of Captain James Callahan's company and others for six weeks. Republic records do not indicate that Captain McCulloch was able to successfully muster in his own ranging company during the summer of 1842. By September, Ben McCulloch would join the company of Jack Hays.[7]

★ ★ ★ ★ ★

Indian Peace Talks of 1842

President Sam Houston had blasted Mirabeau Lamar's Indian extinction policy during his inaugural address before the Texas Congress in December 1841. He believed the ranging service had "failed to achieve the object" of protecting the frontier and therefore refused to appropriate any funds for minute men or rangers during his first months back in office.[8]

President Houston instead opted to grant licenses to three men—Ethan Stroud, Abel Warren and Thomas J. Torrey—to

President Sam Houston, seen wearing a cowboy duster in this early daguerreotype, spent much of his second term as President of the Republic of Texas attempting to negotiate peace with the Texas Indians.
Texas State Library and Archives Commission.

begin trading with the Indians. These traders hired some mixed blood immigrant Indians such as Delaware Jim and Shawnee Jim Shaw to help carry their dialogue of peace. The first chance to negotiate peace presented itself when Sam Houston received letters during March 1842 from Houston County settlers Andrew Jackson Fowler, William M. Crisp and Levi Jordan stating that some of the smaller bands of Indians were willing to listen.[9]

Meetings were arranged by U.S. agents in Indian Territory between Texas authorities and Texas refugee Indians. Agent James Logan met with Wichita Indian leaders on June 1, 1842. Commissioners Stroud, Joseph Durst and Leonard Williams met with Caddo leaders and Kickapoo, Cherokee and Biloxi Indians on August 1 near Holland Coffee's Red River trading post. Cherokee mixed-blood Jesse Chisholm was hired to bring in Comanche leaders but his efforts fell flat. The talks stalled when U.S. agents and the Indians balked at the commissioners inviting a 90-man ranger unit from Fannin County be raised to attend.[10]

Sam Houston continued to try and appease the Texas Indians throughout 1842. He demanded that John Henry Moore send any Comanche prisoners he had previously taken to trading houses for return to their people. He also wrote to Chief Big Mush of the Cherokees and Chief Linney of the Shawnees to inform them that

President Lamar was gone from office and that they could return again to Texas.[11]

On September 26, President Houston gave instructions to Indian agent Louis B. Franks, a former Texas Ranger captain, to persuade the Tonkawa and Lipan Indian leaders on the Upper Brazos to come to the Waco village for a council on October 24. He also quietly appointed frontiersman George Terrell to head the commissioners of peace and to urge mutual friendship, repatriation of captives and no liquor trading among the Indians. Houston gave special orders on October 18 to former ranger captain Eli Chandler to accompany the Indian commissioners to the Waco village to serve as guards and to prevent any Indian-haters from disrupting the council.[12]

Chandler was authorized to raise around "ten or fifteen" men, a force small enough not to excite the Indians. Captain Chandler's muster roll of guards shows that he had two of his former 1841 minutemen—Moses Griffin and Charles Sevier—and 15 other Robertson County citizens: Clark Dunlap, Isaac C. Spence, Granville Arnett, Thomas I. Smith, John Martin, James Martin, A. F. Moss, P. C. Whitaker, T. Kay, ____ Robertson, William M. Wilkinson, John Miles, James B. Powell, ___ Howe and D. W. C. Nerry. Chandler's unit, enrolled on October 20, was paid one dollar per day for services through November 15, 1842.[13]

Terrell's commissioners had trouble carrying out the intended council. The Indians misunderstood the time of the meeting and were late and the commissioners had trouble with high water in the Texas rivers. The Brazos Indian leaders were, however, impressed enough with the peace messages sent by President Houston that they opted to give his word a chance. John Washington Lockhart, an aide to Houston, wrote, "A decided change was noticed on the frontier. Hostilities in a measure ceased among all the warring tribes that these men visited, except the Comanches."[14]

Houston was concerned that depredations carried out by either Indians or rangers had to be stopped as either party conducting a raid only served to bring on a retaliatory raid by the other party. The peace efforts of Houston continued even as the San Antonio rangers continued to have confrontations with raiding Comanches.[15]

★ ★ ★ ★ ★

The Gilleland Family Massacre

The Comanche Indians committed another depredation against the Gilleland family during the time of the excitement caused by the Vasquez invasion. The Gillelands lived near a Mexican village known as the Don Carlos Ranch in Refugio County. The Comanches attacked the home and carried off at least two Gilleland family members as hostages.[16]

Johnstone Gilleland was outside of his home with his wife Mary Barbour Gilleland and their children Rebecca and William M. Gilleland when a party of Comanches appeared. Johnstone ran for his rifle at his home but was cut down before he could reach it. Mary grabbed her children and prayed as the Indians approached and killed her with a spear. Eleven-year-old Rebecca Gilleland later related, "As she pressed us to her heart, we were baptized in her precious blood."[17]

The two children were hauled away by the Comanches after their home was pillaged and their parents were left dying. Word soon reached some of the military forces which had gathered to repel the Vasquez invasion. Among those men in the vicinity of the lower San Antonio River were First Lieutenant Anthony B. Hannum and Dr. A. T. Axsom of the Matagorda Riflemen. Albert Sidney Johnston, the former adjutant general of Texas, was in camp near the tragedy and he called for ten mounted men to reconnoiter the movement of the Comanches. Others who were on hand to help with the cause included Andrew Neill and Alfred S. Thurmond, the town marshal of Victoria.[18]

Lt. Hannum later wrote of his scouting efforts.[19]

> With General Johnston we proceeded about one mile below the town, where I found and pointed out to him an Indian trail leading into the river bottom. Here, after dismounting and making coffee, Gen. Johnston returned to the command, leaving me in charge of half a dozen men and fifteen scouts under Captain Price, who had joined us. We soon discovered the trail of the Indians and were in hot pursuit.

In addition to Price, Hannum listed others who participated in the pursuit of the Comanches to be: Dr. Axsom; Colonel Kerr, former purser of the Texas Navy; and John Dallam. The Comanches rode through the night with their two Gilleland children captives until halting after morning the following day. Soon after they halted, the Texan pursuit party caught up with them a short distance from the site of the 1836 Fannin Massacre.[20]

"After clearing the timber, they formed in line to receive us, while a tall old chief ran up and down the line playing the flute," recorded Hannum. "They had evidently counted us and intended to give battle." The action commenced when Hannum spotted a "gay Indian on a finely caparisoned horse" who presented too much of a tempting target. Hannum fired and knocked the Comanche from his stolen horse.[21]

The other Indians fled for the woods, leaving guns, shields and stolen horses behind. The Texans dismounted and ran for the woods in preparation for a fight from tree to tree. The fleeing Comanches had no time for their captives. Young William Gilleland was lanced in the side and left for dead. His sister Rebecca was knocked on the head and dumped from her horse. She prayed, picked up her wounded brother and helped carry him to the edge of the woods. When she finally decided the approaching horsemen were friendly, Rebecca called out for help.[22]

Lt. Hannum's force recovered the children and Dr. Axsom tended to William Gilleland's deep wound. The latter would recover from his injuries and become a prominent citizen of Austin. Rebecca Gilleland was carried by Albert Johnston to the home of Presbyterian minister Dr. Blain of Victoria. She lived with the doctor for some time and in 1844 would attend Rutersville College, the first Methodist college in Texas. Rebecca Jane Fisher later married minister Orceneth Fisher and was mother of six children.[23]

The Fishers later moved to Oregon, where they founded Corvallis College, where Rebecca headed the female department. When they later returned to Texas, Rebecca Gilleland Fisher was a charter member of the Daughters of the Republic of Texas. Rebecca served as state president of the DRT for her last 32 years. She assisted with saving the Alamo from destruction, was the only woman elected to the Texas Veterans Association, and her portrait hangs in the Senate Chamber of the Texas State Capitol. The former Comanche captive died in Austin on March 23, 1926.[24]

★ ★ ★ ★ ★

Captain Hays' Guadalupe River Battle

Texas historians will long debate some of the actions of Captain Jack Hays' famous ranging company. Sufficient muster rolls and records remain to pinpoint the dates and details of Hays' significant Comanche battles of 1841 at Uvalde Canyon on June 29 and the July 24 Llano battle.[25]

During early 1842 and in the months following the Vasquez incursion, Hays certainly remained in command of a ranging company which covered much of the frontier while operating out of San Antonio. Through the course of time, any muster rolls or battle reports he may have submitted about his encounters with Indian forces have vanished.

There are, however, enough extant accounts from various men that point toward his company having at least one Indian battle during the first half of 1842. The accounts, it must be noted, vary widely on details and the men involved. Some of the stories that have been recorded were passed on second or third-hand, at best.

Hays had recruited some additional rangers during the spring months to his Béxar County ranger unit. William Bugg, with ranger service dating from 1836 which included Colonel John Moore's 1839 Comanches offensive and Major Lewis' 1841 expedition, signed on April 2. Stephen and Matt Jett's younger brother, 21-year-old William Glenn Jett, signed on to ride with the Hays rangers on April 22, 1842. One of the more colorful new hands joining on June 1 was 26-year-old Gustav Elley. Born in the kingdom of Saxony and soon orphaned, young Gustav made his way to the United States in 1836. Once in Texas, Elley had since served in both the Texas Army and Texas Navy before joining the Texas Rangers.[26]

Jim Nichols, a veteran of the 1840 Plum Creek battle with the Comanches, wrote in his journals that he joined Captain Hays two years after Plum Creek to help fight Indians.[27]

> In the spring of this year, the Comanche tribe became very troublesome, especially in the west in and around San Antonio, evidently thinking to take revenge on the people of that place and vicinity for their defeat two years before.
>
> John C. Hays, a popular man and a good Indian fighter, concluded to raise a company for three months' service

Captain John Coffee Hays fought with the Texas Cavalry in 1837 and participated in a number of Indian expeditions and battles during 1839–1840. Jack Hays commanded his first ranger company during 1841 and led his men in several famous battles. His reputation in battle was well known by the time President Houston authorized him to raise a ranger company again in 1842. *UTSA's Institute of Texan Cultures, No. 073-0641, courtesy of the Library of Congress.*

and endeavor to drive the savages from the vicinity of San Antonio as they scarcely ever was out of sight. He saw and talked with some of the government officers and they assured him they would do all in their power to have an appropriation made to pay off him and his men for all services that they would render.

Mission Concepción in San Antonio is the best preserved Spanish mission in Texas and is considered by some historians to be the oldest unrestored church in the U.S. The mission was moved to its present site in San Antonio in 1731 and this stone church was completed in 1755. Nearly 90 years later, Captain Jack Hays' rangers made their camp near the Mission Concepción. *Author's photo.*

> Hays wrote me a note stating that he had the promise of pay for the service and that if I was not engaged he wanted me to join him as trailor and scout. He said he had engaged some Lipan Indians but they were so treacherous he could place no confidence in them without a white man constantly with them.

Nichols therefore set out in the spring of 1842 with companions Calvin Turner and Joe Williams to the place of Captain Hays' rendezvous. They were mustered into service "and went into camp below town near the old mission Concepción." The old Mission Concepción was located on the San Antonio River, south of the Alamo.[28]

Hays rangers remained idle in their camp only a few days before word reached them that a band of 80 Comanches under war chief Yellow Wolf had made a raid in the vicinity of San Antonio. According to Nichols, Yellow Wolf's Comanches were blamed for "driving off horses, killing several Mexicans and one

The journal of James Wilson Nichols (1820–1887) describes an 1842 battle between Comanches and a small group of Captain Hays' rangers. His recollection of the location places this fight in Kendall County—in contrast to previous accounts placing this battle in Bandera Pass.
Jim Nichols portrait, circa 1870s.

negro sheep herder and taking one white man prisoner, a red-haired child of Erin, who was also herding sheep." The Irish man taken prisoner was James Dunn, a Hays ranger.[29]

The Comanche raid occurred in broad daylight but word did not reach Hays' camp until several hours before dawn the next day. "About sunrise there was sixteen of us in our saddles," wrote Nichols. "I was put in front with two Lipan Indians to trail and Hays with fifteen of the boys following close on our heels, the rest of the company being out on detached service, some hauling provision[s], others out on a scout."[30]

Hays' company followed the Comanches rapidly and overtook them on the Guadalupe River at what was called the Pinta Trail Crossing. This crossing was located near the present community of Sisterdale in Kendall County, northeast of Bandera. The Pinta Trail ran northwest from Austin toward Fredericksburg through the hill country approximately 180 miles to a point near present Menard.[31]

Three other early Texans—Benjamin F. Highsmith, Thomas Galbreath and Creed Taylor—later related their experiences to Andrew J. Sowell of fighting with Jack Hays against Comanches. Since neither Highsmith nor Galbreath appears on the muster rolls for Captain Hays of 1841 or 1843–1845, their service period would have to have been in 1842. Both Highsmith and Galbreath claim to have fought with Hays at his battle at "Bandera Pass," located a short distance from the area in Kendall County which Nichols describes.[32]

This battle taking place at Bandera Pass is based on the writings of early Texas historian A. J. Sowell, who collected stories from rangers Ben Highsmith, Creed Taylor and Thomas Galbreath. *(Above, left):* Benjamin Franklin Highsmith (1814–1905) fought at Brushy Creek and in the Cherokee War of 1839, and told Sowell that he fought with Jack Hays against Comanches. Photo originally published in Sowell's *Early Settlers and Indian Fighters of Southwest Texas,* 1900. *(Above, right):* Creed Taylor (1820–1906) was photographed with his friend John McPeters (seated to left of Taylor) and their rifles around the turn of the century. Although Taylor's recollections to Sowell describe a fight at Bandera Pass, he left another battle account which agrees with Jim Nichols that the Comanche fight was on the Guadalupe River in Kendall County. *Photo courtesy of Bena Kirkscey.*

In further support of this battle occurring during 1842 is the fact that Creed Taylor did serve with Jack Hays in 1842. In 1870, Henry McCulloch affirmed in Taylor's pension papers that Creed had served under Captain Hays during the 1842 battle of Salado Creek, where Taylor was wounded. In his recounting of the "Bandera Pass" battle, Taylor's "recollection" to Sowell was that the date was June of 1841, prior to the Salado Creek battle. June of 1842 would be more likely. Highsmith claimed the year to be 1841 and Galbreath said 1843, the latter certainly being a mistake. Between these three men interviewed by Sowell, the size of Hays' force engaged in this action varies between 25 and about 40 rangers. Taylor claimed that his brothers Josiah and Pitkin were with him for the battle.[33]

Another account by Creed Taylor entitled "Jack Hays Fight on the Guadalupe" is a little more specific, although he gave the time as being the fall of 1840 (versus the 1841 he told Sowell).

He agrees with Jim Nichols that the rangers went out in response to a group of about 200 Comanches who "made a raid around San Antonio and drove off a vast number of horses and mules." Taylor stated in this version that he was with his brothers Jim and Josiah Taylor and Sam Walker. Creed Taylor says the rangers were encamped on the Cíbolo near San Antonio and that Captain Hays' force at the time numbered "about twenty-two of us." This number of 22 more closely matches Nichols' recollection of 16 men than the higher numbers Sowell would later relate. "Without waiting for reinforcements, we mounted and were soon in hot pursuit," Taylor related.[34]

The recollections Sowell recorded from Taylor, Galbreath and Highsmith each seem to mix this expedition with the 1844 Walker's Creek fight of Jack Hays' rangers. In the subsequent battle, these stories have five rangers being killed (including a Lee Jackson or George Jackson) and as many as six others being wounded. From the accounts relayed by these three men, the rangers accompanying Captain Hays in pursuit of this Comanche force alternately include: Highsmith, Galbreath, Creed Taylor, Jim Taylor, Josiah Taylor, Kit Acklin, Sam Luckie, Ben McCulloch, George Neill, Sam Walker, Robert "Ad" Gillespie, Mike Chevallie, James Dunn, Peter Bell, Andrew Erskine, Peter Fohr and Lee or George Jackson. Adding in other names given by Nichols as being in the fight (Nichols, Cal Turner, Joe Williams, Jack Pearson and Dave Laurence) the total rangers mentioned by all four men is about two dozen. By dropping a few of the names that were likely confused with another 1844 Hays fight, the total number of men on this scout would fit nicely between the Nichols number of 16 and Taylor number of 22.[35]

The report of this battle taking place at "Bandera Pass" near the Kerr and Bandera county lines appears to come solely from these stories presented by A. J. Sowell. No primary source can be found for Jack Hays fighting Comanches in Bandera Pass. The written accounts by Jim Nichols and Creed Taylor point toward this battle taking place in Kendall County along the Guadalupe River (a relatively short distance from Bandera Pass). Nichols wrote that the battle was fought at the Pinta Trail crossing of the Guadalupe in Kendall County. In Creed Taylor's separate account of the fight he agrees that it took place in Kendall County at "the Guadalupe River about where Waring is now situated."[36]

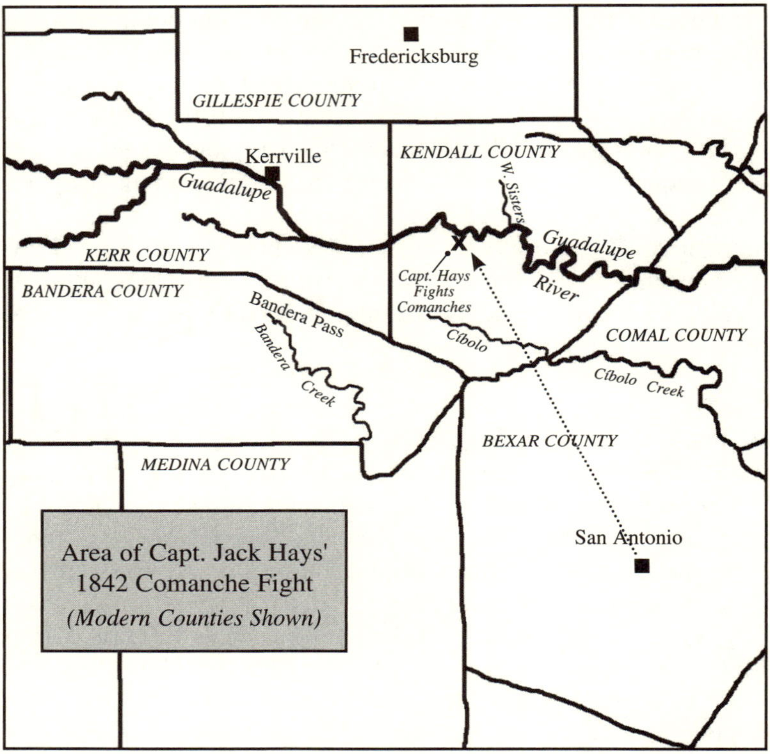

The least tainted account of this 1842 Hays fight comes from the journals of ranger Jim Nichols. Since the statements given to Sowell vary widely in dates and contain elements of the Walker's Creek fight, the more direct version offered by Nichols will be primarily recounted.

Nichols claims that Hays' rangers overtook the Comanches near the Guadalupe and opened fire on them as they headed up the bank on the other side. Several Indians were killed and others who were wounded were helped away. "They moved on to the top and over the hill out of our sight," wrote Nichols. "We crossed over and galloped to the top of the rise."[37]

When the rangers topped the hill, they found that Chief Yellow Wolf's Comanches had halted and formed a battle line. Captain Hays, sensing that his men were riding into a trap, called out in a sharp, clear voice, "Steady there, boys! Dismount and tie those horses. We can whip them—no doubt about that."[38]

Creed Taylor later offered his recollections of Hays' gallant speech to his rangers.[39]

> Capt. Hays called a halt and setting his horse like he was a part of the animal, made us a little talk I shall always remember. In a quiet, conversational tone, he said, "Boys, yonder are the red thieves and there's our horses. The Indians are ten to one against us but we can whip them. What do you all say?"
>
> "Fight 'em!" said the boys. "You take the lead and we'll stay right with you!"
>
> In the meantime, the Indians had discovered us and formed in battle array. We dismounted and tightened up our saddle girths, belts and etc., and while doing this I was struck with the spirit of the dare-devil levity that seemed to have seized every man.
>
> Finally, when all were ready, Capt. Hays said, "Come on boys, and when you shoot, shoot to hit."

Jim Nichols' journal relates the battle which ensued.[40]

> We pored into their ranks another volley and made them scatter. We then retreated back down the hill to reload but before we had finished reloading we looked and saw the top of the hill red with the savages.
>
> When they saw us, they raised the war whoop or yell and charged down towards us but seeing we did not flee but stood our ground, they charged halfway down the hill, discharged their escopets and a perfect shower of arrows at us, wheeled their horses and galloped back, followed by loud yells from the Texians and a volley of bullets.
>
> We reloaded as quick as possible and charged them in return. We charged halfway down the hill that time, receiving their fire as we charged. Arriving within sixty yards of their line, we fired and retreated as before with the savages in full chase as before and they fired and retreated.
>
> Captain Hays then sent half his men to charge and draw them out and while their guns were empty the other half would charge them. That plan worked well as the reserve men ran in and killed several and wounded the chief Yellow Wolf severely.
>
> It was then too dark to charge them again and [we] awaited their charge, as we had two men wound[ed] severely and one

> slightly: Sam Luckie in left thigh slightly, Jack Pearson in the fleshy part of the right thigh with an arrow, [and] Dave Laurence in [the] shoulder with [a] ball.

Creed Taylor noted that Chief Yellow Wolf "mounted on a fine black horse, the property of a prominent citizen in San Antonio, seemed to be everywhere in the fight. He was trigged out in a gorgeously gotten-up head gear and carried a shield of large size and extra fine ornamentation." Taylor says that the Comanches broke formation and fled after Yellow Wolf was shot from his black horse.[41]

Ben Highsmith claimed to have been wounded in the leg by an arrow shortly after assisting his wounded comrade Sam Luckie. Highsmith said the wounded rangers included himself, Luckie, Kit Acklin, Tom Galbreath, and James Dunn. Galbreath, a 20-year-old from North Carolina who had fought at Plum Creek in 1840, was reportedly wounded by an arrow which penetrated his left side near his hip above his pistol belt. He withdrew the arrow and continued fighting. Galbreath told Sowell that he and Luckie were later carried to San Antonio for treatment. The more direct accounts by Nichols and Taylor agree that no Texans were killed in this fight on the Guadalupe—as opposed to the five listed as killed by the less direct recollections taken down by Sowell.[42]

Cal Turner, Joe Williams and Jim Nichols were ordered to the top of the hill to keep watch on Yellow Wolf's Comanches as the wounded rangers were assisted. Captain Hays' men gathered the spoils of war, including about 35 horses which had been abandoned. "In this fight, we recovered nearly all the horses stolen by the Indians in the raid and got off without the loss of a man," recalled Creed Taylor. The San Antonio man captured by the Comanches, James Dunn, managed to escape after this battle. He reported to Hays that the Comanches had suffered 23 men killed in this battle. "He also stated that Yaller Wolf with thirty-six of his men was wounded and that thirteen died from their wounds on their way out," Nichols wrote.[43]

"Red" Dunn had been treated well by his captors after his abduction. His bright red hair was something of amazement to them. Some Comanches even tried scrubbing the "paint" from his hair in the river.[44]

"The Indians' loss we never knew, but considering the close range and the deadly aim of the Texans, it must have been very heavy," recalled Taylor. He said that Yellow Wolfs horse was returned to its lawful owner in San Antonio. Taylor also wrote that the Comanche chiefs "shield was sent to Austin where it remained in the old Capitol until that structure was burned in 1881."[45]

Based on the stories of A. J. Sowell, the state of Texas erected a commemorative marker in the town of Bandera in Bandera County on State Highway 16, on the public square across from the courthouse. The marker describes the "Old Texas Ranger Trail" between San Antonio and Kerrville. This marker states that Jack Hays' company fought a noted battle at Bandera Pass, 10 miles north of town, while his men were "on a scouting mission in the Guadalupe Mountains." The marker states that the battle at Bandera Pass occurred in the spring of 1841 between Hays' rangers and several hundred Comanches. Perhaps future sources will reveal that this marker should likely be moved from Bandera County into Kendall County near the Guadalupe.[46]

Surviving records of the actions of Captain Hays' rangers during 1842 do not pinpoint a date for this battle. Early settler Mary Ann Maverick, however, wrote on May 13, 1842, that "about twenty men under Hays were out west and had overstayed their appointed time, and fears were entertained for their safety—Cornelius Van Ness had been accidentally shot and killed by James Robinson." She gives no indication of what expedition Hays was on but added on May 24 that another group of volunteers rode out from La Grange to track a group of 50 Comanches who had been seen on Peach Creek. These young men returned two days later when they were unable to find a fresh trail.[47]

★★★★★

Ranger Life

Chief Castro and his Lipan Apaches paid a visit to President Houston. After this, the president issued a safe conduct to Castro's Indians on June 21 so that they could safely return to their Lipan camp near Austin. Houston noted that their services might be needed in a future war with Mexico and he cherished his friendship with Castro.[48]

Another report from the Secretary of War and Marine of June 22 shows that Flacco and some Lipans had traveled to San Antonio to join Captain Hays. The rangers and Lipans went out on a scout during the late summer against Mexican spies and bandits who had been troubling the southwest region. While riding out through a valley one day, they spotted a Mexican horseman watching them from a cedar-covered peak in the distance. Hays took two men with him to flank the lookout while his remaining rangers continued slowly forward. Hays hoped to frighten the sentinel and follow him back to his own camp.[49]

Once they had the Mexican scout on the run, the other rangers were signaled to follow. Hays, his own two scouts and Flacco pursued the fleeing horseman toward his camp. Captain Hays shot the sentinel from his horse and his rangers then surprised the bandit camp. They killed other members of the marauders and then turned to head back for San Antonio. During their scout to maintain peace on the frontier, new trouble had been brewing with Mexican invaders.[50]

Relatively little remains in the form of precise documentation of the actions of Jack Hays' 1842 ranging company. His men remained on duty throughout the spring and into the summer, making occasional minor brushes with Mexican marauders and small bands of Indians that went without much notice in the local newspapers. Jim Nichols' journals relate another expedition where Captain Hays' men set out in pursuit of Comanche raiders who had driven off horses from the Béxar area.

Joe Williams and two of Flacco's Lipans found a fresh trail several days later and raced back to alert Hays. The rangers rode hard for six miles and found the Comanches just breaking from camp. "We never even got to fire a gun," wrote Nichols. "They ran into the break, leaving everything." The rangers plundered the camp accoutrements, recovered the stolen horses and made their way back to San Antonio without incident.[51]

Life as a ranger on the Texas frontier was hard and pay for service was not even guaranteed for Hays' men in 1842. The men used their idle time to practice their skills and even bet each other on who was the fastest horseman. Jim Nichols—who soon returned home to Seguin when his original enlistment expired—wrote that Captain Hays' rangers fine-tuned their shooting skills by employing Comanche techniques.[52]

When one would come in, another would go out, and those not on a scout were every day practicing horsemanship and marksmanship. We put up a post about the size of a common man, then put up another about 40 yards farther on. We would run our horses full speed and discharge our rifles at the first post, draw our pistols and fire at the second. At first there was some wild shooting but we had not practiced two months until there was not many men would not put his balls in the center of the posts.

Then we drew a ring about the size of a man's head and soon every man could put both his balls in the circle. We would practice this a while, then try riding like the Comanche Indians. After practicing for three or four months we became so perfect that we would run our horses half or full speed and pick up a hat, a coat, a blanket, or rope, or even a silver dollar, stand up in the saddle, throw ourselves on the side of our horse with only a foot and a hand to be seen, and shoot our pistols under the horse's neck, rise up and reverse.

★ ★ ★ ★ ★

The Battle of Lipantitlán

The only other ranger company in operation during the summer of 1842 was the Corpus Christi company of Captain Ephraim McLean. He had been authorized to raise 56 men but McLean had only 22 men in service at the height of his company's strength in late May. When Adjutant General James Davis was appointed as commander of the southwestern frontier during the spring, he instructed McLean's rangers to report to him for orders. McLean, unable to raise enough men due to the lack of funds from the Texas government, was unable to comply with General Davis' order.[53]

Davis, charged with training and organizing volunteers to be ready for any renewed Mexican invasion, had his hands full maintaining the peace in the southwest region. Thieving parties and independent spy companies roamed the region without submitting to any authority. One such company was that of Captain James P. Ownby, who had been authorized by President Lamar to raise a company of rangers in 1841 in San Patricio County. His renegade cowboys bickered so much over spoils of battle that his company was soon broken up and half of the men were captured by Mexican soldiers. Ownby had escaped back into Texas, where he proceeded to operate his own independent company under no authority.

As General Davis worked to organize volunteer companies coming in from the United States, he received orders from President Houston on May 31. "We cannot permit the rogues any longer to frequent our frontier," he ordered. "We must punish them. You will have Captain McLean and Hays' command put a stop to such atrocious villanies [sic] as have been practiced on our South Western frontier."[54]

Davis began trying to form U.S. volunteer companies into an official army during May in accordance to a proclamation from Houston. Major John J. B. Hoxey, who arrived with a company from Georgia, was elected commander of the First Battalion of Texas Volunteers. Hoxey turned command of his company over to Captain William R. Shivers and another of Hoxey's men, William H. Hughes, was appointed as the battalion's adjutant on June 1 by General Davis.[55]

Mexican traders, who regularly visited Henry Kinney's post on Corpus Christi Bay, encountered troubles with the growing number of Texan forces in the southwest. A group of volunteers under Major Augustus Williams seized a party of 20 traders in May and stripped them of all their property. When General Davis arrived in the area, he held the traders under arrest and informed Sam Houston. The president instructed Davis to release them and to allow their trading to resume for any goods excepting munitions of war. Houston further directed that Captain McLean's Corpus Christi rangers should escort the Mexican traders to the Rio Grande.[56]

Davis released the traders but his men kept their supplies. McLean, disgusted by the jockeying for power among the various forces in the area, wrote a note to General Davis on June 8: "I have been in readiness and willing at any time to discharge any duty to forward the desires of the executive or yourself but everything appears to work backwards. To be called upon 25 or 30 mi. from camp to return and wait the movements of committees to carry into effect the orders of the executive is more than I am willing to stand any longer." McLean threatened to discharge his rangers and return home, although he ultimately changed his mind.[57]

The regional commander of the Mexican Army, Colonel Antonio Canales, received word from his spies in June 1842 that more than 400 Texan troops had assembled near Corpus Christi. Canales feared that the Texan cavalrymen might attack Camargo and opted to hit them first. He assembled an assault force of some 700 cavalrymen and infantrymen, many of whom were volunteer armed rancheros. Colonel Canales' forces marched to confront General Davis' army at the settlement of Lipantitlán.[58]

When the Mexican troops reached Lipantitlán on July 7, James Davis' forces were in poor condition. Few provisions and poor drinking water had compelled many of his men to desert in the prior weeks. Although a force of another 220 men was en route over water from Galveston to join him, Davis had but 192 men on the Nueces River as of July 7. His command of mainly companies raised in the United States included: Company A from New Orleans under Captain H. H. Brower; Company B from Mobile under Lieutenant N. H. Birmingham; Company C from Memphis and the remnants of Company E from Mississippi, commanded by Captain Henry W. Allen; Company D from Galveston under Lt. E. T. Fox; Company F from Georgia under Captain William Shivers; and the mounted gunman company of Captain Ewen Cameron from the Corpus Christi area.[59]

The muster rolls for Cameron's gunmen have not survived but men known to have served under him during July 1842 include: first lieutenant Alfred Allee, second lieutenant Alfred S. Thurmond, orderly sergeant John S. Browning and privates Nathan Burkett, Beverly C. Greenwood, Gideon K. Lewis, John Lowe, Exum Luter, Peter Rouche, William Rupley, Achilles Stapp, Thomas P. Tatum, Robert W. Turner, A. Walker, Henry D. Weeks, James Wilkinson and Melville Wilkinson.[60]

As Canales' troops approached the Texan camp on the afternoon of July 6, General Davis abandoned his camp and fortified his men in a high bluff on the Nueces River. The Mexican forces opened fire on the Texans after daylight on July 7. The Texans withheld their fire until the cavalrymen were within 60 yards before shooting a number of them from their saddles. The ill-trained Mexican rancheros caused little casualties with their muskets and the cavalry charge was soon repulsed.[61]

In mid-afternoon, Colonel Cayetano Montero's four-pound cannon was advanced to within 250 yards of the Texans on the

Nueces. A Texan named Ferguson scored a lucky shot with a long rifle which downed the Mexican artillery detachment's commander. The Mexican cannon broke free from its carriage after its first shots and was finally withdrawn from the battlefield at 4:00 p.m. The Mexican infantry opted not to pursue the Texans into the woods and the brief battle of Lipantitlán was ended. Colonel Canales claimed that his men had killed 22 Texans, but Davis' men had suffered only one Texan slightly wounded. The Mexicans claimed only four soldiers killed and two wounded but blood trails on the battlefield and three bodies left behind made the Texans believe that they had killed or wounded at least 30.[62]

Colonel Canales' men had plundered the abandoned Texan camp but even these supplies were not enough to sustain a single company. The Mexican forces therefore began their march from the vicinity of Lipantitlán toward Camargo on the morning of July 8. Captain Cameron's cowboy gunmen had handled themselves well in this fight and Colonel Canales would later make him pay dearly for his bravado.[63]

The Mexican forces fell back toward the Rio Grande and General Davis' battalion began to fall back toward Live Oak Point, where they arrived on July 15. Captain Cameron and his 50 mounted rangers took up a station at Refugio to monitor the movements of Canales. General Davis returned to Houston, resigned from service on July 28 and his companies were soon disbanded.[64]

San Patricio County remained a troubled area during the summer and the citizens around Victoria pledged to defend their own ground without moving away in fear. Captain Cameron's 50-man ranger unit was encamped a few miles above Victoria at Governor's Pass on the Guadalupe River as of August 24. Ewen Cameron's mounted gunmen grew in size from less than 30 men at one point to more than 70 by September 1842. He had resisted Mexican forces in southwest Texas since first joining Captain John Price's rangers in January 1841.[65]

John Henry Brown, who served with Captain Hays' rangers during the summer of 1842, later wrote that Captain Cameron's company ranged "in the country from Victoria to the Nueces in the southwest. They were called cowboys, as they subsisted on such wild cattle, deer and other game as they could kill. Cameron was a fine specimen of the old Highland chiefs of Scotland."[66]

Captain Ewen Cameron (1811–1843) commanded a company of Corpus Christi mounted gunmen during the summer of 1842. Born in Scotland, Cameron came to Texas in 1836 and became known as a famed leaders of "cowboys" who protected the southwestern frontier in the early 1840s. His company participated in the battle of Lipantitlan and was taken prisoner following the battle of Mier. Cameron was later executed in 1843 by his Mexican captors. *"Shooting of Captain Cameron" frontispiece illustration from General Thomas J. Green's Journal of the Texian Expedition Against Mier, courtesy of Texas State Library and Archives Commission.*

By the late fall of 1842, talks became serious of making an offensive into Mexico and Captain Cameron's gunmen were ready for the challenge. The *Telegraph and Texas Register* praised the veteran ranger in its September 14 edition as "a bold and chivalrous leader who already by his valor and military skill promises to become the Bruce of the West, a soldier worthy of the most heroic of his Scottish ancestors."[67]

★ ★ ★ ★ ★

Ranger Actions: Summer 1842

The poorly-disciplined and half-starved soldiers of the volunteer Texas Army were allowed to return to their homes soon after turning back Canales at Lipantitlán. President Houston and the Texas Congress did not make any immediate efforts to set up an efficient military system to handle any further incursions by Mexican forces. By the end of summer, the frontier was protected by only a handful of companies which ranged from Corpus Christi to San Antonio.[68]

Captain Cameron's Corpus Christi mounted gunmen continued to operate in the southwest throughout the summer as unpaid volunteers. Captain Jack Hays' San Antonio rangers continued to make scouting expeditions and monitor the peace in their region. During June, several other companies were in operation under Colonel Clark L. Owen of Texana. Six companies of mounted volunteers had been organized in March in response to the Vasquez invasion. Their captains were John P. Gill, Albert C. Horton, John S. Menefee, John Rugeley, John M. Smith and Lafayette Ward. The companies of captains Horton and Rugeley were discharged on April 13, but the other four remained under Colonel Owen's direction through June 6.[69]

San Antonio remained largely abandoned during the summer of 1842 aside from Hays' rangers, small numbers of Tejanos and some town officials. Even the town's artillery had been removed during the Vasquez invasion. Béxar's brass six-pounder and another cannon acquired from the United States were still in Gonzales as of late June according to a report given by Secretary of War George Hockley on June 23.[70]

Many of the Anglo-American families refused to return to San Antonio during the summer due to the marauding by both Anglo and Mexican forces through the area during the preceding months. Tejanos who remained in Béxar were confident that former mayor Juan Seguín would revisit their town soon with a large detachment of Mexican troops. Dissension ensued in town council meetings during the summer between the Anglo-Texans representatives and the Tejano representatives. At the July 16, meeting the three Tejano and five Anglo aldermen voted to dismiss two Anglo councilmen. New major John Smith declared the vote moot since two of the Anglo aldermen had moved out of the city and he opted to call for a vote for two new councilmen.[71]

For the first new position, Anglo John Twohig (a recent Hays ranger) was posed against Tejano Francisco Granada in the voting. The vote was again split, with the three remaining Tejano councilmen voting for Granada and the three Anglos voting for Twohig. Smith sided with the Tejanos to help ease tensions and Granada became a San Antonio councilman. For the second seat, the voting was between Twohig and another Hays ranger, Cornelius Van Ness. This time, one of the Tejano councilmen joined the Anglo in giving Twohig the majority vote. Twohig, however, declared himself unable to serve at the swearing in and yet another vote ensued in which Van Ness (favored by all four Tejanos) won out over former Juan Seguín rival James Goodman.[72]

The Anglo and Tejano councilmen remained divided over

other issues during their July meeting. Alderman Cayetano Rivas introduced a bill aimed at cutting taxes in half for merchants bringing their carts into San Antonio. Rivas was a proud citizen of San Antonio, having been born in that city in 1810, who had fought for Texas during the revolution years earlier. The four Tejano councilmen all voted for the tax decrease while three of their Anglo cohorts voted against it. Such close voting was indicative of the strained bonds between the Anglos and Tejanos remaining in Béxar during the summer.[73]

Edward Burleson returned home to the Bastrop area from the capital in Houston during July for a few weeks. Small parties of Indians had committed raids on the Colorado River settlements and the indomitable frontiersman opted to take a party of volunteers into the field on expedition until the next Congress was called to session. Around August 5, Burleson took about 80 men out to scour the upper Colorado for Indians.[74]

Bartlett Sims was later paid as orderly sergeant of Burleson's command for the period of August 5–September 20, 1842, "on an expedition up the Colorado River." Interestingly, Burleson signed this voucher as "Comdt. of Rangers." Reuben Hornsby and George J. Durham's pension papers, also signed by Burleson, were for service as a "ranger" on this expedition.[75]

Burleson's muster roll has not survived but extant public debt papers show some of the other men who made this expedition to be: Robert G. Anderson, Jonathan Burleson, David C. Cady, William R. Cannon, George J. Durham, Joseph Gray, Thomas J. Green, George Hancock, Anderson J. Harrell, John Harrell, Reuben Hornsby, Alfred W. Luckett, James H. Matthews, Cicero Rufus Perry, Hutchinson Reed, James Rogers, Asa Savery, Josephus Scott, Charles Shepherd, William Simmons, Donald Smith, James Smith, Noah Smithwick, Achilles Stapp, John Taney, Horace L. Upshur, Thomas F. Webb, Martin Jones Wells, Samuel C. Whiting Jr., William Wilkes, and Thomas M. Woolridge.[76]

The expedition went up the Colorado to the San Saba River. Horace Upshur wrote a letter to Matthew Woodhouse in Austin on August 27 from the expedition. "Some 13 of us gave the Indians hell the other day in a chase of two days over this level country just about Austin—delightful ride," Upshur wrote. "Genl. Burleson with some 60 or 70 men has gone up after them and I am in hopes will do 'something for his country.'"[77]

Burleson's volunteer rangers "scoured the whole country watered by the Pedernales" without finding any serious Indian encampments or getting any battles. His command returned to Bastrop and were discharged on September 20.[78]

Rufus Perry later wrote that he "started with Ed Burleson on an expedition against Indians, found but one party, ran them thirty miles, but could not catch up with them. We was out one month and the day that we got back to Bastrop we found all of the men gone to meet the Mexicans under Woll who had taken San Antonio."

★ ★ ★ ★ ★

By early July, Clark Owen still had a number of volunteers operating under his direction and he was ordered to collect all the ammunition and government supplies along the Victoria-Refugio-Corpus Christi frontier from the breakup of General Davis' expedition. Late in July, Jack Hays made a quick trip to the temporary capital of Houston, where the youthful-looking 25-year-old leader checked into a hotel. Some of those who encountered the much-praised ranger leader were surprised by his young appearance and unbearded face. Hays left the hotel, met with President Houston, and was on his way back toward San Antonio the following day.[79]

Hays' short meeting obviously had its desired effect of raising more rangers. The Texas Congress passed another joint resolution on July 23, directing President Houston to accept one company of volunteers to range the frontier on the Trinity and Navasota rivers. These rangers were to equip themselves for a tour of not less than two months. The same resolution authorized two ranging companies for the southwestern frontier and set aside two thousand dollars to keep these companies in operation.[80]

Jack Hays was promoted to the rank of major commanding two companies: his own and that of Captain Antonio Menchaca, who was to act between the San Antonio River and the Rio Grande. Menchaca could not find enough volunteers to even fill one small spy company. Menchaca, a San Jacinto veteran, had commanded a spy company in 1836–1837 under the direction of Juan Seguín. Audited claims of Antonio Menchaca show that he was paid $271.86 as "Captain of Cavalry" from July 1 through

September 11, 1842. His costs included clothing, rations, one servant and forage for only three horses, indicative of how vain his efforts were to raise rangers. Any muster roll that may have existed for his small Tejano ranging company appears to have been lost over time.[81]

San Antonio, like other western settlements of Texas, was still suffering from the effects of the earlier raid on the town. Settlers were still apprehensive of another raid by Mexican forces and many of the frontier families had not elected to return to this area. When it became clear that Menchaca was unable to raise a ranging company, the Secretary of War and Marine instructed Major Hays to increase his own company to 150 men, all well mounted and armed, to defend the entire country south to the Rio Grande. Hays, however, found it almost impossible to raise a sufficient force of rangers. Men who had served under him during the past 18 months were literally destitute. They had lost horses, clothing and weapons while in service and had received no payments in return. Men who might be able to enlist were too poor to pay for the horses and arms required for them to be accepted as rangers.[82]

Hays tried recruiting more men as he rode from Houston back to San Antonio, moving through the Guadalupe County settlements. He found that the western settlers had little interest in ranging when there was no immediate crisis. Hays found his own company as difficult to bring to full muster as Menchaca had found. The September 7, 1842, edition of the *Telegraph and Texas Register* reported that Major Hays' company scarcely totaled 50 men, only one-third of his allowed strength.[83]

Sam Houston wrote to Clark Owen on September 2, giving him instructions that Owen and Major Hays at San Antonio were to look after the peace and safety of the frontier. The president encouraged these leaders to open the frontier to trade with Mexico. The movement of such traders would help the people of the frontier and afford the rangers the opportunity to obtain reliable information about the movements and intentions of Mexican troops.[84]

Peter Hansbrough Bell would write a letter in October 1842, calling for ranging companies to operate between the Nueces and Rio Grande, from the Agua Dulce, "or even from the Coast" to handle the movements of Mexican forces. Bell recommended that the government should support these rangers, but no actions were taken to help create the desired units.[85]

The Secretary of War would note in his November 12, 1842, report of the difficulties faced by the ranging service.[86]

> Few men could be found at once able to mount and equip themselves and willing to enter a service which promised little else than fatigue and danger. Those who were willing to enlist were for the most part utterly destitute of means to fit themselves for the field; the government was equally so—it could neither furnish the means to equip and mount a force, nor sustain them for any length of time when in the field.

★ ★ ★ ★ ★

Comanche Empire

The absence of a clear and present danger posed on the Texas frontier by the various Native American tribes only added to the woes of Ranger commanders who desired to recruit new men. Aside from the occasional reports of a depredation attributed to them, the Comanches maintained relative peace during 1842. By this time, there were four main Comanche divisions on the southern plains: the Kotsotekas (Buffalo Eaters), the Yamparikas (Yampa-Root-Eaters), the Hois (Timber People), and the Tenewas (translated roughly as "those who stay downstream").[87]

From their early days in Texas, the Tenewas were led by an influential Comanche named Chief Paruakevitsi (Little Bear), an influential man who had exerted considerable energy toward peace with the Mexican government in earlier years. In 1829, Paruakevitsi had met with high-ranking Mexican officials in New Mexico to accept gifts for his people in exchange for peace. By 1830, however, the gifts were reduced and peace was lost to violence in New Mexico and neighboring Chihuahua to the point that Mexican authorities soon cut all commercial ties to the Comachería and declared a general war with the Comanches.[88]

During the late 1830s, Hois and Tenewas had suffered major losses to Lipán and Texas raiders, while the Kotsotekas and Yamparikas had faced their own threats from central plains raiders. By 1840, however, Comanches and Kiowas had made peace with their former Cheyenne and Arapaho enemies, exchanging guns, beads, ammunition, horses, blankets and other goods in signs of their new friendship. The four key Comanche divisions had also cooperated at times with Tawakoni and Shoshones on the southern plains to maintain their territorial security. By September 1840, the allied bands began plundering across the Rio Grande into Mexico to steal horses and mules for trading. The Comanches and Kiowas sent twice as many large raids below the Rio Grande between 1840 and 1847 as they had in the previous eight years.[89]

The most prominent Hois raider to emerge from the campaigns into Mexico was Chief Potsanaquahip, whose Comanche name "male buffalo" was commonly translated as Buffalo Hump. More than one Comanche war leader had been called Buffalo Hump, as evidenced by the chief of the same name who had been slain in Captain John Bird's Comanche fight of 1839. Potsanaquahip—who was also known to Texas frontiersman as Buffalo Hump—was in his early thirties by 1842 and he had long enjoyed a reputation for sound leadership and bravery in combat. Following his tribe's bitter losses in the Council House Massacre of 1840, Buffalo Hump had led the large campaign which plundered the Victoria and Linnville areas and fought at Plum Creek.[90]

Buffalo Hump's Hois division of the Comanche would be the most prominently intertwined with Texas frontiersmen during the early 1840s. Following the death of Chief Muguara at the 1840 Council House Massacre, the senior leaders of the Hois were Chiefs Pahayuco (Amorous Man) and Mopechucope (Old Owl). These two elders eventually saw the value of maintaining a dialogue with Texas leaders while Potsanaquahip favored a different approach.[91]

The other prominent Hois war leader to emerge in the 1840s aside from Potsanaquahip was Chief Pia Kusa, whose name translated to "Big Leggins." Pia Kusa had been involved in various conflicts with Texas frontiersmen and during the late Republic years he became known to Mexicans and Texans as "Santa Anna," perhaps because it was a name his people thought Texans would hold in dread. Like Buffalo Hump, Pia Kusa would remain staunchly opposed to treating with the Texans although most of his warlike reputation was earned during his leadership of raids into Mexico during the 1840s.[92]

Comanche population likely peaked at forty thousand in the late 1770s but warfare and epidemics claimed thousands of lives in the decades that followed. By the 1840s, the Comanchería's population was closer to twenty thousand people.[93]

The decline of bison on the southern plains due to overhunting increased the Comanche campaigns into Mexico during the early 1840s. The herds of captured horses and mules kept on the southern plains by the Comanches and Kiowas added to the difficulties of the bison to find sufficient grazing areas to sustain life. One New Mexican official would comment in 1843 that the increasing Comanche raids into Mexican territory was due in large to the vanishing bison herds.[94]

CHAPTER 3

Woll Seizes Béxar

August–Sept. 1842

President Santa Anna was intent on restoring the territory of Texas to Mexico during the summer of 1842 and he urged his Congress to approve a new campaign. He sent orders on June 5 to the new commander in chief of the Army of the North, General Isidro Reyes, to prepare for another attack upon San Antonio. The July battle at Lipantitlán against Texan forces delayed this initiative but Reyes was active during late July and August in recruiting men and supplies to carry out these orders.[1]

General Adrian Woll, a French-born senior officer of Mexico's Army of the North, would lead a division of the army to retake San Antonio. The 47-year-old, now a naturalized Mexican citizen, had fought in many independence fights for his new country, including the Texas Revolution. Woll crossed the Rio Grande at Presidio with his Second Division and made his way toward Béxar. Woll issued a proclamation on August 30, 1842, to a Mexican force camped on the left bank of the Rio Bravo, in which he called for the second invasion of Texas of the year. He asked these troops to march to San Antonio and reclaim the former province. These Mexican forces moved toward San Antonio with ease as there were no ranging units operating at the time to intercept them.[2]

William "Big Foot" Wallace knew most of San Antonio inhabitants by sight and he reported to Major Hays at this time that there had been at least a dozen strange Mexicans about town.

One of these Mexican spies was Cristobal Rubio, a villain who was wanted for crimes in both Seguin and San Antonio. Wallace reported that Rubio was rumored to be hiding 9 miles down the river at the Mission San Juan Capistrano.[3]

Major Hays gathered 20 of his rangers and rode for the Mission to arrest Rubio and his companions in early September. Two of Rubio's spies were captured at the Mission San Juan Capistrano. When Hays returned with them, the San Antonio townspeople called for their execution. Hays instead said that his prisoners were to be taken to Seguin for trial for their crimes in that settlement. The San Antonio citizens were irate and confrontational with the rangers.[4]

Major Hays sent the two prisoners toward Seguin with two of his trusted rangers, John Lee and William Hesskew, guarding the prisoners. Hays' company followed as an escort until the company was well away from town. Lee and Hesskew then proceeded alone toward Seguin with their two prisoners. They halted after midnight and tied their prisoners securely. Hesskew's prisoner, a wily ranchero, managed to untie himself during the night as the rangers slept near their horses.[5]

The ranchero quietly untied Hesskew's horse, led it away and then mounted it. John Lee awoke the next morning to the sound of approaching horsemen. Hesskew also discovered that both his prisoner and horse had disappeared during his slumber. The rangers, at first fearful that San Antonio citizens were intent on taking their prisoners, quickly realized that the approaching riders were Mexican marauders who had been alerted by their own escaped prisoner. Lee decided they would have to flee for their lives and give up their other prisoner. Lee drew his pistol, shot the Mexican bandit through the chest, and the two rangers raced for San Antonio on his horse.[6]

Three other Mexican spies were captured near the Guadalupe and one gave the startling information that at least 50 San Antonio Mexican-born citizens were conspiring against the white settlers. The informant claimed that the Tejanos had helped conduct raids in the vicinity of Austin, Gonzales and Bastrop, blaming each on marauding Indians. Further evidence of Mexican loyalty was the fact that by late summer, men of Mexican descent could obtain ammunition freely from traders while Anglo-Americans could not. The Vasquez raid had compelled the San Antonio merchants to destroy all of their powder, so Hays dispatched two of his rangers—Bigfoot Wallace and Nathan Mallon—to the government arsenal in Austin for powder, caps and lead.[7]

Wallace and Mallon reached Austin, where they helped bury the bodies of two men—Captain William Y. Pyron, who had commanded a company in 1836–37, and Donovan—who had been killed by Indians outside of town. The rangers could only procure small quantities of lead and caps and one barrel of gunpowder in Austin. Mallon rolled the caps and lead in a blanket and Wallace did the same with the powder barrel, strapping each precious bundle to the pommels of their saddles. The rangers rode the 70-odd miles of open country back toward Seguin, stopping in Seguin in order to acquire corn for their horses.[8]

In San Antonio, former ranger Antonio Perez warned Mayor John W. Smith on September 9 that a Mexican force of 1,500 soldiers was approaching town. Another San Antonio Mexican received similar intelligence which was communicated to Antonio Menchaca—who spread the word to Judge Anderson Hutchinson and Captain Hays. In a town meeting on September 10, the people decided to fortify the town and temporarily halt the case of *Shields Booker vs. the City of San Antonio*. The former Texas Army surgeon was suing former San Antonio mayor Juan Seguín for a fee of 50 pesos which had been promised him.[9]

The reports of approaching Mexican forces were alarming enough to cause the citizens to organize their forces. The able-bodied men were split into two forces, with Captain Salvador Flores commanded approximately 100 Tejanos and Captain Chauncey Johnson commanding 75 Anglo-Texans. Jack Hays assumed overall command of the forces, stationing Flores' Mexican group in the old courthouse and Johnson's men in the Samuel Maverick residence at the northwest corner of the Alamo mission quadrangle. Flores sent out a group of spies that day who reported on the approach of Woll's advance guard.[10]

The muster roll for Captain Flores' company, if one was formally drawn up, has not survived to preserve the names of the Tejanos who joined him. José María Rodríquez, however, would later write that his father Ambrosio Rodríquez—a veteran of the battle of San Jacinto—joined Antonio Menchaca in this Tejano company, which was stationed "in the old court house on the corner of Market and Main Plaza."[11]

Capt. Johnson's San Antonio Volunteers Captured on September 11, 1842 and Held Prisoner by General Woll

Captain:
Chauncey Johnson
First Lieutenant:
Archibald Fitzgerald *
Second Lieutenant:
William Bugg *
First Sergeant:
Robert S. Neighbors *
Second Lieutenant:
James L. Trueheart *
Third Sergeant:
John Lee *
Fourth Sergeant:
Nathaniel Harbert *

Privates:
Isaac Allen *
Horace Alexander Alsbury
Truman B. Beck *
Shields Booker
Edward Brown
James H. Brown *
Ludovic Colquhoun
Joseph [Jose] A. Cruz
John R. Cunningham
John Dalrymple
David J. Davis
Gustav Elley *
John Forester
Simon Glenn
French Strother Gray
Thomas Hancock *
George C. Hatch
Anderson Hutchinson
William E. Jones
John Lamon *
A. F. Leslie
Francis McKay
Samuel Augustus Maverick
David Morgan
Joseph C. Morgan
Andrew Neill
S. A. Nobles
Samuel G. Norvell *
Duncan C. Ogden
William H. O'Phelan
John Perry
Cornelius W. Peterson
Marcus L. B. Rapier *
John Riddle
Wilson Irwin Riddle
James W. Robinson
George Schaeffer
John Smith *
Samuel Stone
John C. Trapnell *
John Twohig
George Van Ness
Johann George Andreas Voss *
John Young *

* Served as a ranger under Captain Jack Hays during 1841 or 1842 prior to Woll's capture of San Antonio.

Source: Nance, *Attack and Counter-Attack,* 600–603.

Note: Author has been unable to locate a muster roll for Captain Salvador Flores' 100-man Tejano unit.

Around 7:00 p.m., Jack Hays and five of his rangers departed town to reconnoiter Woll's troops while another messenger was sent toward the Guadalupe settlements to raise men. As other scouts went out during the night and early morning of September 11, Captain Johnson's Anglo-Texan company was reduced from 75 men to less than 60 men in town as Woll approached.[12]

Jack Hays' scouts went out south along the Laredo road, but Woll's troops had outfoxed him by first going west and then circling through the rough country north of San Antonio, staying off the main roads. While Hays was scouting south of Béxar, the Mexican troops slipped quietly in from the north on September 10 and prepared to invade San Antonio.[13]

On the morning of September 11, 1,300 cavalrymen and artillerymen under Woll surrounded San Antonio, and took the city with only a few shots being fired. District court was in session and Woll took the entire court—including the lawyers, clerks and judges of Captain Johnson's unit—as prisoners. The citizens and some of the volunteers under Salvador Flores surrendered with little resistance. Antonio Menchaca was angry to see that many of the Flores Tejanos fled the city as the Mexican Army marched in. The remainder of Captain Flores' men and 52 of Captain Johnson's company were soon taken prisoner.[14]

Jack Hays reconnoitered the Mexican forces in company with James Robinson. The famed ranger leader reportedly put on a Mexican blanket to disguise himself and rode near the Mexican lines in the early morning to count their forces. Hays then dispatched Robinson to ride east to other Texas settlements to carry the news that Woll's army had come in force.[15]

When Woll took possession of San Antonio, he had six scouts he had captured. One of them was Jesus Hernandez, who had gone out to scout under Captain Hays' orders. Hernandez and his five companions "were all taken prisoner, tied with rope and brought back to San Antonio to be shot." They were thrown in the city jail but later managed to escape during the confusion as Woll's troops took over the city.[16]

Woll released some of the Tejano loyalists to warn others. Word reached Hays, who began gathering troops at Seguin, 30 miles east of San Antonio. Hays wrote two reports on September 12 concerning the capture of San Antonio. He said that he had gone to find the enemy, failed, and returned to find that Woll had taken the city and taken 53 citizens prisoner. Hays pledged to keep scouting for other Mexican forces and called for well-mounted men to join him for the purpose of spying. Hays said that he had captured a Mexican that day who told him that the Mexican forces planned to fortify San Antonio and wait for reinforcements.[17]

Hays recommended that Texan reinforcements should rendezvous at Seguin and attack any raiding parties that the Mexican troops might send out. In a second letter written from Seguin on September 12, Hays detailed that he and five of his scouts had approached San Antonio the previous day but were unable to enter town. He had therefore left his spies stationed near town and had ridden to Seguin to help organize other forces.[18]

Mayor Smith had managed to escape his Mexican captors and he sent a message to Mathew Caldwell at Gonzales, who personally rode out to begin spreading the word for volunteers. Couriers were sent to begin spreading the word to Seguin, La Grange, Houston and other towns, calling for citizens to come to the defense of San Antonio. Blacksmith William Small, who lived eight miles below Béxar and had lost his wagon and oxen to Mexicans, rode to spread the news to La Grange.[19]

Reverend Zachariah Morrell—who had only returned to his hometown in Gonzales the previous week—was gathering corn from his fields on the Guadalupe that morning when Mathew Caldwell rode up with an express from San Antonio. The note, from John W. Smith, stated, "General Woll has arrived at San Antonio with thirteen hundred men. The court—judge, jury, lawyers—and many citizens in attendance, are prisoners in the hands of the Mexicans. I made my escape, and came round under the mountains to Seguin."[20]

"Something must be done quick," said Caldwell, "and you must go with me."

Leaving his son James to head east with their wagon load of corn, Reverend Morrell reluctantly consented to join Mathew Caldwell "on another perilous expedition." Ammunition was gathered at Gonzales and the able men from the town left with Caldwell for Seguin, leaving word for additional recruits from the east to follow their trail.[21]

Caldwell sent word that he had 125 men and wanted to double his forces before he marched against San Antonio. That size force had retaken San Antonio in 1835, he reminded people.

Caldwell called for lead and powder to provision his men and urged settlers to remain in their homes instead of fleeing. Concerning Woll's Mexican troops in San Antonio, Caldwell closed his dispatch with, "The enemy must be whipped. We have them where we want them."

CHAPTER 4

Salado Creek Battle: "Give Them Hell!"

September 18, 1842

When Reverend Zachariah [or Zacharius] Morrell reached Seguin on Monday, September 12, he assisted the volunteers in gathering ammunition to use in their attack on General Woll. Recruits poured into Seguin during Monday night. On Tuesday morning, Colonel Caldwell—the acting commander of all volunteers by their common consent—led his forces to within 20 miles of San Antonio. Caldwell had been vigilant in organizing men to assist San Antonio. "Capt. Caldwell himself came to my house after me," said Robert Hall, a veteran of the 1840 Plum Creek battle. "I joined him next day. He was camped on a creek about eighteen miles northeast of San Antonio."[1]

On Tuesday, September 12, Caldwell made a call for ten of the best horses and lightest riders to race ahead to meet Captain Hays on the Salado. One of these ten, Reverend Morrell, recalled, "He had notified us, by express, that he was there watching the enemy and needed reinforcements."[2]

The volunteers rode hard through the night from Seguin. They reached the rendezvous spot before dawn on September 13 and gave "a keen whistle," which was quickly responded to by Jack Hays. They found Hays and two rangers in camp 8 miles east of Salado Creek with nothing but a small supply of cold flour to eat. Mayor John Smith had been able to sneak back in town to find that the citizen prisoners had been moved. He believed that Woll's Mexican troops were in no hurry to depart San Antonio.[3]

Hays' 13 horsemen reconnoitered the Mexican forces during the next two days, attempting to see if other Mexican troops were coming in to reinforce Woll. Colonel Caldwell remained in camp with his volunteers about 20 miles east of San Antonio to insure that Mexican forces did not attempt a forced march on Gonzales. Hays' men were pursued by Mexican cavalrymen on the afternoon of Thursday, September 15, but Hays was unable to compel his opponents to fight when he had his rangers charge against them.[4]

On Friday morning, September 16, "a mutiny arose in our little camp, in consequence of the condition of our commissary department," Morrell wrote. "Plenty of deer and turkeys were in sight all the time, and we were all hunters; but our leader thought it best to fire no guns, and keep our position concealed from the enemy." After five days of nothing but rationed flour, the rangers were feeling "very lean. Now that the flour was out, our men began to swear vengeance on the game at all hazards."[5]

Hays asked Reverend Morrell to make a speech to calm his scouts. He mounted his horse and rode in front of the other dozen men, trying to assure the men that their starvation was not in vain. "Our situation this morning is critical," Morrell said. "The Mexicans, we fear, have gone toward Gonzales. Secrecy, surely, is the best policy and we ought to report the situation, if possible, to Colonel Caldwell tonight."

The men agreed to kill some game that night and then report their situation to Caldwell. En route to the main camp, Hays' men met Henry McCulloch and 13 other men. With their number now at 27, Hays' scouts soon learned from Caldwell's men that Woll's cavalry had retreated back into San Antonio. McCulloch's men had fresh beef hanging from their saddles. A new company was organized on the spot that day, with Captain Hays in command and Henry McCulloch voted in as the unit's first lieutenant. At the nearest watering hole, Morrell and his companions "refreshed ourselves with this delicious beef and a good night's rest" while encamped some 5 miles from San Antonio.[6]

Bigfoot Wallace and Nathan Mallon, returning from Austin with powder and lead, stop at Antonio Navarro's rancho to rest their horses. They found two of Hays' rangers, James Rice and Jack Johnson, who were sitting on the ground as Mexican women pulled cactus thorns from their feet. They learned from Rice and

Johnson that the Mexican cavalry had chased some of Hays' spies through the chaparral and prickly pear during their advance on San Antonio. Wallace and Mallon hurried on to Seguin to join Hays and McCulloch with their supplies.[7]

In his camp, Jack Hays received a message from President Houston, penned on September 14, which mentioned Houston's own friendship with Hays' father—a fact that likely had kept Hays on constant good terms with the president. "The situation of our frontier is very unhappy," Houston stated. He asked Hays to look into the possibility of reestablishing trade in the southwestern region and wrote another letter to Hays the following day requesting more details. "If possible, send me intelligence repeatedly, for I can hear nothing of what is going on at Béxar, or of what your prospects are."[8]

Before dawn on Saturday, September 17, Hays sent Morrell and three other scouts to go within sight of the city before daybreak. Hays took three other men and made another attempt to circle the city. Hays' men managed to capture a Mexican spy as their prisoner while Lt. McCulloch watched both roads leading to Seguin and Gonzales. Morrell's group also managed to capture a Mexican spy and they rode rapidly back to Colonel Caldwell's camp to report in.[9]

"The poor Mexican felt confident we intended to kill him, and on arrival at camp he recognized John W. Smith, and commenced begging for his life," Morrell reported. Hays and McCulloch had also ridden into Caldwell's camp, bringing in Hays' other captured Mexican horseman. By interrogating their two prisoners, the Texans learned the composition of Woll's forces. The entire Texan force numbered 202 men and they would be going against as many as 1,600 Mexican troops and Indians.[10]

Around 4:00 p.m. on Cíbolo Creek, Caldwell's Texas volunteers formed in line to elect general officers. Colonel Mathew Caldwell, a signer of the Texas Declaration of Independence, was overwhelmingly approved by the volunteers as their leader. Former ranger Canah Colley received 20 more votes than John Henry Brown to be the unit's adjutant and Dr. Caleb S. Brown from Gonzales was selected as surgeon. The other men were organized into companies under the captains of their choice, generally grouped by regions. Captain James Bird had 60 men from Gonzales; Captain Ewen Cameron took charge of 40 cowboys from Victoria whom he had commanded in June against Antonio Canales; Captain Daniel Friar led 35 men in from Cuero (Friar had been a ranger captain during the Texas Revolution and had commanded a company for six weeks under Burleson during the Vasquez campaign); and Captain Adam Zumwalt had 25 from Lavaca. Captain Hays had another 40 men with the best horses who were serving as scouts.[11]

Colonel Caldwell marched his forces closer to San Antonio on Saturday night, September 17. Nate Burkett of Cameron's company recalled, "We were soon on our way to a point on the Salado River about six miles east San Antonio, and made distance of some thirty-five miles during the night." While the troops were being organized, other reports were coming in from groups of Texans who were watching for signs of the Mexican forces. James D. Owen reported from Victoria that 40 Mexican troops had been spotted in the abandoned town of Goliad.[12]

Caldwell's volunteers first reached the Salado in the later afternoon on September 17, where they came upon scout John Smith and two of his companions. "Smith gave Caldwell the details of his reconnoiter in the enemy's camp," recalled Jim Nichols, a long-time ranger veteran. Caldwell then relayed the details from Smith concerning Woll's troops.[13]

They made camp around midnight about 6 miles northeast of San Antonio, fully expecting action the next day. Camp was made on the east bank of the Salado Creek adjacent to a ravine two miles above the Old San Antonio Crossing. One of Caldwell's men, Jim Nichols, recalled the casual atmosphere in the Texian camp that night: "After supper some of the boys had their blankets down and were playing cards. Others were in groups singing war songs and ditties. Others there were wrestling, running foot [races] or jumping. It was a fine moonlit night when [all at] once the bugle sounded for us to come together."[14]

That night, Caldwell called his forces together for a council of war and explained that he expected action with the Mexican forces in the morning. One of Captain Cameron's men was 21-year-old Nathan Boone Burkett, whose family was among the earliest settlers of DeWitt's Colony in Texas. He noted Colonel Caldwell, with a red handkerchief tied around his head, begin to roll up his sleeves. Caldwell then addressed his men by saying that the test had come for them.[15]

Battle of Salado: September 18, 1842
Gonzales, Seguin, Cuero Volunteers

Major General Commanding
Mathew Caldwell
Adjutant:
Canah C. Colley

Company Officers:
Captain James Bird
James H. Callahan, First Lt.
Captain Daniel Boone Friar
George Allen, First Lt.
Arthur Swift, Second Lt.

Volunteers:
Augustus C. Allen
Richard T. Barnett
Miles Squire Bennett
C. Bracher
Solomon W. Brill
Dr. Caleb S. Brown
G. S. Brown
William O. Burnham
Sam Callahan
Rev. Daniel Carl
James M. Clark
R. Clark
Simon Cockrill Jr.
James R. Cook
William Gordon Cooke
H. L. Conn
John A. Cummings
W. H. Cushing
David S. Darst
James Milford Day
Henry Clay Davis [1]
Rolla M. Davis
Samuel J. Denyer
Clinton E. Dewitt
Miles W. Dikes
Nicholas W. Eastland
James Edmondson
Horace Eggleston [1]
Andrew A. Erskine
John P. Erskine
Stuart Tucker Foley [1]
James T. Foster
Alfred L. Friar
James Gibson
Philip Golden
John A. Green
Robert Hall
George Hancock
John Hemphill
Mark B. Hemphill
William Hesskew
David Hodges
John S. Hodges
Josephus Hornsby
Memucan Hunt
Van B. Irion
Stephen Jett [2]
Archibald Jones
Isham G. Jones
Daniel J. Kiger
Henry B. King
John R. King
William G. King
____ Lavala (from VA)
William Lindsay
Byrd Lockhart
William R. Lockhart
Samuel Luckie
Morris May
Green McCoy [1]
T. N. Mentor
Lewis Moore
Thomas A. Moore
Zachariah N. Morrell [1]
James Wilson Nichols
John W. Nichols
Benjamin B. Peck
William Polk [1]
Ben Powers
Joseph Powers
James Ramsay
Barney Randle
Wilson Randle
James O. Rice [1]
B. C. Robertson
Byrd Smith
Ezekiel Smith
French Smith
John W. Smith
Peter D. Smith
Andrew Sowell
Daniel C. Sullivan
James Taylor [1]
Josiah Taylor [1]
Pitkin Taylor [1]
Rufus Taylor [1]
William Taylor
William D. Thomas
William Tomlinson
Calvin S. Turner
J. Hardin Turner
William Turner
William A. A. Wallace
_____ White
Ozwin Willcox
John Wilson
Simeon P. Witt
Robert S. Woolfolk
Jesse Zumwalt

[1] Joined Capt. Hays as volunteer on 9/18/42.
[2] Killed in battle.

Capt. Hays' Rangers: September 1842–January 7, 1843

Captain:
John Coffee Hays
First Lieutenant:
Henry E. McCulloch
Second Lieutenant:
Ephraim Walton McLean
Orderly Sergeant:
James W. Henderson
Privates:
Christopher Blck Acklin
Andrew Adams
William Adams
Powhatan Archer
Marshall B. Bennett
Harrison W. Berry
Tilman Berry
William Bowen
James H. Brown *
Julian C. Calhoun
George Wilson Clark
Antonio Coy
Gustav Elley *
John P. Erskine
Archibald Fitzgerald *
Thomas Galbreath
Peter Gallagher
Archibald Gibson
Robert Addison Gillespie
Eli S. Hankins
Nathaniel Harbert *
Jesus Hernandez *
William Alexander Hesskew
Eli C. (Clem) Hinds
Riley Jackson *
John Richard (Jack) Johnson
Augustus H. Jones
John Lee *
Nathaniel Mallon
Benjamin McCulloch
John McMullen
Zachariah N. Morrell
Robert Simpson Neighbors *
George Jefferson Neill
William Sanders Oury
Franklin L. Paschal
Marcus L. B. Rapier *
James O. Rice
Montrevell C. Roundtree
Arthur Sherrill
John Smith *
William Smothers
Guy S. Stokes
Creed Taylor
John Twohig *
William A. A. Wallace
George W. Walton
John C. Yates

Joined Capt. Hays after Salado:
William Alsbury
Henry Bridger [1]
John Henry Brown
Rufus Cannon [1]
H. G. Catlett [1]
Nereus Dufner [1]
James Dunn [1]
Horace Eggleston
H. Stuart Foley [1]
Mason B. Foley [1]
Beverly C. Greenwood [1]
Hudson A. Greenwood [1]
John W. Hinch [1]
William Hudgeons [1]
P. W. Humphreys [1]
George E. Hunter [1]
William C. S. Hunter [1]
James Matthew Jett [1]
John Himes Livergood [1]
D. H. Lyons [1]
Isaac N. Mitchell
Amos Moore [1]
Cicero Rufus Perry [2]
Thomas S. Pinckney [3]
William R. Rector [1]
S. T. Slater [1]
Jacob Woodward [1]
Edward D. Wright [4]
Isaac K. Zumwalt [1]

* Captured at San Antonio on 9/11/42.

1 Enrolled October 25, 1842.
2 Enrolled October 17, 1842.
3 Enrolled October 24, 1842.
4 Enrolled Oct. 17, 1842. Transfer to Capt. Cameron's company 12/19/42.

Source: Author's study of audited military claims of the Republic of Texas.

Capt. Cameron's Victoria Company: September 1842 (40 men)

Captain:
Ewen Cameron
First Lieutenant:
John Reagan Baker
Second Lieutenant:
Alfred Allee

Privates:
John S. Browning
Nathan Boone Burkett
Thomas Washington Cox
Cyrus Washburn Egery
Beverly C. Greenwood
George W. Guthrie
Samuel Highsmith
Gideon K. Lewis
George Lord
John Lowe
Patrick H. Lusk
Exter Luter
Peter Rouche
William Rupley
Solomon Simmons
Joseph F. Smith
Achilles Stapp
Thomas P. Tatum
Alfred Sturgis Thurmond
Robert W. Turner
A. Walker
Henry D. Weeks
Henry A. Whalen
James Wilkinson
Melville Wilkinson

Source: Incomplete roster is based on author's study of audited military claims of the Republic of Texas and secondary published sources, including John Henry Brown's *History of Texas*, II: 217.

Capt. Zumwalt's Lavaca Company: September 1842 (38 men)

Captain:
Adam Zumwalt
First Lieutenant:
Oliver H. Stapp
Second Lieutenant:
Nicholas J. Ryan
Orderly Sergeant:
John Henry Brown

Privates:
Charles Bradley
John Bradley
Henry Bridger
Anthony Brown
James S. Brown
Joshua D. Brown
Rufus E. Brown
James Lawrence Cherry
Samuel G. Cherry
George Wilson Clark
Henry Cleveland
Nereus Dufner
"Gutter Face" Green
Beverly C. Greenwood
Hudson A. Greenwood
Thomas W. Hunt
Russell Jones
David B. Kent
Isaac Kent
John V. Law
John Himes Livergood
William M. Phillips
Henry Ryan
Joseph Ryan
Jonathan Scott
John Pius Smith
William Smothers
Stapleton Townsend
Wilson Vandyke
George W. Walton
Wingate Woodley
Andrew Zumwalt
Isaac K. Zumwalt
Thomas B. Zumwalt

"Boys, I have longed to see the day when I would have a chance to fight these rascals, ever since I spent some time in a Mexican prison," said Caldwell. "Now boys, the time has come, and I do not want you to shoot until you can see the whites of their eyes. If every one of you will pick your men and make a sure shot, we will whip hell out of them before they know it."

Reverend Morrell wrote that Caldwell and his men decided in the council of war that it would not be prudent to attack Woll's forces in their fortifications. They would instead try to decoy the Mexicans and Indians onto more neutral ground before attacking, "although the enemy outnumbered eight to our one."[16]

A guard detail under Sergeant Isham Jones was detailed to stay on duty through the night while the other Texans rested. "The rest of us spread our blankets and the camp was soon wrapped in that silent slumber so much enjoyed by a tired soldier," wrote Jim Nichols.[17]

On the morning of Sunday, September 18, Major Caldwell sent Hays and some of his scouts to look over San Antonio and see if they could draw out some of the Mexican horsemen. Hays found 38 men with able horses out of the 200-odd Texans present. Other men would continue to join Hays' command during the month and Ephraim McLean became Hays' second lieutenant.

Caldwell claimed in his report that he had 225 men at the start of the day. Those riding out with Hays included Henry McCulloch, Bigfoot Wallace, Ad Gillespie, Kit Acklin, Sam Luckie, Mike Chevallie, Creed Taylor and Andrew Sowell. They rode out from camp and had reached a point a half mile from San Antonio's old powder house by 10:00 a.m. Hays and Lieutenant McCulloch then took six riders and moved toward the Alamo.[18]

Hays' rangers taunted the Mexican cavalry and soon turned to flee when hundreds of Mexican horsemen raced out of San Antonio in pursuit of them. General Woll sent 25 cavalrymen under Captain Perez, and 60 presidial soldiers under Captain Francisco Castañeda to challenge the rangers. As the Texans fled, Perez's cavalry was reinforced to 150 men.[19]

Hays rode hard to where the balance of his company had been stationed, yelling ahead, "Mount!" According to Zach Morrell, "We moved off briskly through the timber, and as the Mexicans went around an open way, we were about a half mile ahead when we reached the prairie."[20]

Hays would report that Woll's 1,300 invaders had been reinforced by another 300 soldiers. His feint to draw the Mexicans from town proved more successful that he would have imagined. Mathew Caldwell later reported that the rangers' efforts "had the desired effect and Capt. Hays was pursued by about 600 cavalry."[21]

When Hays turned to have his men fall back for Caldwell's camp, he moved ahead with others. He left Lt. Henry McCulloch with ten other horsemen—William Polk, Green McCoy, Stuart Foley, Kit Acklin, Clay Davis, Josiah Taylor, Creed Taylor, Pitkin Taylor, Rufus Taylor and James Taylor—to cover their retreat. During their ride back into camp, the Texans dodged the Mexican forces who were endeavoring to cut them off from the main Texan forces. Midway between the Alamo and Salado Creek, Augustus Jones' horse began to fail and he fell behind. Captain Hays, mounted on a dark bay war-horse, threw a large portion of his company behind Jones to offer protection to his comrade.[22]

McCulloch ordered various riders off at points along the way to courier messages ahead. By the time he neared Salado Creek, McCulloch had only Creed Taylor riding beside him and both men were under heavy fire.[23]

Reverend Morrell recalled that he and his 37 companions fled for their lives on horses which "were considerably worn with the labor of the past seven days. During the first four miles we kept out of their reach without much difficulty." Henry McCulloch, bringing up the rear of the fleeing rangers, noted that they left hats, coats and blankets scattered in their wake. "The race was an earnest one," said Morrell. "The Mexicans, toward the last, began to fire at our rear guard, doing no damage."[24]

Hays led his detachment to a ford about a half mile above the hidden Texans, crossed it, and then rode down the east bank to the main defensive position before his men could be run down. The ground ahead of the 200-odd Texian volunteers was heavily wooded with pecan trees and the pursuing Mexican troops wisely held up before they were in range of the Texan rifles.[25]

Jack Hays was much relieved when he reached Caldwell's camp and found all of his men to be unharmed. The Mexican cavalry passed around to the rear of the Texan camp but kept their distance—waiting as General Woll's ground forces advanced. In the half hour that intervened, Hays' rangers quickly refreshed themselves and their horses with water before sparring with their enemy. Morrell gave this description.[26]

> Captain Jack Hays, our intrepid leader, five feet ten inches high, weighing one hundred and sixty pounds, his black eyes flashing decision of character, from beneath at full forehead, and crowned with beautiful jet black hair, was soon mounted on his dark b[a]y war-horse and on the warpath. Under our chosen leader, we sallied out and skirmished with the enemy at long range, killing a number of Mexicans.

According to Jim Nichols, the Texans had carefully selected positions of cover in the banks of the creek as they awaited the return of the rangers leading Woll's cavalrymen. The Mexicans remained in formation about 400 yards from the creek. The cavalry commander sent back word to Woll of the Texan location and an estimate of Caldwell's numbers. The Mexicans made no effort to scout the Texan flanks. Sporadic skirmishing occurred during the two hours following the return of Jack Hays' scouts. Woll arrived after 1:00 p.m. with at least 400 infantrymen, artillerymen to serve two cannon, 40 rebel Cherokees led by Vicente Cordova, and 100 Mexican-born volunteers from San Antonio.[27]

Perhaps the most notable of the Mexican officers among Woll's troops was Juan Seguín, the former Alamo defender, Texas cavalryman and mayor of San Antonio. The valiant frontiersman had been forced to resign as mayor on April 18, 1842, due to "the turbulent state" of affairs in his county. Seguín, exiled, traveled to Laredo, where the military commander threw him into prison. General Arista later interceded in his behalf with President Santa Anna on the condition that Seguín join Woll's troops in attacking Texas citizens to prove his loyalty to Mexico.[28]

The Mexicans deployed their forces and the newly-arrived men took a rest. Caldwell's volunteers had positioned themselves along the Salado after arriving that morning. "We were awful hungry, and French Smith ran a fat cow into camp and shot her down," recalled Robert Hall. After slaughtering four cattle around 8:00 a.m., the Texans roasted their meat as they watched the Mexican troops assemble. "On account of the distance we did not pay a great deal of attention to them, and kept on roasting and eating our beef, without any bread," recalled Nate Burkett. "I had a messmate by the name of Sol Simmons, and after roasting four large portions of rib we devoured the whole of them."[29]

James Ramsay from Gonzales added, "Hungry men are not very particular. Some had fires kindled and boiling meat before the animals were skinned and before any had time to eat, the alarm of the enemy coming was given. For some fifteen or twenty minutes, want of order and excitement prevailed."[30]

Jim Nichols was not feeling at ease with the impending battle as he watched his fellow Texans roast beef during the morning hours. His father, two brothers and two brother-in-laws had been by his side when he had fought Comanches at the battle of Plum Creek in 1840. Worrying that he could be killed at Salado Creek without a relative fighting at his side this time, Nichols later admitted, "On the occasion, I confess I was not in a very merry mood."[31]

One of Caldwell's men, Miles Bennett, later offered his assessment of the Mexican forces before them.[32]

> We retained the place of our guard fire, the guard being a detail of two or three men from each company posted at the extreme right on the edge of a hollow that covered the enemy's left, and this proved one of the hottest places of the battle. Cameron's company was on the right, Bird's on the right center, and the other companies on the line to the left. I was in Bird's company and before the cannon opened fire upon us I had a good opportunity to count the enemy's detachment under Cordova of 85 Cherokee Indians and renegade Mexicans who crawled Indian fashion into the hollow on our right.

James Ramsay felt that the sounds of the Mexican buglers approaching sounded "almost like cat squealing." Camp fires were left burning with beef cooking as the Texans hurriedly formed up for battle. "Keep cool, men, and fall into lines," Major Colley ordered.[33]

The Texans took position under a light bluff that ran along Salado Creek. Colonel Caldwell offered a short war speech to his men as they prepared for battle. He told his men that he would never surrender to General Woll. He had just returned from the

Santa Fe Expedition and he felt it would be death to any Texans who were taken prisoners. "He urged us to make up our minds to fight it out, and even if it required a hand-to-hand combat, the white flag would not be raised."[34]

During the mixed sounds of whooping Texans and distant gunfire, Ramsay only made out Caldwell's concluding sentences, "Fight for your homes and families and give them hell!"[35]

Ramsay noted that Colonel Caldwell, shirt sleeves rolled up, was solemn and courageous. He found Caldwell to be "above the common height of men, a little slim, dark hair now mixed with white patches more particularly in the beard by which he got the sobriquet of Old Paint." Ramsay saw his leader clutching his rifle in his right hand while gesturing considerably to take various positions along the creek banks.[36]

After giving his motivational speech, Caldwell invited Reverends Carroll and Morrell to address the men. Morrell encouraged his fellow Texans to "keep cool" and make every shot count at close range, particularly against anyone wearing an officer's hat or sword. "Let us shoot low, and my impression before God is, that we shall win this fight."[37]

As if to punctuate the end of these war speeches, Woll's men opened fire on the Texan position with their cannon. Fortunately, the canister and solid shot merely ripped the trees above the Texans' position. "The Mexicans opened fire on us with grape canister and round shot, cutting the limbs and brush from the timber at least thirty feet above our heads but to the great annoyance of our horses," recalled Jim Nichols. "The falling limbs, some of which was as large as a common man's thigh, falling on and around them caused them to rear and plunge and some few broke loose." The high shots were corrected by the Mexican artillerymen lowering the barrels of their cannon and shooting into the ground. The Texans dropped into the creek beds as dirt and rock were blown over their heads.[38]

Woll ordered 50 of his infantrymen to advance. Ten Texans with double-barreled shotguns were detached to the edge of the creek bank to discourage this effort. The Mexican infantrymen advanced to within 30 paces of Salado Creek before the close-range firing commenced. The Mexican smoothbore muskets had a shorter range and Woll's men were vulnerable in their advance. The Texans fired in relays and dropped below to reload while others fired. Zachariah Morrell said that the first firing caused Woll's infantry troops to drop to the ground with heavy loss of life.[39]

General Woll was in sight, but remained at some distance near his cannon while his foot soldiers skirmished along the Texan lines throughout the afternoon. "In the beginning, the enemy would come out of the densest part of the woods and daringly open fire against our entire front," Woll wrote the following day. "The game was critical; there was no time to lose."[40]

The only Texan wounded during the early skirmishing was Jess Zumwalt of Caldwell's volunteers. At one point, the Mexican commander did attempt a flanking maneuver, but his troops were spotted. Shotgun-wielding Texans moved to cover this exposed position. Miles Bennett later described these charges.[41]

> Our men at the center and on the left laid low until after the discharge of the cannon. Then, upon the charge of the enemy in close quarters, the firing became general and the foe was compelled to fall back to their cannon, leaving the ground strown with their dead and wounded, their bugles and even their muster rolls falling into our hands. These charges were repeated and the fighting severe. On our right, the enemy was strengthened by a band of Carrizo Indians [who] charged us repeatedly but failed to drive us from our position.

The small Cherokee group posed the greatest threat during the battle. Cordova brought his men in close to the Texans and the fight became hand to hand as men were caught with rifles uncharged. "At the first fire the Indians rose to their feet, yelling and fought like demons," said Jim Nichols. "We had the advantage of the ground [and] as we could, part of us [would] be behind the bank. They charged to the top of the bank and sent a shower of arrows at us but [they] was shot down so fast, [they] came no more but fell back and tried to gain our rear and a desperate fight ensued."[42]

Bigfoot Wallace was attacked by a Mexican infantryman who shot at him from close range with his escopeta. The ball grazed Wallace's nose. Henry Whalen of Captain Cameron's company, standing nearby, cried out, "Damn such shooting as that!" Whalen shot the Mexican soldier with his rifle and watched the man crumple against a mesquite tree.[43]

One of Wallace's fellow rangers pointed out a Mexican soldier who was assisting a wounded man away from the action. "Bigfoot, yonder is a Mexican who has on a pair of pants large enough to fit you," he said. Wallace, a conspicuously tall man, had lost his spare pair of long pants when Woll's forces seized San Antonio. Wallace shot at the long-legged Mexican man and missed. Ben McCulloch, however, made his shot count and he ran out to strip the man's pants. The long trousers, made of fine material, were worn by Wallace for the next two years.[44]

The Mexican cavalrymen darted back and forth across the battlefield, pausing for a time on a hill a short distance up the creek. Green McCoy and his buddy Andrew Sowell led their horses up the Salado a short distance, tied them off and then slipped to within easy rifle shot of the cavalrymen. Mexican infantrymen, however, cut off this attempt and Sowell and McCoy narrowly raced back to the main camp with their lives. The battle was not continuous, as Woll's troops took long breaks between each charge for the Mexicans to collect their own dead and wounded. For some unknown reason, the Mexican cavalrymen were not effectively used during this battle.[45]

Robert Hall was impressed with the courage of commander Caldwell throughout the day's fighting.[46]

> No man who ever stood on Texas soil was his equal in battle. As soon as the bullets began to whistle he seemed to grow taller and look grander. I don't think it ever occurred to him that he might be hit. He rode over a battlefield as unconcerned as if he had been out corn shucking. His nerves must have been made of iron; nothing disturbed him.

The Mexican infantry resumed its frontal attack, advancing, halting, firing, reloading and moving forward again. The well-sheltered Texans carefully fired and reloaded during each advance and managed to turn away each new advance farther away from the creek bank. Robert Hall alternated shooting while another Texan loaded his rifle. The two then switched positions, with his companion standing to fire while Hall reloaded.[47]

At one point in the battle, Colonel Caldwell sent Hall up

Salado Creek to insure that Mexican troops were not attempting to surround the Texans. "I climbed up a tree and saw a Mexican slipping on another scout named Hill," Hall related. "I got my gun and shot at him. He dropped over on the horn of his saddle. We found him next day seated against a tree with the gun across his lap."[48]

Parson Carroll, the Methodist preacher who had given such motivational speeches to the troops prior to the battle, was equally inspiring in battle. He stood upon the bank of the creek and shouted at his opponents, "God take your souls!"[49]

During one of the halts, the Mexican cavalrymen departed the field and left their infantry in position. Distant rifle fire and cannon fire was heard as if they were now firing on some other supporting troops who were approaching out in the open. Jim Nichols later wrote of the artillery's movement: "They had not been gone but a short time before we heard a furious cannonading on the flat. It was then that Dawson's mas[acre] was enacted."[50]

General Woll's most serious charge against the Texans at Salado Creek came late in the afternoon. Cordova and his rebel Cherokees moved through a dry creek bed to confront some of the Texas guards and men of Captain Cameron's company. During the sharp action which ensued, Cordova—the leader of the 1838 rebellion in Texas—was killed. Some men would later give credit to Wilson Randle of Seguin, but John Henry Brown says it was actually John Lowe, "who belonged to the adjoining company on our right and stood about thirty feet from me, while I was loading my gun. I watched the affair closely." Cordova was in the process of firing his gun when Lowe shot him down with a Yeager ball from 90 yards.[51]

At that moment, Brown said that "no one knew it was Cordova till his men were driven from the position by Lieut. John R. Baker of Cameron's company, when old Vasquez, a New Madrid Spaniard in our command, recognized him." Augustus C. Allen of Houston, who had known Cordova while a resident of Nacogdoches, also confirmed the identity of the rebel leader's body.[52]

Several Cherokees were killed during this intense fighting, which was only ended when Cordova himself was killed. Eleven Cherokees were killed in this sharp action, with the balance retreating after the death of Cordova. Only one Texan, Calvin

Turner, had been slightly wounded by a musket ball which grazed his head, cutting some skin and hair from his temple. His brother William Turner assisted him and Calvin soon recovered. The Texans then turned their attention back to defending other Mexican charges and each attack was repelled.[53]

During the last, half-hearted charge, some of the Texans moved atop the creek bank and fired from behind the cover of trees. This bold move caused the Texans to suffer several men wounded. Creed Taylor was shot in the shoulder and Solomon Simmons received a painful shot through his lower bowels. When the battle had commenced, Simmons was in the process of cooking large chunks of beef over the camp fire. He had hurriedly stuffed large quantities of meat in his mouth and swallowed much of it with little chewing. When the bullet ripped through his intestines, Solomon was in mortal agony according to company mate Robert Hall. "He roared that he was a dead man, and began to throw up that beef. It looked as if he had enough cow inside of him to have killed him. He was hit in the stomach and the bullet was never found, yet the man got well."[54]

As the Mexican forces began retreating, Andrew Sowell took careful aim and dropped one of Woll's soldiers with his rifle. "That's the way to do it, Andrew," Miles Dikes called out to his companion.[55]

Rolla Davis (who had served under Burleson at San Antonio earlier in the year during the Vasquez raid) was shot in the arm, John Law of Zumwalt's company in the thigh and Sam Callahan through both hips. All would recover except Callahan, who died several days after his return to Seguin. The Mexicans finally called a truce until 6:00 p.m. to carry off their wounded.[56]

Caldwell struggled with keeping his men in place during this time as the Mexicans began retreating back toward San Antonio. He worried about the enemy's artillery and their superior numbers. In addition to those wounded who were carried off, the Mexicans left 60 dead and seriously wounded on the battlefield. Most of the wounded died during the night. Officially, General Woll listed his casualties in a report the next day as " 29 dead and 58 wounded."[57]

Caldwell's forces had only suffered a few Texans slightly injured and one killed during the day's fighting. Some horses had been killed and others had fled during the cannon fire which had dropped tree branches down on them. Jim Nichols recalled William Hesskew, Calvin Turner and John King being successful in recovering their horses that night, "leaving Stephen Jett and Simon Cockrill still in search of theirs.[58]

Jett had been in attendance in the San Antonio district court when Woll's men captured the entire court. He managed to escape his captors later when the Mexican forces had been caught in the confusion of preparing for battle on the Salado. He fought in the battle and afterwards was endeavoring to reclaim his lost horse when the remnants of the Mexican cavalry happened upon Jett and Cockrill.[59]

Jett was chased down a creek by some of the Cherokees, who killed and scalped him. Cockrill was shot in the shoulder with a rifle ball and two arrows, but he managed to hide under a creek embankment until his pursuers finally moved on. Miles Bennett later related that Cockrill "concealed himself beneath a leaning tree on the bank of the Salado, keeping entirely underwater only leaving his nose and mouth above water." Painfully wounded, wet and muddy, he made his way back to Caldwell's camp that evening. "The body of Jett was brought up and William Hesskew taken charge of the body as they had worked on the same ranch together," Jim Nichols wrote.[60]

According to Nichols, the Salado battle and its aftermath had killed Jett and wounded eight others: Simon Cockrill (shoulder), Sol Simmons (bowels), Creed Taylor (shoulder), Jesse Zumwalt (shoulder), John Law (thigh), Sam Callahan (both hips), Calvin Turner (temple), and Rolla Davis (arm).

★ ★ ★ ★ ★

"I Would Rather Die Than Retreat"

Colonel Caldwell had no knowledge of the forces that had helped draw the attention of the Mexican troops this day. Even as he lay in his defensive position writing a battle report that night, other Texans were dying a short distance away. The small arms fire and cannon fire that his men had heard had been directed toward a newly-arriving volunteer force under Captain Nicholas Dawson.

Dawson was a veteran Texan fighter who had fought at San Jacinto and served in the cavalry of the Texas Army during 1837.

He had served as first lieutenant of Captain William Eastland's La Grange company during John Henry Moore's 1839 Comanche campaign. When Moore made a second expedition against the Comanches in the fall of 1840, Dawson was captain of the Colorado County company.

When news reached him of the Mexican capture of San Antonio, he quickly assembled 15 men under the historic oak in La Grange. His original Fayette County volunteers included: Jerome B. Alexander, John Beard, John Church, William Coltrin, Lewis W. Dickerson, Robert Moore Eastland, Low Farris, Nathaniel W. Faison, George Hill, John Higgerson, David Smith Kornegay, Edward T. Manton and Joseph Shaw and at least one other man.[61]

The Dawson company crossed the Colorado River on a ferry and proceeded toward San Antonio along the Old Seguin Road. Their numbers increased along the way. Among the first to join were 70-year-old David Berry and his son-in-law Harvey Hall, a veteran of Major Mark Lewis' 1841 Indian expedition. Another eleven volunteers joined the La Grange company near West Point at the Ivy School House, including: Zed Barkley with sons Richard and Robert Barkley; 69-year-old Zadock Woods with sons Henry Gonzalvo and Norman B. Woods; and brothers William James and Edward Trimble. Henry Woods had made Colonel Moore's 1839 and 1840 Comanche expeditions and had fought under Ned Burleson at the 1839 Mill Creek Fight.[62]

By the time the La Grange men had passed through Gonzales, others had bolstered their numbers. Joe Griffin, a slave of Samuel Maverick, arrived heavily armed and bearing a ransom note from Mrs. Maverick for the release of her husband. In the vicinity of Nash's Creek, some 15 miles west of Gonzales, scout Alsey S. Miller from Captain Jesse Billingsley's company caught up with them. Billingsley sent word that Dawson should wait so that their combined forces could march against Woll in San Antonio. Dawson, however, opted to press on and Miller joined the unit. In camp near Nash's Creek, the company elected Nicholas Dawson as their captain, Jerome Alexander as their first lieutenant and Robert Eastland as the second lieutenant.

The unit included many seasoned Indian fighters. Dawson, Henry Woods, Lewis Dickerson, Nathaniel Faison, Thomas James, and David Kornegay had all fought Comanches under

John Henry Moore during late 1840.

During the early evening, courier John Wilson from Colonel Caldwell's forces reached Captain Dawson. His call for more volunteers and descriptions of the Mexican forces compelled Dawson to have his men make a forced march through the night. By daybreak on September 17, they had reached Seguin, about 45 miles from Caldwell on the Salado. Undaunted, Dawson continued to move at a fast pace until his men reached the Cíbolo on the morning of September 18.[63]

The few men with horses which were not completely broken down at this point moved ahead to scout for Caldwell's forces. Alsey Miller and others found only Mexican troops and Miller raced back to alert Dawson that a battle was already underway between Woll and Caldwell's forces. Dawson's men soon ran afoul of the rear guard of General Woll's troops. He soon found that his company faced around 200 Mexican cavalrymen and one of the Mexican cannons.

Captain Dawson called a hasty conference of his men to vote on whether they should attack or fall back to await the volunteers under Jesse Billingsley. His men voted to face Woll's troops while attempting to join up with Caldwell's main body. Zadock Woods, the oldest member of the company, voiced his sentiment: 'We have marched a long way to meet the Mexicans, and I do not intend to return without meeting them. I would rather die than retreat."[64]

Dawson's men were out of view of the action with Caldwell, which was taking place about 1.5 miles away on the Salado. Two groups were seen to be approaching between 3 and 4 p.m. One of Dawson's scouts mistook one of these groups to be friendly Texans. They soon proved to be Mexican cavalry under colonels Cayetano Montero, José María Carrasco, and Pedro Rangel. Dawson ordered his men to dismount in a mesquite thicket where Fort Sam Houston now stands and face the approaching riders. The Mexican riders split and approached the La Grange company from two sides. The Texans held off the first cavalry charge and inflicted injuries on the Mexican soldiers.

Carrasco had his men fall back so that his artillery could open fire on Dawson's company. The cannon began taking its toll on Texans and their horses. Their rifles picked off some Mexican soldiers from a distance but the Mexican grape and canister cut down Dawson's men. He continued to urge his men to take careful aim as he strode up and down the lines. The Mexican cavalry, now dismounted, soon began a spirited charge that proved costly for the Texans. When Captain Dawson found that more than half of his men had been killed or wounded, he made an attempt to surrender. His own hip shattered, he limped into the open to surrender, waving a blanket tied to his rifle.[65]

The attempt failed—either due to Mexican forces who refused to accept the surrender or due to Texans who panicked and fired on the Mexican troops during the surrender attempt. The Mexican forces then began cutting down and massacring Dawson's men with sabers and lances.

General Woll gave an analysis of the destruction his men carried out on Dawson's volunteers. "Our dragoons dismounted, encouraged by their chiefs and officers, particularly the Brevet Colonels Cayetano Montero, Pedro Rangel and José Maria Carrasco, and entering the wood, started cutting down every enemy they encountered. A quarter hour later all was finished."[66]

Zadock Woods tried to come to the aid of his wounded son Norman but was hit by a bullet and fell dead on top of his son. Zadock's other son, Henry Woods, had been wounded in the shoulder and received several hacks at his head with Mexican sabers. He finally concluded that his only chance at survival was to surrender. A Mexican soldier, however, refused to accept Henry Woods' surrender and turned his pistol on the young Texan. The gun misfired and Woods quickly realized he had best flee. A Mexican horseman pursued him and swung at him with a lance. Woods snatched the weapon as it swung past his head and managed to pull the rider from his horse. He drove the lance through the Mexican cavalryman, sprang upon his horse and made his escape. Woods rode until he met up with John C. Wilson, who helped wash and treat Woods' wounds and lead him back to La Grange.[67]

Another who managed to escape was Alsey Miller, whose horse was killed early in the action. When he saw Captain Dawson killed while waving the surrender flag, Miller took up the flag and tried riding toward the Mexican forces on another horse he had secured. The Mexicans began firing on Miller so he gave up the surrender option and fled to the Cíbolo, where he met Edward Burleson and other arriving volunteers.[68]

(Left) The remains of the Dawson company victims were buried in a common tomb on what is known as Monument Hill in Fayette County, Texas. This 48-foot marker with murals was erected near La Grange by the state in 1936. *Courtesy of Marion Daughtry.*
(Right) Texan scout Alsey Silvanus Miller was one of only two Texans not killed or captured during this engagement. *Courtesy of Mrs. Lucy Ainsworth, Luling, Texas.*

In the meantime, the balance of Captain Dawson's men fought valiantly until their deaths. Among them was Joe Griffin, the African-American slave of Samuel Maverick. Mexican Colonel Carrasco later commented on the brave fighting of "that valiant black man." Mary Ann Maverick wrote of Joe Griffin several days after the battle.[69]

> He was a man of powerful frame and he possessed the courage of the African lion. And this faithful and devoted African performed prodigies that day. When his ammunition became useless because of the proximity of the enemy, he fought with the butt-end of his gun and when the gun was broken, he wrenched a limb from a mesquite tree and did battle with that until death closed his career. He received more than one mortal wound before he ceased fighting.

Capt. Dawson's Company: September 18, 1842

Captain:
Nicholas Mosby Dawson [1]
First Lieutenant:
Jerome B. Alexander [1]
Second Lieutenant:
Robert Moore Eastland [1]

Privates:
_____ Adams [1]
James Alley [1]
Richard A. Barkley [4]
Robert Barkley [1]
Zed Barkley [1]
John Beard [1]
David W. Berry [1]
John Bradley [4]
Francis E. Brookfield [1]
Thomas J. Butler [1]
T. John Church [1]
William Coltrin [4]
Robert Cummings [1]
John Dancer [1]
Lewis W. Dickerson [1]
Nathaniel W. Faison [4]
Lowe Farris [1]
Charles S. Field [1]
Elijah S. Garey [1]
Joe Griffin [1]
Harvey W. Hall [1]
Milvern Harrell [4]
John Higgerson [4]
George A. Hill [1]
Thomas D. James [3]
Asa Jones [1]
John F. Jones [1]
Davis Smith Kornegay [4]
Patrick Lewis [1]
William Linn [1]
Winfield S. Lowe [1]
Edward T. Manton [4]
John McCrady [4]
Richard McGee [1]
Alsey S. Miller [3]
Allen H. Morrell [4]
William D. Patterson [4]
John Wesley Pendleton [1]
Thomas Rice [1]
Joseph C. Robinson [4]
William Savage [1]
Elam Scallorn [1]
John Wesley Scallorn [1]
Thomas D. Simms [1]
Richard Slack [1]
Edward Trimble [1]
William James Trimble [4]
Norman Miles Wells [1]
Henry Gonzalvo Woods [3]
Norman B. Woods [4]
Zadock Woods [1]

1 Died in battle Sept. 18, 1842.
2 Enrolled October 17, 1842.
3 Escaped from the battlefield.
4 Taken prisoner after battle.

Key sources: http://www.rootsweb.com/~txfayett/dawson_expedition.htm, accessed April 3, 2008. See also Nance, *Attack and Counter-Attack,* 621–23.

Colonel Carrasco and other Mexican officers did finally gain control of their men, but not until 36 of Dawson's 54 volunteers had been killed. Norman Woods, a young man born in Missouri in 1805, was among the wounded. His father, Zadock Woods, perished while his brother Henry Woods escaped and his nephew Milvern Harrell was taken prisoner. Norman later wrote to his family:[70]

> I was shot across the hip at the time that Captain Dawson ran out with the white flag. It was Carrasco's order for his soldiers to disarm us then put us to death. We were released from this order by General Woll. I was left on the ground as dead until they came to stripping us and tearing the clothes off of me. I had recovered enough to ask for quarters, which was granted by a sergeant who kept off the soldiers with his sword. I had received five wounds with the sword. Four on the head and one on the left side, which nearly proved fatal.

Only Thomas D. James, Alsey Miller and Gonzalvo Woods were able to escape the deadly attack. Another 15 men were taken prisoner. Of these 15, John McCrady, William Patterson and John Higgerson would later die in escape attempts. Three others—William Coltrin, William James Trimble and Norman Woods—would later perish in Perote Prison near Mexico City. Only Richard A. Barkley, David Kornegay, John Bradley, Nathaniel Faison, Milvern Harrell, Edward Manton, Allen Morrell, Joseph Robinson and Joseph Shaw would later be released from Perote Prison in 1843-1844.[71]

The three dozen Texan lives lost in this battle could have been averted had Nicholas Dawson waited to unite with Jesse Billingsley's company. His courage in following his men's wishes to engage the Mexican troops and the subsequent slaughter they endured upon attempting to surrender would only further fuel the desire of Texans to avenge such atrocities.

★ ★ ★ ★ ★

Ben McCulloch, Clem Hinds, and Eli Hankins of Hays' unit made a scout at dusk and found the site of Dawson's battle. It was

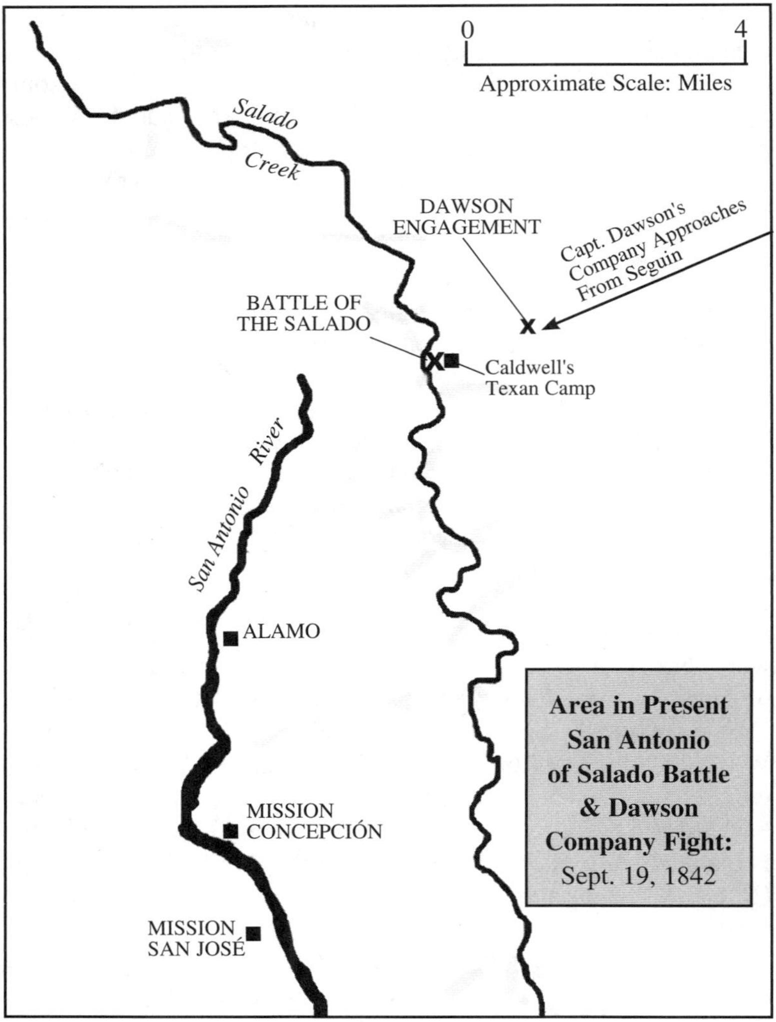

becoming too dark to identify any of the mutilated bodies. The men had hoped to try and identify the body of Reverend Morrell's son, who had ridden with Dawson.[72]

Mathew Caldwell sent H. L. Conn and Robert Hall out into the moonlight to scout for the Mexican troops. "We found that the enemy had fallen back on San Antonio," Hall wrote. "We found a great many dead and wounded."[73]

During the night of September 18, one hundred men from Bastrop reached Caldwell. This included Captain Jesse Billingsley's 75-man company. Among his men was Sam Walker, soon to become famous among the Texas Rangers. When darkness and uncertainty as to Caldwell's location halted Billingsley's company, he sent Walker ahead to scout for the Texans. He found Caldwell's men near the battle scene and returned to guide Billingsley's reinforcements to the area.[74]

One of Billingsley's scouts, Rufus Perry, had gone out with Walker, Luther Flint and a Tonkawa Indian ahead of the company. "We four reached the top of a hill and from there could see the battleground, just in time to see that Dawson had raised the white flag," Perry later wrote. Perry sent Walker back to Billingsley's company, which was still some three miles away from the battle which they could hear in the distance. After briefing his captain, Walker returned to the battlefield with four other men. They, in company with Flint and Perry, took on the grim task of burying the mutilated victims of Captain Dawson's company.[75]

Capt. Billingsley's Company: September, 1842

<u>*Captain:*</u>
Jesse Billingsley
<u>*First Lieutenant:*</u>
William H. Garrett

<u>*Privates:*</u>
John Adams
George Allen
Richard Anderson
James Barber
David Barnett
William B. Billingsley
Theodore Bissell
Thomas Brite
Desha Bunton
J. W. Bunton
John Caldwell
William Cannon
William R. Cannon
Stephen Cassidy
_____ Chapman
Greenup Christian
William A. Click
Preston Conley
Leander C. Cunningham
James Curtis
Gordon Dies
James S. Dodd
Greenlief Fisk
Luther Flint
____ Frazier
George A. Gambell
William Gammell
George D. Glasscock
Charles J. Grainger
Robert H. Grimes
George Hancock
John Hancock
William L. Hancock
William R. Hancock
Samuel A. J. Haynie
Cornelius M. Hemphill
Benjamin F. Highsmith
Middleton M. Hill
John Hobbs
Allen J. Holderman
William S. Holton
John H. Jenkins
Philip W. Jobe
____ Kelley
Garrett Moppin
Francis Nash
George J. Neill
Julien J. Nichols
James Nicholson
Nelson F. Owen
Robert B. Owen
William E. Owen
James M. Patton
Cicero Rufus Perry
William M. Perry
William R. Redding
C. Seabaugh
Michael Sessum
Benjamin Smithson
Charles Spalding
John Talk
Campbell Taylor
Richmond Thomson
Richmond Townsend
Hiram Turner
Stephen Turner
Samuel H. Walker
R. F. Whitaker
John W. Wilbarger
William Williams
Alford H. Wood
Nicholas Wren
John C. Yates

Source: Jesse Billingsley PD, R 137, F 280–89.

CHAPTER 5

Hondo Creek Skirmish

September 19, 1842–January 1843

Colonel Caldwell's volunteers spent a dark, anxious night camped on the Salado following their battle with General Woll's troops. Reverend Zachariah Morrell received word that Captain Dawson's forces had been overrun and massacred. He was deeply worried about the fate of his son, Allen Morrell. At sunrise, Colonel Caldwell and Captain Hays allowed Morrell, William Burnham, Griffith Jones, John Henry Brown and Dr. Caleb S. Brown to leave camp to scour the battlefield for survivors of the Dawson engagement.[1]

The men were guided to the scene by a number of wounded horses found around the grove where the battle had taken place. At the scene of Dawson's surrender, Morrell and company found 35 bodies of men he knew well. They "lay scattered and terribly mangled among the little clusters of bushes on the broad prairie." Brown wrote that the bodies were "entirely naked, so mutilated with cannon shot, sabre wounds and lances as to be unrecognizable. The heads of several were nearly severed from their bodies. The cold rain of the previous night had cleaned them of blood and given the bodies a marble-like appearance. It was simply a horrible sight." The body of Robert Cummings, who had run about 400 yards before being killed, was not immediately found.[2]

Reverend Morrell examined each Texan, many of whom were friends, neighbors and young boys he had known. When he encountered a man whose face or body was particularly mangled, Morrell examined their feet for a scar that his boy had carried since childhood. He was soon "satisfied that he had either escaped or was among the prisoners."[3]

Steve Jett, the former ranger who perished in the previous day's fighting, was buried with the honors of war that Monday morning, September 19. His companions dug a grave for him with their bowie knives. Miles Bennett later stated, "Our brave frontiersman Steve Jett we buried on the battlefield on the bank of the Salado."[4]

Ezekiel Smith, a veteran of the Plum Creek battle, returned to Caldwell's camp after daybreak with a wounded Mexican soldier who had been shot in the mouth. "The ball knocked out three of his upper teeth and the same of his lower teeth and [came out] on one side of his neck bone," recalled Jim Nichols. Although the elder Texan was intent on killing his captive, his son French Smith, admonished him with, "Father, you ought to be ashamed of yourself."[5]

Nichols talked with the wounded Mexican soldier and offered him coffee and a cigarette. The prisoner was allowed to live and was very thankful of Nichols' intervention, thanking him profusely when the two men encountered each other in San Antonio again three years later.[6]

In all, some 50 men had surrendered to the Mexicans and had been taken prisoner. This included 13 men from Captain Dawson's company and several of Captain Hays' former rangers who had been captured when San Antonio was overrun. Reinforcements began arriving at San Antonio that day, the first being Jesse Billingsley's men. He took his company back to recover the bodies of the fallen Texans and return them to their families for burial. Among the veteran frontiersmen who made their way quickly to San Antonio were Ben McCulloch and William Eastland.[7]

Colonel Caldwell maintained his camp on September 19. The following morning around 10 a.m., scouting intelligence reached him that Woll had begun his retreat from San Antonio that morning. After a short meeting with his commanders, Caldwell led his combined forces, now more than 250 men, in pursuit. He paused at noon at the head of the San Antonio River, where he anxiously waited in hopes of more reinforcements. When no others arrived, Caldwell set marched his troops forward again on the afternoon of September 20 and arrived at the Presidio crossing of the Medina (present Castroville) around midnight.[8]

On the morning of September 21, Caldwell moved up the valley about 6 miles and then halted while Jack Hays' scouts went out to reconnoiter. "About noon Hays returned bringing in four prisoners, and stating that Woll was encamped 8 miles above," wrote John Henry Brown.[9]

Captain Hays and Ben McCulloch—who had arrived in camp shortly after the battle of Salado—had actually made two successful ventures out in which they apprehended Mexican soldiers this morning. During the overnight hours, the pair had eased up on the outskirts of Woll's camp, tied off their horses, slipped on Mexican blankets from their saddles and pulled their hats down low. According to an associate of Hays, the rangers "took observations of everything and saw the position of the enemy. Some of the Mexicans were asleep, some sitting around smoking their cigaritos, but none of them discovered the spies."[10]

McCulloch and Hays slipped away from Woll's camp before sunrise and reached their horses. At that moment, a Mexican sentry appeared from the dark of the moonless night and called, "Who goes there?"[11]

"Texans, God damn you!" shouted Hays.

McCulloch held a pistol on the Mexican soldier while Hays took him prisoner. The rangers slipped away with their prisoner and rode back to Caldwell's camp, urging their companions to prepare for an assault on Woll's troop during the daylight on September 21. Hays and McCulloch found that Caldwell's troops were divided on the question of attacking the Mexican army that morning. While the debate continued, Captain Hays reconnoitered Woll's position again that morning and returned at noon with four more straggler prisoners.[12]

Around 4:00 p.m. on September 21, another group of about 100 men reached Colonel Caldwell's camp. This included roughly twenty men from Lavaca and another 80 from the Colorado River settlements, all under the leadership of Colonel John Henry Moore. Most of the Texan volunteers were on foot, with Hays' rangers acting as scouts and advance guards. Woll had loaded his wounded men on carts in San Antonio, and took everything of value from the town. Woll's forces continued their slow retreat, rightfully suspecting that Caldwell's Texans would be pursuing him. Woll's losses were never accurately determined, although Morrell claimed he later heard Woll admit to 600 killed or wounded.[13]

Woll claimed that his forces were now divided, with a good number of men escorting the Texas prisoners toward Mexico. His main division was "considerably reduced" to "barely 500 men" after leaving San Antonio and heading west for the Medina River. Texan volunteer Thomas Jefferson Green later wrote that Woll left San Antonio with some 200 wounded, many of whom died en route to Mexico.[14]

Lt. Henry McCulloch of Hay's ranger company was charged with the wounded Texan men, who numbered about a dozen. Fortunately, Solomon Brill had managed to capture a cart and team from Woll's forces and in this vehicle the wounded men were hauled back toward the nearest settlement. The casualties were first taken to Seguin, escorted by some of Captain Zumwalt's company. The balance of Zumwalt's men remained with Caldwell and reorganized their unit with Captain Oliver Stapp in command and John Henry Brown as their first lieutenant.

Reverend Morrell rode into San Antonio with Judge Hemphill to learn what had happened to his son. Some of the ladies in town had seen the Texan prisoners which Woll's forces had captured and brought back into town. They told Morrell that Allen had been wounded by a lance in the fight under Captain Dawson but he had escaped death when a Mexican colonel decided to take him as a prisoner.[15]

★ ★ ★ ★ ★

Hays Takes Cannon at Hondo Creek

With the arrival of Colonel Moore's 100 men at Caldwell's camp at 4:00 p.m. on Wednesday, September 21—and other volunteer groups which had joined him—John Henry Brown wrote that Caldwell now had 489 men. Zachariah Morrell gave a similar estimate of 500 men whom the Texans had to pursue Woll. By general consent this force was split into two battalions, with Mathew Caldwell as colonel, John Moore as lieutenant colonel and James S. Mayfield as major.[16]

After nightfall, Colonel Caldwell moved his troops up the Medina River to a point 2 miles beyond the present site of

Castroville. Scout John W. Smith found that Caldwell's men were within 4 miles of Woll's forces but Jack Hays reported at midnight that the Mexicans had broken camp and moved out. Caldwell's men immediately began a pursuit but were delayed in crossing the river.[17]

Hays' rangers moved forward rapidly and caught up with the Mexican rear guard around 3:00 p.m. on September 22. Scout Reverend Morrell recalled, "Our spies were out, right and left of the road and in advance. The rear-guard of the Mexicans was in the bottom, in a bend of the creek, and concealed. The Mexican general had offered five hundred dollars for the head of Captain Hays, and just at this time he came very near losing it."[18]

When the Mexican troops suddenly opened fire on the rangers from their place of concealment, one of their shots narrowly missed Captain Hays. The musket ball ripped through the breast of ranger Sam Luckie—who was riding beside Hays—and passed out of his right shoulder. Luckie was thrown from his horse when it suddenly bolted away.[19]

Other rangers charged into a dry branch of Verde Creek, where they spotted a fleeing Cherokee who was believed to be Luckie's shooter. Luckie, severely wounded, was carried in a litter to the Medina and from there back to San Antonio in a cart. He lay on the brink of death for days but finally recovered and lived another ten years in San Antonio.[20]

Jack Hays and his other rangers dismounted and formed for battle near the site of their ambush. Caldwell's main army was a mile and a half behind. During the half hour that Hays waited for an attack, General Woll pushed forward toward the Arroyo Hondo, located about 50 miles from San Antonio. When Hays learned that Woll was still fleeing, he sent word back to Colonel Caldwell. Woll began crossing the Hondo just below the mouth of Quihi Creek, where he set up a defensive position. He placed a cannon with 20 artillerymen and additional infantrymen on a bluff on the east side of the river while his troops crossed to the west side of the Hondo.[21]

Mathew Caldwell hurried forward with his men to make up the mile-plus difference between his forces and Hays' rangers. A call was made for volunteers to help increase Captain Hays' horsemen by another 100 men. William Eastland was called out by Caldwell to take the additional horsemen to support Hays but John Henry

Moore ordered him back into the ranks. James Mayfield then made a speech for volunteers, but not a man responded in spite of his good talk. Caldwell, wisely thinking that Mayfield was not known well among the men of central and southwest Texas, called on Reverend Morrell to make another speech.[22]

His son Allen Morrell was a prisoner of the Mexicans and the Baptist preacher admitted that his "soul was fired as it never had been before." He rode down the lines and asked for help. "My dear boy was upon the hill, perhaps in irons, and unless that cannon was charged and silenced, the sad news must be borne to his mother, that our Allen was in chains."[23]

The preacher's word had the desired effect, as dozens of men stepped forward to join Captain Hays and Henry McCulloch for a charge on the cannon on the hill. Once assembled in front of the main Texian forces, these 100 men moved forward at the shrill call from Jack Hays, "Charge!"[24]

The volunteers raced across the Hondo Creek ford and advanced up the ascent toward the Mexican cannon. The Mexican artillerymen failed to take the sloping ground into account and they overshot the charging rangers and volunteer horsemen. The Texans responded with a loud war cry that greatly excited the Mexican infantrymen who nervously opened fire on Hays' advancing men. Several Texans were shot but the charge continued. The cannoneers only managed to fire off a second high shot before Colt pistols were doing their damage at close range.

The Mexican infantrymen scattered and the artillerymen were killed and wounded in close quarter fighting. During the charge up the hill, Nicholas Wren's horse was killed and the former ranger was thrown from his mount. Another horseman, Bill Morrison, was also thrown from his mount during the charge into the chaparral. Anderson J. Harrell suffered the loss of his horse—later valued at $100 by Ned Burleson—during the charge on Hondo Creek.[25]

During the charge, Kit Acklin leaned from his horse and killed a Mexican cannoneer by shooting through its wheels. Reverend Morrell recalled another ranger beside him who was wounded during the charge against the Mexican cannon.[26]

> My friend Arch Gibson, one of my nearest neighbors on the Guadalupe, who was riding on my right, lost his

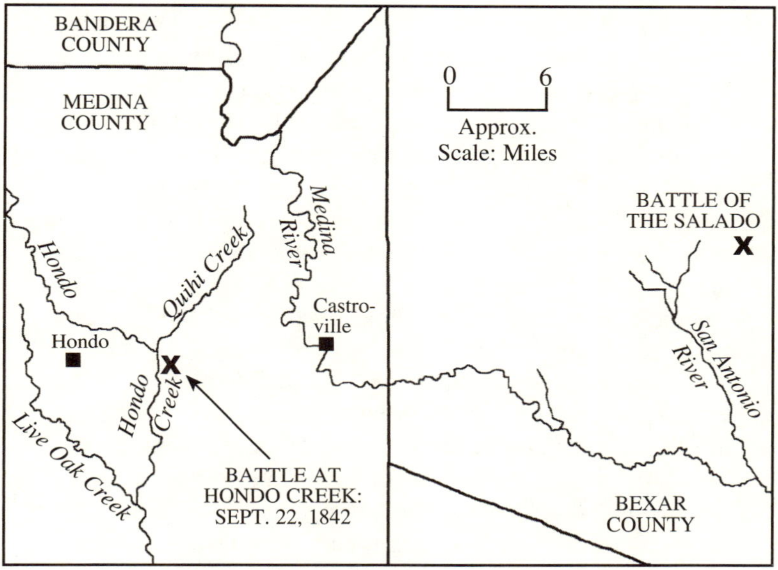

> right cheek bone. To prevent him from falling and being trampled to death, I threw my right arm round him, seizing the rein of his bridle with my right and guiding his horse and mine at the same time, [and] bore him safely to the rear, in a speechless fashion. His first cry was for water, which was furnished as quickly as possible. He recovered from his wound.

Four Texans were wounded at Hondo Creek: Arch Gibson in the face; Hurd "Dutch" Perry, badly wounded in the bowels; John Castleman; and William G. Cooke, who received a slight wound from grape shot. Woll reported that his forces had suffered five men killed and others wounded.[27]

Jack Hays' men succeeded in capturing the Mexican cannon on the east side of the Hondo but they were only able to hold it for about ten minutes. The other Mexican cannon on the west side continued to fire and a large number of Woll's infantrymen advanced on Hays' small group of men. Hays fell back, even as Colonel Caldwell was arriving on the scene with the bulk of the Texan volunteers. Shots were exchanged as dusk began to fall.[28]

Adrian Woll gave a report of his encounter with the Texans on the Medina River and Arroyo Hondo several days later. He said that he had turned back to engage Caldwell's forces when he learned that the Texans hoped to capture Mexican officers.[29]

> I immediately countermarched with 100 infantrymen, a light cannon and 50 horsemen, leaving the camp under command of Colonel Sebastian Moro del Moral, while sending ahead Capt. Agatón Quiñones with ten of his scouts, to open fire against the Texans as soon as he saw them, but with the expressed order of retreating and drawing the enemy toward me. Said officer complied exactly with my orders, and the Texan advance guard of some 100 men, emboldened by the retreat of said Captain Quiñones, was already charging with great vehemence, when the fire of our Infantry and of the cannon compelled them to flee in haste, leaving behind some dead horses and carrying five wounded off with them, among them a Captain who, as I learned, died on reaching the bulk of the enemy force. The said crowd of Texans, terrified, split up in small fractions, and retreated fleeing in all directions toward their homes.

Woll no doubt hoped that the captain was Jack Hays. Lt. Col. Moore's failure to allow William Eastland to bring out more horsemen had crippled Hays' efforts to hold the Mexican cannon. The differences of opinion between Moore and Caldwell would soon drive a wedge between the Texians. The balance of the Mexican rear guard fled as nightfall approached, bringing an end to the brief skirmish at Hondo Creek.

Just after dark, Henry McCulloch found his old friend Arch Gibson lying on a blanket beside a tree. Gibson's brother Jim was attending to him while Hurd Perry lay moaning for water on another blanket nearby. McCulloch's ranging companion Clem Hinds "heard their pitiful moans and cries for water." He gathered canteens, went out into the night and soon returned with ample water for the wounded men.[30]

The Mexicans made camp for the night a short distance away, blazing numerous camp fires that were easily spotted. The Mexicans instead slipped away during the night, leaving their fires burning. When ranger scouts eased up on their camp, they found their foes had fooled them.[31]

Colonel Caldwell held another council of war after daybreak on September 23. "Feeling anxious to overtake the enemy early in the day, lest the coming night might interfere with the capture, as on the evening before, I did all I could to assist both Hays and Caldwell to get the men ready," Zachariah Morrell testified.[32]

Morrell, eager to recover his captured son, soon found that Woll's forces had moved about six miles away onto a prairie where they could use their artillery fire to full advantage. Morrell, Caldwell, Hays and other men like Judge Hemphill spoke eagerly about continuing the pursuit of Woll. Others were not willing to fight again. Major Mayfield, who had tried unsuccessfully to rally Texans to support Jack Hays in his cannon charge the previous afternoon, considered it futile to pursue Woll any further.[33]

As Mayfield spoke about the overwhelming numbers of the Mexican force, Morrell "was absolutely furious." He interrupted Mayfield and said that he, for one, was more than willing to make another fight against Woll's troops. To his chagrin, he found that many of the Texans were tired, and were discouraged by their worn-out horses, dwindling ammunition and lack of supplies. Many of the men who had fought with Caldwell were receptive to the prospect of returning home to check on their families. Some felt that their victories on Salado Creek and in the Hondo Creek skirmish were enough.[34]

Disagreements among command arose and the volunteers voted Moore to be their commander in place of Caldwell. Jim Nichols noted that many of Caldwell's supporters were upset with John Moore taking over from their leader. "A goodly number of Caldwell's men turned back from here," Nichols wrote. "When we resumed our march, I joined Hays' spy company."[35]

About 300 of the volunteers retraced their steps to San Antonio with Edward Burleson, arriving on September 24. On the following day, a meeting was held in front of the Alamo. According to John Henry Brown, "Burleson addressed the crowd, then increased to about twelve hundred. He recapitulated the repeated outrages of the Mexicans within the last year or two, and outlined a plan for a retaliatory expedition into Mexico. He advised those present to return home, recruit their horses, procure suitable clothing, supplies, arms and ammunition and rendezvous at San Antonio a month later." Major Mayfield then appealed to the volunteers from Fayette County to follow him to the site of the Dawson battle to bury the bodies of the fallen Texans. The Dawson victims would remain interred on the battlefield until 1848, when they were exhumed, removed and buried on what is called Monument Hill near La Grange.[36]

Reverend Morrell, for one, never forgave Mayfield for breaking up the Texan forces. "Five hundred such Texans as ours could easily have killed and captured the whole army," he wrote. "This was certainly one of the most disgraceful affairs that ever occurred in Texas." His own son Allen and the other Texan prisoners of war were thus carried off back into Mexico for a lengthy imprisonment.[37]

Scout Robert Hall later assessed the breakdown of the Texian forces.[38]

> I think there were about a half dozen men who wanted to have command of the army, and they were constantly caucusing and trying in some way to remove old Paint Caldwell. Woll began to retreat again. We skirmished with his rear guard. Our officers constantly differed with each other, and many wanted to play the general; consequently Gen. Woll marched away from us.

Woll's invasion further unnerved Tejano residents of Béxar. They had faced reprisals from Anglo-Texans following the earlier Vasquez invasion, so as many as 200 San Antonio-area Tejano families left their homes as Woll retreated. They went with Juan Seguín to live south of the Rio Grande, almost halving the number of Tejanos living in San Antonio by October. Most would return within six months, however, explaining that they had left in fear of Mexican reprisals. In reality, their fears had been based more on Anglo-Texan reprisals.[39]

The Woll invasion was over and finger-pointing would prevail for some time. Caldwell was blamed for not retaining command of the men he had commanded in the Salado fight, letting Moore and Mayfield take over from him. Caldwell was troubled by this turn of events and in being blamed for giving up the pursuit. He would die on December 28, 1842, soon after returning to Gonzales.[40]

CHAPTER 6

The Somervell and Mier Expeditions

September 23, 1842–January 1843

The Somervell Expedition

The Texans had allowed Woll's troops to escape, but they did not give up the plans for revenge and for recapturing their own men. Mathew Caldwell's report indicates that many of his men had returned home but that he planned to reassemble forces in 30 days. Ned Burleson set October 25 as the date for men to rally in San Antonio. Volunteers began drifting into town during October, among them a Washington County company under Captain Samuel Bogart. Many weeks would pass before an effectively organized force of men would be able to set out toward Mexico.[1]

President Houston wrote to one of his militia leaders, Brigadier General Alexander Somervell of San Felipe, on October 3, 1842. Houston advised Somervell to "proceed to the most eligible point on the southwestern frontier of Texas, and concentrate with the force now under your command." Somervell was directed to advance into "the enemy territory" if necessary and if he could maintain an element of surprise. He told the general to maintain discipline and control of his troops while observing the rules of civilized warfare. Somervell was also advised to "rely upon the gallant Hays and his companions" to cooperate with his efforts. Among the troops which eventually marched to San Antonio were the companies of two regiments of militia which had been ordered out by President Houston.[2]

While volunteers assembled in San Antonio during October, Sam Houston continued to exert efforts toward diplomacy with the Texas Indians. He sent commissioners to make a treaty with the scattered eastern Indians in October with a meeting held at a Waco village. He wrote a letter to Eli Chandler to raise a detachment of rangers to escort the commissioners. One of the Indian commissioners wrote on the back of Houston's letter to Chandler that it might be wise to increase the ten or 15 proposed men to twenty. Chandler was able to raise 17 men who served for 25 days and brought everyone home safely.[3]

Jack Hays' rangers remained in operation around San Antonio as Alexander Somervell attempted to organize his expedition against Mexico. Captain Bogart's volunteer company also existed in San Antonio during this time. He wanted to send a patrol of his men out toward the Nueces River to watch for Woll's men and he asked Captain Hays for a guide. Hays did not furnish a man but Bogart sent his forces nonetheless, following Woll's route to the river. Bogart thereafter kept his spies out on patrol to watch for Mexican forces.[4]

Hays' rangers were not involved in any significant actions or scouts during October which have been recorded. As the days passed idly while awaiting incoming troops, Somervell sent out spies to keep a watch for Mexican activities. On October 27, Captain Hays sent out spies down the Medina Road while Sam Bogart sent out Harvey Alexander Adams and Marshall Bennett from his company to cross the San Antonio River. Adams wrote that they were ordered to proceed "by the old Mission San Juan on to the Labadia Road till we cross Salado, crossing about one-half mile so that we could see over the surrounding country in order to discover fires, if any. We were out there until about 7 p.m. when we returned campward, having surprised no one during our march and returned to camp about 11 a.m."[5]

As October passed into early November, the gathering Texan companies were ordered to concentrate at the old Mission San José on the San Antonio River for the purpose of forming a permanent organization. During this time, Captain John Goodloe Warren Pierson rode out of town on November 6 on a scout with his volunteer company. The former revolutionary ranger returned to San Antonio several days later. Three of his men had a brush with Comanches. One man made his way independently back into town on November 10 after being separated from his two companions during the excitement. No further encounters with Indians were noted during the early days of November.[6]

The proposed invasion of Mexico got off to an ill-fated start as General Somervell leisurely spent his time about San Antonio entertaining himself and casually organizing his forces. The Texans in town numbered about 1,200, which Somervell split into two brigades of properly formed companies on November 11. Colonel Joseph L. Bennett commanded the First Brigade and Colonel James R. Cook and Lt. Colonel Jesse B. McCrocklin of Washington County took command of the Second Brigade.[7]

In addition to the regular troops, two scouting companies remained unattached to either brigade. The first was the ranging company of Captain Hays, which numbered 18 men at the time Somervell was organizing his forces. His officers were first lieutenant Henry McCulloch, second lieutenant Ephraim McLean and orderly sergeant James "Smokey" Henderson. More men arrived daily until Hays' company had about 60 men.[8]

Young Chief Flacco and a small group of his Lipan Apaches operated with Hays. In recognition of his past service to Texas, Flacco had been given the honorary title of "Colonel" along with a full colonel's uniform, plumed hat and a sword. Flacco's men included one Lipan named Luis from New Mexico who had been smuggled out of a Mexican prison by the Santa Fe prisoners.[9]

Hays wrote to Secretary of War and Marine George W. Hill on November 12, informing him of the $400 in company expenses he had incurred personally during the year. He also reported with pleasure that the Texas frontiers had for several months enjoyed "almost an immunity from the incursions of Indians. The only source from which danger is now apprehended is the robbing parties of Mexicans that have, until recently, been employed by the Mexican government on the frontier."[10]

In reality, the larger danger now posed for Tejano settlers was the unruly army assembled by Somervell. Many of his men were new to Texas and the less scrupulous members of this expedition would turn down no opportunity to gather plunder on either side of the claimed borders of the Republic of Texas.[11]

The other scouting company was the mounted unit under Captain Bogart from Washington County. On Sunday, November 13, Bogart's company was paraded and 17 men were ordered to join Somervell's regiment. Bogart refused to give up any of his men, reminding the general that he had been given the privilege on November 7 of operating his men as an independent spy company. Somervell then tried ordering Bogart's spies to join Jack Hays' company but Bogart again refused, saying he would go home if his men were not given equal status to that of Captain Hays' unit.[12]

Bogart's 60-man spy company was thus allowed to remain as a separate unit. Private Harvey Adams of Bogart's scouting company noted on Monday, November 14, "Captain Bogart obtained an order from the Commanding General [Somervell] to the effect that he should move on with Capt. Hays and when any spies were sent out from the main body, than an equal proportion should be detailed from each company." When Hays was absent on scouting missions, Bogart could command both units. Although neither man was satisfied with this arrangement, Bogart declined other offers to take on a regimental command.[13]

General Somervell's expedition finally departed San Antonio on November 13 for the Medina River. He then set up camp for another two weeks awaiting a promised cannon. When it did finally arrive, the casual commander then refused to take it along, much to the chagrin of his disgusted troops.[14]

On November 15, Jack Hays set out with several men to reconnoiter the ground close to camp. After spotting three Indians or Mexicans in the distance, he raced back to camp and called for 15 or more men with the best horses to follow. "The men were promptly in the saddle," wrote Harvey Adams. "They went on the trail until darkness put an end to the pursuit and returned to camp, but saw no more of them. They came up with a loose American horse but he was wild, and it being so late in the evening, they failed to capture him."[15]

The expedition struck out across country instead of following the Laredo road. The Texans floundered through mud and cold weather for three days before reaching firmer ground. What could have been a seven-day march turned into 17 days, and Sterling Hendricks for one felt that the blame lay somewhere between the poor leadership of General Somervell and the piloting of Jack Hays. In fairness, Hays was often well out ahead of the expedition with Henry McCulloch, Flacco and two Lipan scouts in search of trouble.[16]

Capt. Bogart's Scouts: September 25, 1842–Jan. 20, 1843

Captain:
Samuel Bogart
First Lieutenant:
John M. Dickson
Second Lieutenant:
Sterling B. Hendricks
First Sergeant:
Jabez D. Giddings
Second Sergeant:
John Ashmore
Third Sergeant:
William B. Cody
First Corporal:
Rufus Charles
Second Corporal:
Henry Day
Third Corporal:
Thomas Bailey

Privates:
Harvey Alexander Adams
William W. Allen
John Atkinson
Francis Hall Ayers
William P. Ayers
William Bates
Thomas S. Baxter
Thomas W. Bell
Marshall B. Bennett
Kernan Brenan
A.S. Brooksher
William Brown
John Campbell
B. W. Chamberlain
Benjamin L. Cheek
Lewis C. Clemons
C. W. Crawford
John W. Crawford
William B. Dean
George H. DeMoss
W. Trimmier Dobson
Newton J. Edney
James W. Foster
William Gilleland
George W. Harbour
Horace Hogan Helfer
Thomas Hood
John Ivy
William E. Jackson
Dan R. Jones
Edward H. Kemp
James H. Kinney
James Knight
William H. Kuykendall
Elisha D. Little
Joseph T. Marshall
John A. McDade
William McIntire
Thomas J. Middleton
John Mitchell
John M. Payne
Williamson Price
William P. Rutledge
William A. Santy
John E. Sherrod
James B. Stephenson
John M. Stevens
Thomas Stevens
James H. Stribling
B. Edward Tarver
William A. Temple
John Trimmier
Thomas Trimmier
John T. Violett
Edward Walker
A. G. Williams
William H. Woodard
Thomas Wooldridge
Charles Young

Source: Texas State Archives muster roll and author's search of Republic records.

Rufus Perry, who had joined Captain Hays' company after the Salado battle, recalled that Somervell received much ridicule for his poor efforts to guide his men. "The boys raised the cry, 'Where was Gen. Somervell in 1842? Up to his ass in mud, god-damn him.' But old Somervell just laughed and said, 'All right, boys, we will come out all right yet.' When we got through, our horses was about played out."[17]

Tempers flared when the Texans finally emerged from the bog and made camp. With Hays absent on a scout, Captain Bogart ordered the remaining men in the spy company to bivouac with his company. Lieutenant Ephraim McLean, in acting command of Hays' remaining rangers, refused to let his men move and several of them cursed Bogart. When Hays returned, a meeting was called between Hays, Bogart, Somervell and others. Some of the rangers who attended the meeting began berating Bogart, including Lt. McLean and Guy Stokes. Bogart left the meeting and later threatened to court martial McLean and Stokes, although this never materialized.[18]

Acting Secretary of War Morgan C. Hamilton wrote a blistering letter to General Somervell on November 19, in which he criticized the commander for not communicating on his actions thus far. Reports of mismanaged troops compelled Hamilton to order Somervell to assess his situation and determine if he had a reasonable force to continue his campaign. Hamilton explained that Captain Hays had broad powers to act as commander of the western frontier and should act independently. If Somervell moved his forces, Hays should report to him and act under his orders. If Somervell disbanded his troops before crossing the Rio Grande, Hamilton said that Hays should revert to his old status and could raise three ranging companies, if necessary.[19]

Somervell ultimately decided that his forces—now reduced to about 750 men—were not strong enough to successfully attack the town of San Fernando de Rosas. Intelligence indicated that about 800 Mexican troops under General Isidro Reyes were stationed at San Fernando, a town equivalent in size to San Antonio that was situated about 38 miles west and slightly north of Presidio del Río Grande. The Mexican troops at San Fernando and at Santa Rita de Morelos possessed artillery, while a smaller military force of less than one hundred soldiers was reported to be at the small garrison of Laredo. Due to his own dwindling numbers and the fact that this latter town was less heavily fortified, General Somervell thus held a council of war in which his officers unanimously decided to march against Laredo instead of San Fernando.[20]

The army of occupation under General Somervell finally marched out from the west bank of the Medina on the morning of November 25 down the Presidio Road. Flacco's Lipan scouts led the procession with the two scouting companies under Hays and Bogart. Mrs. Eleanor Elliott of San Antonio had fashioned a new flag that was flown by Hays' company this day which was stitched with the motto, "We give but ask no quarter."[21]

The expedition moved toward the Presidio Road with the hope of confusing any spies who might be watching them that their intention was to cross the Rio Grande along that road. Their guide chose the wrong road the next day, however, and much time was lost before Captain Hays was able to make a reconnaissance mission to determine their correct course. A heavy rain set in during the night which only further complicated their movements on November 27. Tempers flared again as men struggled to move their horses and pack mules through the boggy mire. By mid-afternoon of the 29th, the army had only managed to cover 50 miles from their Medina campground to Pilot Knob near the Laredo Road.[22]

By November 30, Somervell assigned Captain Hays' unit as the spy company for his expedition and designated Captain Bogart's company to be the leading company within the column, a position of honor. When the column started out the following morning, however, Bogart's men refused to follow Hays' spy company. They galloped after the rangers and trotted side by side with Hays' men for several miles until an exasperated General Somervell could catch up to them. One of the expedition volunteers, Sterling Brown Hendricks, wrote that the Hays and Bogart companies were "trying to outstrip each other for the highest post of honor." Somervell ordered Bogart's mounted men back into their proper secondary position, at which time many of the Washington County men threatened to return home. Bogart's company did finally agree to stay on for the sake of the expedition.[23]

During the ensuing days, Hays' company operated in conjunction with his old companion Flacco and a small group of his

Lipan Apache scouts. Hays stayed ahead of Somervell's main force, spying for signs of Mexican troops and sending back intelligence. Hays sent back a message to Somervell on the night of December 2, with Flacco and another Lipan. He said that he had gone on ahead to scout the Mexican border while leaving the rest of his men on the west bank of the Nueces. Crossing the swollen Nueces was no small chore. Ranger Bill Oury feared that his horse would go under at any moment and get snagged on a submerged tree trunk in the cold, swirling waters.[24]

The Nueces was in flood stage at this time and Captain Bogart's men had to build a makeshift bridge for all of the troops to use for safe crossing of their provisions. Swimming their horses over proved to be adventurous, as Harvey Adams recorded:[25]

> We were obliged to stand in the water about waist deep 3 hours before all things were safely over, then we swam our horses over. No accident occurred except the drowning of a horse of one of the men belonging to our company. He had tarried behind with some 5 or 6 others trying to recover a pair of saddle bags which an old man lost a day or two before, containing $100 in gold and silver, with some paper and other valuables.

When this group of men attempted to cross the Nueces River on November 3, the man and his horse were both nearly lost to their inability to swim. The man drifted down river until he caught himself on a pile of driftwood, where his companions soon rescued him with ropes.

The Washington County company of Captain William S. Fisher and the Lavaca company of Captain Isaac N. Mitchell were detailed to build the brush bridge across the Nueces. John Henry Brown, first sergeant of Mitchell's company, recalled:[26]

> Men with hatchets swam over and from both sides trees were felled into the stream, their tops meeting and overlapping. Then came large bushes worked in, getting smaller and smaller until finally the bridge was floored with layers of reed cane and long grass, so that next morning all the horses and pack mules passed safely over.

Somervell's expedition camped on the west bank of the swollen river, drying their baggage while awaiting word from Jack Hays. During the night of December 4, a heavy rain and cold wind set in and about midnight a general stampede of Texan mules and horses took place. "It was a fearful time," wrote Sergeant Brown. "Dark as pitch and nearly a thousand horses and mules rushing blindly, furiously over the men." Reverend Edward L. Fontaine, a grandson of Patrick Henry, fell into a bed of cactus while escaping the stampede and his captain, Dr. Jerome B. Robertson, spent many hours extracting the thorns from Fontaine.[27]

Bogart's company was finally sent forward on December 5 with some of the Lipan scouts to locate the ranger commander. Flacco and another Lipan returned the next day to report that Captain Hays had gone toward Laredo and captured two Mexican rancheros. Hays' men had not found any sign of Mexican forces along the river and Flacco said that Hays had injured his horse chasing down the prisoners and he was camped about 18 miles away.[28]

En route to Hays' camp, Bogart's scouts were overtaken by the rest of Hays' men. They told him that the entire Texas horse herd had been stampeded but that Bogart's men and the other spies were to continue. One of Hays' two prisoners managed to escape from a careless guard, William Alsbury, and the rangers made a forced march toward Laredo to try and prevent their escapee from alerting the Mexicans in town.[29]

Laredo, established in 1755, was located on the northeastern bank of the Rio Grande, the river which was generally considered to be the southern boundary of the new Republic of Texas. The roughly 2,000 residents of Laredo, however, still considered themselves to be citizens of the Mexican state of Tamaulipas. From the time that Texas declared its independence in 1836, Laradoans rightfully felt that they were never truly under the jurisdiction of Texas until 1846, during the Mexican War.[30]

When word of the escaped prisoner reached General Somervell, he sent the spies of Hays and Bogart with other troops to cut off any Mexican forces which were trying to reach Laredo. When the main body of troops reached the swollen Rio Grande, they refused to cross without boats or rafts. Hays sent out Rufus Perry, Thomas Jefferson Green, Ben McCulloch, Ad Gillespie and Sam Walker to steal all of the Mexican boats and secure them across from Laredo for the Texans' use. "You ought to have heard the Mexican women laughing at us," Perry recalled. "I told the boys when I heard them laughing that the jig was up and that the birds had flown."[31]

On December 7, Somervell ordered Colonel James Cook to cross the Rio Grande with six companies of his best mounted men to cut off the escape of the Mexican garrison. Cook, however, failed to find a place to safely cross the river due to the heavy rains. He instead opted to set up his men on the outskirts of Laredo, on the Republic of Texas' claimed side of the border, that night to wait for Somervell's main body to catch up with them. The two spy companies of Hays and Bogart were also on hand, so they were sent forward on foot around 4:00 a.m. on December 8 to seize the town.[32]

The advance scouts remained on horseback in a half-moon formation around the outskirts of Laredo in the hours before daybreak. Ben McCulloch captured a young boy before dawn who had come down to water his mule. The Texans learned with disappointment that the approximately one hundred Mexican soldiers in town, aware of their advance, had already retreated across the Rio Grande with many of the citizens. The scouts thus rode into town to find only women, children, dogs and a few old men that had been left behind.[33]

The remaining townspeople shouted praises of, "¡Buenos hombres, buenos Americanos!" and offered the Texans cakes and other items to eat. Disappointed at the results of their "siege" of Laredo, Bogart and Hays' men retired to a ravine to sleep and rest their horses. The town's alcalde surrendered his town to the Texans, who had their flag flying in the town square fifteen minutes before General Somervell marched in with the balance of his troops. The general requisitioned meat and supplies for his troops and set up his camp about a mile above town.[34]

The Laredo alcalde did offer eight or ten cattle and some meager supplies for the Texans around noon, but Somervell's men were not impressed. Groups of soldiers slipped out of the Texas camp without orders and returned to loot the town. Justifying their lawless acts by considering the Laredo townspeople to be under Mexican rule and thus fair game for plunder, Somervell's troops became lustful criminals who kicked in doors and helped themselves to whatever they could find. Somervell

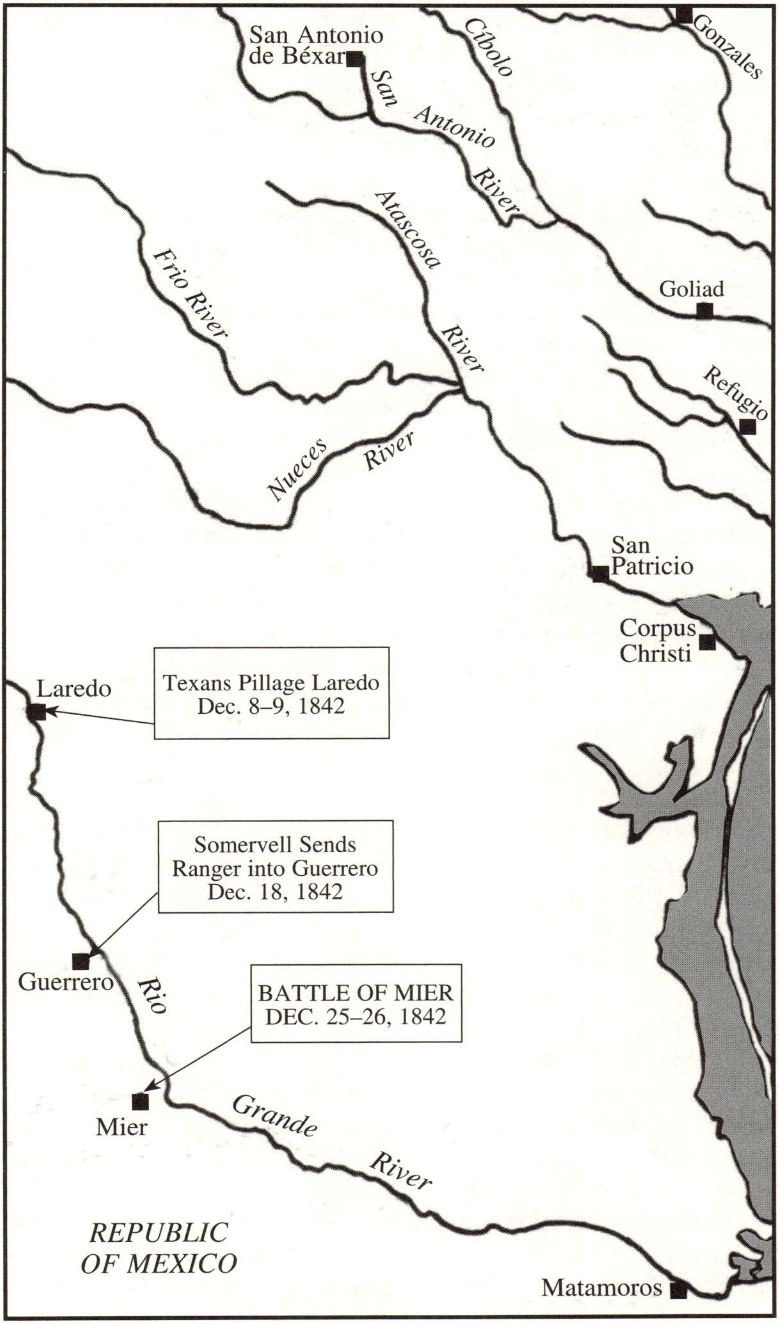
San Antonio
de Béxar
Cíbolo
Gonzales
San
Antonio
River
Atascosa
River
Frio River
Goliad
Refugio
Nueces
River
San
Patricio
Corpus
Christi
Laredo
Texans Pillage Laredo
Dec. 8–9, 1842
Somervell Sends
Ranger into Guerrero
Dec. 18, 1842
Guerrero
Rio
BATTLE OF MIER
DEC. 25–26, 1842
Mier
Grande
River
REPUBLIC
OF MEXICO
Matamoros

finally resorted to moving his camp about three miles from town to try and put a halt to the looting.[35]

Thomas Jefferson Green took five men and crossed the Rio Grande at dusk. They rode into the little Mexican town of Galveston, planted the Texan flag and demanded five mules. When Green returned to the Texas camp near Laredo, Somervell did not punish him for stealing but did pass strict order to forbid men from leaving camp without orders from their company commanders. The following morning, many captains allowed their men to "examine" Laredo and as many as two hundred rode back into the town to continue their looting.[36]

The scene turned ugly as one-third of Somervell's army ransacked the town, stealing everything of value and harassing the townspeople. They used logs to break down doors and they removed everything from cigarettes to women's underwear. They looped a rope around the neck of alcalde Florencio Villareal and had a gun to his head, demanding to know where he had hidden the town's silver, when Major Henry Davis arrived and demanded his release. Davis was so disgusted with the behavior of the Texans that he resigned and headed for home. Some soldiers claimed that General Somervell condoned this behavior on December 9 until the pillaging became too rampant. He then sent officers into Laredo and ordered his men to return immediately.[37]

As the looters returned to camp from town, they were ordered to pile up their plunder of clothes, hats, blankets, saddles and cooking utensils. The soldiers argued that their stealing was justified, particularly since some of the items they collected even belonged to San Antonio citizens who had been similarly plundered earlier by Woll and Vasquez's troops. Somervell apologized to Villareal and allowed his citizens to bring carts to haul away much of the stolen goods.[38]

Somervell moved his forces forward through thorn bushes and prickly pear to avoid being confronted by the Mexican army in this countryside. He marched his troops in a circuitous route the next morning to find water after a cold night with only a few campfires allowed. Men began to realize that their leader did not seem willing to continue with the campaign into Mexico. Some were convinced that Somervell had orders from Sam Houston to break up the campaign. "It was said that he had secret orders from Genl. Houston to drag the men round till they would be glad to get home again, and if nothing else would do them, to cross the Rio Grande, but not disturb the [Mexican] people," Harvey Adams wrote in his diary. The brigade's inspector, Colonel Tom Green of Fayette County (not to be confused with Hays scout Thomas Jefferson Green), resigned in disgust on December 10 and joined Captain Hays as a private soldier.[39]

By December 11, there were about 737 men in Somervell's force but after a discussion some 187 of these men decided to return home that day with Colonel Joseph Bennett. Somervell decided nonetheless that he would proceed down the east banks of the Rio Grande, cross the river and capture the Mexican town of Guerrero, located some 54 miles below Laredo. The Texans had marched to within six miles of the town by December 14, when they captured some shepherds on some ranches and learned that there were no Mexican troops in Guerrero.[40]

From the two scouting companies, 17 of Captain Hays' rangers and 35 of Captain Bogart's men swam some of their horses across the Rio Grande and used canoes to move men and some of their supplies. Mexican cavalrymen were soon spotted racing toward them and the spies took up a defensive position in gullies at the foot of a slope. Other Texans on the other side of the Rio Grande saw the Mexican forces arriving and most of Somervell's men began crossing over to join the action.[41]

Somervell, however, could not be convinced to engage the Mexicans and by the following morning they had vanished. He instead submitted a request for provisions from the Guerrero town the next day so that his troops could feast in the snow, sleet and freezing temperatures that had settled on them. The bitter conditions and the refusal of Somervell to go on the offensive compelled most of the troops to cross back over into Texas the following day. "The whole command was sullen, indignant and mutinous," wrote Sergeant Brown. Hays and Bogart's men were ordered into town to demand $5,000 for new horses. When they reached Guerrero, the curious townspeople offered all that they had—cigars, sweets, corn for the horses and all their money, which amounted to only $381. When the rangers returned with these meager offerings to confer with Somervell at the river, he flew into a rage. He sent town officials back to Guerrero with the people's money and issued orders on the following day,

December 19, that effectively ended his ill-fated campaign. Somervell ordered his army to march to the junction of the Frio and Nueces rivers and then on to Gonzales to be disbanded.[42]

Some two hundred men struck out for home, leaving 307 behind who still wished to invade Mexico. Among the many turning for home were Colonel James Cook, Captain Peter Bell, Adjutant General John Hemphill, Lt. Colonel George Howard, Major David Murphree, Captain John Shelby McNeill, Captain Mitchell, Captain Bogart, James A. Sylvester (who had helped to capture General Santa Anna at San Jacinto), and Sergeant John Henry Brown.[43]

Five company commanders—Ewen Cameron, William S. Fisher, William Eastland, William A. Ryon and John G. W. Pierson—went to Somervell and announced that they would be continuing the campaign without their general. The remaining men of the Mier Expedition were organized into six formal companies. Six of Jack Hay's rangers—Henry Bridger, John Livergood, John Twohig, Bigfoot Wallace, George Walton and Isaac Zumwalt—opted to stay for the expedition and enrolled in Captain Charles Keller Reese's Company F. Two other Hays rangers, Edward Wright and John McMullen, joined Captain Ewen Cameron's Company A. Thomas Jefferson Green also broke from Hays' spies to become second-in-command of the Mier Expedition. Colonel William Fisher took acting command of the remaining men who wanted to continue the expedition. Many of those who broke from Somervell still wanted horses that he had promised them from the spoils of captured Mexican goods. Many of their own horses were broken down and were in no condition for the long ride home.[44]

Jack Hays and the majority of his rangers opted not to affiliate with Colonel Fisher's expedition in a formal manner. He had never been counted on any of Somervell's musters and he was not about to take on an official status with the remaining men. Hays did promise to remain with Fisher for a few days to perform voluntary scouting services.[45]

Captain Hays parted with his Lipan friends as Flacco had opted to return home toward Gonzales in company with General Somervell's men and Sam Bogart's scouting company. The nearly-starved men were forced to scavenge roots and herbs and even ate their horses en route home. The Somervell Expedition had thus ended and those continuing on became part of what was labeled the Mier Expedition.[46]

★★★★★

The Battle of Mier

While many of Alexander Somervell's men made their way back home, William Fisher took the rest of his group on into Mexico. The force crossed the Rio Grande on December 20 on boats that Thomas Green had seized below Guerrero. During the next three days, Hays and his rangers led the Texans down the river toward the Mexican town of Mier, a small village situated in a bend of the Rio Alamo, which flows into the Rio Grande. Upon entering the desolate town with his scouts, Hays found no soldiers there and dispatched a courier to notify Fisher of his findings.[47]

Hays' company remained overnight at Mier until Colonel Fisher's forces caught up with them. The ranger captain felt that he had completed his obligations of leading the troops to Mier and that service on the southwestern frontier of Texas was his proper duty. He advised Fisher of his plan to leave and warned him that a large Mexican force was said to be assembling to oppose the Texans. Hays and most of his company departed Mier in the early hours of December 24.[48]

As Hays was returning toward San Antonio some 100 miles along his journey, he found that one of his prize horses had gotten loose and headed for the Rio Grande. He finally located his lost horse in the stable of a Mexican ranch on the river where Somervell's forces had camped before entering Guerrero. Hays slipped in after dark and retrieved his horse from the Mexican ranch without a shot being fired.[49]

During the return, Hays sent Rufus Perry on ahead to find something for the men to eat. "The first thing I killed was a lot of turkeys," he related. "I dressed them and hung them up, putting the name of Hays and George Neil on them. The next thing was a large work steer which I found by himself as wild as a deer." Perry slaughtered the steer as well. The rangers ate well for the first time in weeks. Perry moved ahead to the Medina River and slaughtered some cattle for Hays' company. "We then rested up for a few days then split up and lit out for home," he said. Hays'

This sketch by Mier prisoner Charles McLaughlin shows the execution of Texans who were unfortunate enough to draw one of the deadly black beans at the Mexican prison at Hacienda del Salado. Among the 17 Texans executed on March 25, 1843, were three former Texas Rangers. McLaughlin sketch from Thomas Jefferson Green's Journal of the Texian Expedition against Mier *(1845). The University of Texas at Austin, Center for American History.*

rangers would be a week longer in making their return to the settlements than Somervell's men.[50]

Somervell's men endured their own trying conditions while marching back through Texas in cold, wet weather without sufficient food or rest. Captain Hays' rangers apparently moved on back toward San Antonio on their own. Sam Bogart's spies became lost and did not reach San Antonio until January 4, 1843, after a prolonged period of suffering.[51]

In his reports of the campaign, Somervell did not count Jack Hays' ranging unit as being part of his command. He did account for Captain Bogart's spies but Somervell apparently never considered Hays' men to be officially attached to his expedition. Hays, for his part, resumed his role as frontier commander and simply moved on from the disappointing experience of Somervell's expedition.[52]

Hays suffered one final indignity during the return home.

Sometime after warning the Texans about a possible ambush, his trusted Lipan friend Flacco was murdered. The true murderer was never discovered, although the Lipans would blame someone in San Antonio for his death. Despite damage control efforts made by President Houston, the Lipans were thereafter hostile in nature when dealing with San Antonio townspeople.[53]

President Houston wrote a letter to Flacco's father on March 28, 1843, in which he praised the Indian ranger's service to Texas. "Your chiefs look down upon the earth and groan in trouble. Your warriors weep—the loud voices of grief are heard from your women and children. The songs of the birds are silent...Flaco was a friend to the white brothers. They will not forget him."[54]

Shortly after the departure of Hays' rangers, Fisher's troops fought a battle with Mexican troops at Mier on December 25–26, 1842. Although outnumbered ten to one, the Texans killed and wounded hundreds of Mexican soldiers against their own losses of about 16 killed and 17 severely wounded. Injured in battle, Colonel Fisher finally agreed to a surrender. The remaining Texans surrendered when promised that they would be treated as prisoners of war. Among those captured were at least eight rangers who had previously served under Jack Hays who had decided to continue with the expedition. Tom Green angrily smashed his rifle rather than hand it over to his Mexican captors. Bigfoot Wallace was equally bitter, remarking, "Never shall I forget the humiliation of my feelings."[55]

The prisoners endured a long captivity in Mexico and were marched from Matamoros toward Mexico City during early 1843. On February 11, the Texan POWs managed to escape from their prison at Hacienda del Salado. Ewen Cameron and Sam Walker wrestled two guards to the ground while other Texan prisoners seized the guards' guns as they ate their breakfast. Five Texans and five Mexican guards were mortally wounded during the escape. The escapees headed for the mountains and soon became scattered. Mexican forces pursued and captured most of the Texans during the next two weeks. John Alexander and Major William Oldham survived a perilous journey through the mountains and across the Rio Grande, arriving back at San Antonio in mid-April. Only two other Texans from this escape party were known to have made it back home alive, Thomas W. Cox and John L. D. Blackburn.[56]

Captains John Pierson, William Ryon, John Baker and two other Mier prisoners wrote a letter on April 27, in which they described their recapture.[57]

> Some days after our flight from the Salado when we were completely exhausted from climbing the lofty mountains near Salado under a broiling sun without water for nearly a week, we were surrounded in the night by the enemy's cavalry to whom we surrendered only upon the expressed condition that we should be treated as prisoners of war. Notwithstanding this pledge to men literally dying from the cause above assigned, we were marched into camp and tied with raw hides in couples and told if one man misbehaved the whole should be instantly shot.

President Santa Anna was not pleased with the conduct of the escaped Texans, who were marched back to a new prison at Saltillo. By decree of Santa Anna, every tenth man of the 176 who were recaptured was to be shot to death. In order to determine their fate, each Texan was forced on March 25 to reach into an earthen pot to draw a colored bean. The 159 who drew a white bean would live; the unlucky 17 who pulled a black bean were to be executed. Ewen Cameron, the leader of the escape, was ordered to draw first. He thrust his hand to the bottom of the jar and pulled a white bean. Captain Eastland, one of the officers who followed Cameron, pulled a black bean.[58]

Bigfoot Wallace, watching the proceedings, noticed that the black beans which were pulled by the unfortunate Texans appeared to be larger than the white ones. Wallace reached in, sifted several beans through his fingers and pulled out a small one with an indeterminable grayish color. Good fortune shined on the Texas Ranger when the officer in charge declared it to be a white bean.[59]

Among the 17 who drew black beans of execution were three former Texas Rangers: James Decatur Cocke, a veteran of Plum Creek; William Mosby Eastland; and Jasper Newton McDonald Thomson. One of the condemned men, Henry Whaling, insisted on a last meal and a cigar—which the Mexicans soldiers provided to him. Robert Dunham, another of the condemned men, wrote a last note to his mother, "I hope with firmness may God bless you, and may He in this last hour forgive and pardon all my sins."[60]

After the 17 Texans had been executed, the remaining Mier Expedition prisoners were marched deeper into Mexico. On April 24, Ewen Cameron was ordered to be executed as well for his part in leading the prison escape and for his past efforts to carry on the warfare with Mexico. Some believed that the order came from Colonel Canales, who had a great hatred for the former Ranger leader. Whatever the rationale, the great Scotsman Ewen Cameron faced his executioners without a blindfold and bared his breast toward the Mexican riflemen. He died instantly, struck squarely by eight musket balls.[61]

William Fisher and Tom Green were marched to the little village of Perote, lying some 160 miles from Mexico City. They were added to the 40 Texan prisoners already contained there who had been captured by General Woll in San Antonio or after the Dawson company battle in September 1842. One of these prisoners was Judge James W. Robinson, the former lieutenant governor of the provisional government of Texas in 1835. The prison at Perote was an old castle called San Carlos de Perote, built by the Spanish in the 1770s.[62]

On the night of July 3, 16 Texan prisoners escaped from the Perote castle, although half were quickly rounded up. Tom Green and seven others made it to the coast and sailed from Veracruz to New Orleans aboard an American steamer. Among the other seven escapees was former Jack Hays ranger John Twohig. "I remained a prisoner in chains until the night of the 3rd July 1843, when I made my escape from the castle," he related.[63]

In spite of the best diplomatic efforts by Texas and the United States, Mexico continued to hold the various Texan prisoners for many months. Disease claimed 20 Texans in the Perote castle prison by February 1844, including Dawson company survivor Norman Woods. It was not until March 24, 1844, that the last 35 men captured by General Woll some 18 months prior were finally escorted out of Perote as free men. The remaining 104 Texan survivors of the Mier Expedition remained imprisoned until September 14, 1844, before they were finally freed to begin their journey home to Texas.[64]

Among the former Texas Rangers who were finally freed in August and September were John Reagan Baker, John Bate Berry,

Jacob J. Humphreys, John McMullen, William B. Middleton, Lawson F. Mills, William Sanders Oury, John Pierson, Daniel Sullivan, Bigfoot Wallace and Isaac Zumwalt.

The Mier Expedition had been a failure but the sacrifice of the Black Bean victims and the other Texans who died in Mexican prisons would long be remembered by the frontiersmen who did return home. Bate Berry, whose Texas Ranger veteran brother Joseph Berry had died in Mexican captivity, was later reprimanded by General Zachary Taylor during the Mexican War when Berry vengefully scalped his Mexican victims.[65]

★ ★ ★ ★ ★

The Archives War

While Somervell and Fisher were carrying out their tragic expeditions into Mexico, short-term companies that might be considered as rangers had been called on to handle special duties. One such responsibility involved moving the archives of Texas back to the proper capital in Austin. Governmental functions had moved from Austin earlier in the year due to the Vasquez raid. Later in the year, President Houston had ordered that the archives be moved to a safer location in Washington-on-the-Brazos.[66]

Houston had given orders to former ranger captain Eli Chandler and Thomas Ingles Smith—who had both recently served as guards for George Terrell's Indian council—to carry the archives from Austin. Chandler and Smith met land commissioner Thomas W. Ward on the night of December 30, 1842, and began loading the archives papers on three wagons with 20 volunteers. Vigilantes in Austin, however, decided that the governmental papers would not be moved. Mrs. Angelina Eberly, who ran a local boarding house, spread the word and helped citizens roll a loaded cannon from Congress Avenue to the Land Office. Mrs. Eberly applied the torch and the cannon lobbed shot into the archives building. Chandler's men hurriedly took what papers, ledgers and books they had gathered and set out from town with their wagons.[67]

Another former ranger captain, Mark B. Lewis, gathered men and started in pursuit of Chandler's archive wagon with a cannon. Lewis' men caught up with the other former ranger captain at the crossing on Brushy Creek. After a few warning shots from the cannon, Chandler was compelled to surrender his wagonloads of archival papers to Lewis. The republic's papers, after the brief "Archives War," were thus returned to Austin by the vigilantes and stored for some time in Mrs. Eberly's boarding house.[68]

The House of Representatives of the Seventh Congress of Texas, in reviewing the events of the Archives War several weeks later, decided that the local citizens acted appropriately in their actions—despite claims made by Sam Houston. "The citizens of Austin, in resisting the armed force despatched by the Executive to execute his commands, unauthorized as they were, neither acted as a 'mob,' or were they 'in a state of beastly intoxication,' as His Excellency chooses to represent them," representatives Tod Robinson and John Caldwell ruled. Instead of facing the ire of the president, these citizens were said by the Congress to "deserve the thanks of the country for their conduct" in protecting the republic's archives.[69]

The only other scouting action of 1842 of any significance happened in mid-December when a company from Victoria made a raid into the disputed Nueces territory. Armed men had been seen at New Bahia—also known as Carlos' Rancho—during the times of the Vasquez and Woll invasions. New Bahia was believed by Texan travelers to have become a spy center for Mexican troops. Captain James P. Ownby therefore gathered a volunteer company of 120 men to investigate this ranch.[70]

Ownby's company gave the people there the choice to gather everything they owned and move to Mexico or they would be driven out forcefully. The New Bahia residents did not attempt to resist. Most packed and moved to Matamoros, while one family loyal to Texas moved to Victoria. There were rumblings for some time that another Mexican raid would come to punish Victoria for Captain Ownby's actions, but it did not materialize.[71]

The Republic of Texas had struggled through the year 1842, allowing two Mexican forces to briefly invade San Antonio. Their own counteroffensives had been poorly executed and during the course the Texans had suffered casualties and numerous men captured, some of whom would themselves be soon executed. One of the reports by the secretary of war late in the year detailed the problems he saw with the volunteer militia system. President Houston had no intentions of maintaining a true army, leaving the ranging system under Jack Hays as the only viable force to maintain order in between periods of crisis.

CHAPTER 7

"Active, Vigilant and Efficient"

1843

The Texas Congress was taxed with creating a new system for protecting its frontiers in the wake of the Mexican incursions of 1842. Citizens from the eastern portions of the state had not been of benefit to the more sparsely settled western counties during the times of crisis. Deciding that reestablishing a formal Texas Army was futile, the Congress opted to organize a new militia with designated commanders in order that the Republic of Texas would be able to be better organize itself in the event of another invasion attempt.[1]

The Seventh Congress passed a new frontier act on January 16, 1843, which declared a state of martial law between the Nueces and Rio Grande while hostilities existed between Mexico and Texas. The major general of the Texas Militia, once again Thomas Jefferson Rusk, was authorized to organize his militia throughout Texas into six brigades of up to six companies of 56 men each. Rusk was able to organize his militia should he "deem it expedient" and take his command into the field. Congress even dictated where the militia companies were to be stationed if they were raised: "two companies at the crossing of the Presidio road of the Leona River; two companies at the White House on the Nueces River; one company at Tumlinson's Blockhouse; and the remaining company to be posted in the West, at the discretion of the commanding officer." A sum of $50,000 was set aside to pay any militia forces which should be mobilized during 1843.[2]

Capt. Hays' Spy Company: March 1–April 30, 1843

Captain:
John Coffee Hays

Privates:
Donley, John
Eschalara, Manuel (guide)
Gillespie, Robert A.
Jett, James Matthew
Jett, William Glenn
Luckie, Samuel *
McKennon, Thomas
Paschal, Franklin L.
Perry, Cicero Rufus
Perry, William M.
Ross, Shapley Prince
Small, William B.
Stokes, Guy S.
Threadgill, Joshua
Woolfolk, Robert Shapley

* Enrolled February 20, 1843.

Source: Texas State Archives.

The Seventh Congress passed an additional act on January 16 which authorized the formation of a new spy company to protect the southwestern frontier. Five hundred dollars was set aside to pay this company until such time as the new militia act could be passed. In the end, President Houston disagreed with the locations of the militia units and he refused to sign the act.[3]

The new ranging company had no company commander designated by Congress, but Jack Hays soon took control of this unit's organization. As events would come to pass, no other formal military force was authorized for all of 1843, and the rangers Hays would organize were the sole formal military force in Texas that year, as authorized by law. Houston would forbid any armed forces to operate in the Nueces-Rio Grande country during 1843 except for those commanded by Captain Hays.[4]

Within a few weeks of the passing of the new scouting company law, word reached Jack Hays in San Antonio. He had recently reached town after passing through Gonzales, where he acquired "one new strong bridle" from Valentine Bennett on January 29, 1843. Hays began recruiting volunteers for his ranging unit during February 1843, but enlisting men into his new command proved to be tougher than he would have imagined. The invasions of 1842 had caused many families to leave San Antonio. After his first nine days in command of his company, Hays had only two privates under his direction, Sam Luckie and Frank Paschal. By March, however, his company had grown to 15 men, including Rufe Perry, Matt Jett, William Jett and Ad

Gillespie. Tejano Manuel Eschalara is shown on his rolls as the company's guide. Shapley Prince Ross (later a ranger commander and Indian agent) and his 25-year-old nephew Robert Shapley Woolfolk were also new enrollees into the Hays company.[5]

★ ★ ★ ★ ★

Frontier Depredations of 1843

Sam Houston's continuing efforts to negotiate peace between the Texas settlers and the Native Americans did not prevent random acts of violence and retaliation between the two groups. In the vicinity of Austin, the Comanches and their associated bands made at least several attacks on isolated groups of settlers.

The first recorded depredation of 1843 occurred on January 2, 1843, about 2 miles south of Austin. William Bell and Alexander Coleman had accompanied Mrs. William M. Thompson from her residence in town to the farm of James Smith, promising to return for her in the late afternoon. They started from Austin about 4:00 p.m. in a carriage to fetch Mrs. Thompson and her daughter. They crossed Waller Creek and were about a quarter mile from town when a party of about fifteen Indians on horseback appeared about one hundred yards ahead of them.[6]

Coleman and Bell were both unarmed, so Coleman "whipped the horse for the purpose of making my escape," toward the nearby home of Nolan Luckett—who lived about a half mile from the place where the Indians were first discovered. "Unfortunately, however, part of the harness broke and the horse got loose from the buggy," Coleman later related. He and Bell were left "perfectly afoot and unarmed." The Texans jumped out of their buggy and hopped over a fence to their right.[7]

The duo managed to flee only about three hundred yards before the Indians caught them. "They speared me," Coleman wrote, "and shot me with an arrow and hit me with something like a club. As soon as they shot me with the arrow, I stopped, and they immediately pulled out the wood part of the arrow, and then stripped me. At the same place they were stripping me they were scalping Mr. Bell, within forty yards of me, but they did not strip him." When the Indians forcibly ordered him to remove his clothing, Coleman pulled off his coat vest and shirt. "I very politely asked them in Spanish if they would have my pantaloons, to which they replied, 'yes' in Spanish," he recalled. "My own opinion is that they took me for a Mexican, as my hair was very long and [I was] dressed rather in Mexican garb. They, however, took all my clothes and left my boots and hat, but took the band of my hat, which had a very large silver buckle on it."[8]

While Bell and Coleman were being attacked, five of the Comanches from the party proceeded on toward Nolan Luckett's farm. Luckett's young son and three young black boys were driving the family's cattle when the Indians attacked them. One black youth fled and raced to alert Luckett. The Comanches overtook Luckett's young son, shooting him and one of the young black men, while carrying another off as a hostage. He was shot in the back with an arrow and died within a few days of his wounds.[9]

Bell was killed and scalped but Coleman's life was spared for the moment. He said that five of the Indians had overtaken him and a similar number had killed Bell. Nine of the Indians then started back to the place where the buggy had been abandoned, leaving only the tenth Comanche to guard Coleman in his naked, wounded condition. "I think he was the one [who] shot me, and he was afoot," Coleman related. The Indian "told me in Spanish to go, and pointed to the place where we started from. I done so, and when within about one hundred yards of the main body of Indians, I discovered some Americans in full speed approaching the main party of Indians."[10]

The Comanche with the spear urged Coleman forward. "I looked back at the Indian who appeared to claim me, and invariably he would pull his spear and tell me in Spanish to go faster," he recalled. "At this time, my only chance to escape presented itself to me, and I looked back at him again, and he was looking up at the Americans coming down the road. As soon as I discovered his attention drawn off from me, I turned directly to the right and ran." After running about twenty yards, Coleman looked back, "and to my great satisfaction," he noticed that the Comanche guarding him was running in the opposite direction. The Indians were mounting their horses as Coleman's fellow Texans approached. His captor "had barely time to reach his horse before the Americans were upon them."[11]

Fortunately for Coleman, the Comanches that had captured him had been spotted by Josephus Hornsby and James Edmundson. The two young men were traveling on the same road

Reuben Hornsby (1793–1879), an early Texas Ranger and frequent pilot of ranger expeditions during the republic years. His son Josephus Hornsby, another veteran ranger, participated in two Indian fights near Austin during 1843. Reuben, patriarch of the Hornsby's Bend settlement, would lose another son, Daniel Hornsby, to an Indian attack in June 1845. *Courtesy of Hugh Hornsby.*

near the Colorado River which Bell and Coleman had taken. Both men were veteran rangers. Edmundson had first served in Captain Tumlinson's 1836 ranging company while Hornsby at age 20 now had already seen action with the 1837 Bastrop Rangers, in the Flores fight of 1839, at the battle of Brushy Creek, at the battle of Plum Creek, and in the Vasquez and Woll campaigns. Edmundson and Hornsby had only one pistol between them but they decided they must attempt somehow to save their comrade. The day was growing late and there was no time to ride back to round up a pursuit party. As they rode to engage the ten Comanches, Hornsby and Edmundson were joined by their brothers, William Hornsby and Crawford Edmundson, and Enoch Johnson. The latter three only had two rifles between them. The five-man party was "very poorly armed," according to Coleman. Nonetheless, they bravely charged the Indians.[12]

The five young men spurred their horses and raced toward the Comanches, firing their only pistol while screaming at the tops of their voices. The Indians were so taken by surprise that they left Coleman behind and raced for cover. The yelling and firing of the pistol was heard by other citizens who spread the alarm. The Indians fled along the eastern part of present Austin as citizens gathered their firearms and pistols from around the Austin area and the Reuben Hornsby settlement on the Colorado. Hornsby and Edmundson continued their pursuit of the Indians even after they had emptied their pistol, shouting loudly all the while for the benefit of the Texans coming to their aid.[13]

One of the Austin-area citizens who joined the pursuit party was Judge Joseph Lee, who later praised the courage of the former rangers who doggedly chased the Indians from Austin. The pursuit party moved up Waller Creek and intercepted the Comanches about dusk some 2 miles from Austin. The Indians halted and made a brief fight before a strong volley from the Texans forced them to race for the security of the high hills. Josephus Hornsby had his horse killed in the fight. Three horses, complete with their saddles and equipment, were captured from Comanches who had been killed or wounded in the brief fight.[14]

Hornsby and Edmundson were hailed as heroes for their brave chase to save their fellow man. Coleman secured one of the horses and saddles captured from the Comanches. Lucky indeed to have survived his near-fatal brush with these Indians, Alexander Coleman would go on to become commander of the Travis County Rangers. He considered his January 1843 attack to have been one of "the last Indian depredation[s] on the Southwestern frontier, and is the most miraculous escape ever made from the savages."[15]

Josephus Hornsby was involved in another Indian scrape just months later in the spring of 1843 (one source says April 1844). About twenty Caddo Indians came down from the upper Brazos mountains and killed three men—Dr. Thomas W. Kenney, Henry Castleberry and John Courtney—on Salado Creek who were killing buffalo. The men were stripped, scalped and their bodies were horribly mangled. A fourth Texan, Hamilton W. Merrill, narrowly escaped with his life on a fast horse. Settlers later formed a grave site of stones in the northern edge of Williamson County about 14 miles from present Georgetown.[16]

The Caddos next proceeded to the Colorado River, reaching it about 12 miles below Austin at what was known as Moore's Prairie. They collected a large number of horses belonging to a Mr. Puckett and were in the act of driving them off when they were discovered. Josephus Hornsby was among the five riders who had gone out in search of these horses. He and companions William C. Reager, William S. Hotchkiss, Nathaniel Gilleland and Dow Puckett (son of the man who owned the horses) were unarmed. Once again, Hornsby and his companions decided to make a bold charge against these Indians, as they noted that the Caddos were armed with only bows and arrows.[17]

The Texans quickly dismounted and cut heavy mesquite clubs before leaping back onto their horses. The Indians were on foot, driving the horses toward a prairie. The Texans closed on them as they ran the horses down a long descent. The Caddos began firing arrows at the Texans as they attempted to get between the horse rustlers and their horses. Six of the Indians suddenly dropped to their knees and began rubbing their arrows across their bow strings so as to produce an eerie sound like yelping coyotes. The yelping sounds succeeded in spooking the Texans' horses, who wheeled and dashed away as the young men attempted to restrain them. Each time Hornsby and his companions attempted to move in close to the Caddos, they "fiddled" upon their bow strings and managed to spook their horses with the coyote-like sounds.[18]

Another Austin-area settler armed with a gun soon joined the chase but was similarly thwarted in his advances by the clever Caddo technique. The Indians continued advancing over the prairie and they were joined by six of their companions in the process. A party of armed settlers joined the pursuit a short while later but they did not arrive until the Caddos had entered the edge of some timber. William Hotchkiss was shot under the left shoulder with an arrow during one of the many advances against the horse thieves. He was so anxious to overtake the Indians that he continued riding for some time before having the arrow painfully extracted from his body. In the end, this resourceful band of Caddos escaped into the thickets near Brushy Creek after eluding the Texans for some twenty miles.[19]

Another group of Indians attacked a young Georgia native named Leroy Williams in Bastrop County in the spring of 1843. Williams was plowing some ground for land owner Michael

Young and he made the mistake of laying his rifle down while plowing one of his rows. As soon as he had proceeded down a row without his gun, several Indians raced from behind the cover of some bushes and seized it. He was shot with his own gun and then killed by their arrows. The pursuit party which tracked these Indians the following day was unable to overtake them.[20]

★ ★ ★ ★ ★

The Snively Expedition

The most significant military effort of 1843 was the so-called Snively Expedition, the last of the invasions and counter invasions between Mexico and the Texas Republic. Jacob Snively, former paymaster general of the Texas Army, petitioned the Texas government on January 16, 1843, for permission to fit out an expedition for the purpose of capturing the property of Mexican traders who might pass through territory claimed by Texas on the Santa Fe Trail.[21]

Snively considered all property of Mexican citizens to be a lawful prize and President Houston on February 16, notified Snively that his request had been granted. He was to raise up to 300 men, who would equip and provision themselves. Volunteer Steward A. Miller felt that such hardy frontiersmen would make the positive effects of the campaign "almost beyond doubt."[22]

Spoils of the campaign, to be taken only in honorable warfare, were to be divided equally between the government and the members of the expedition. Interestingly, the expedition was not to be considered a governmental undertaking. The appointed place of the rendezvous was in Fannin County (now Grayson County) at Fort Johnson at the little settlement of Georgetown near Coffee's Station on Red River.[23]

The first 150 volunteers were organized into three companies on April 24, and other men joined Major Snively's Expedition in early May before it crossed the Red River. At least one former ranger captain, Eli Chandler, was an important leader. The Texans followed a northwestward course across present Oklahoma, and on May 27 reached the Arkansas River and the Santa Fe Trail in the vicinity of present Edwards County, Kansas. Snively's expedition finally engaged a force of about 100 Mexican soldiers on June 20 along the Santa Fe Trail, killing 17 and taking 82

President Sam Houston counciled with Caddo and other Indian leaders near Washington-on-the-Brazos in April 1842. Originally published in 1912 in DeShields' *Border Wars of Texas*.

Mexicans prisoner without loss to the Texans.[24]

The Mexican prisoners were ultimately released a week later and dissension among the volunteers soon set in. Colonel Snively resigned his command on July 9 and Eli Chandler was elected into leadership. In the end, this expedition never managed to intercept any significant trading party. After crossing into American territory, his men ran upon a U.S. Army unit which was protecting the Mexican traders. Some of the Texans gave up their weapons and those unwilling to fight Americans simply turned back for home. Disputes over the expedition ensued again and Snively's expedition quickly splintered as Chandler headed for home with some of the men.

On July 13, approximately 70 men remained under Charles A. Warfield. These men soon found their numbers to be too small to effectively challenge Mexican forces who were guarding a Mexican caravan which was making its way along the Santa Fe Trail. Warfield's men ultimately gave up on trailing the Mexican forces and he resigned. Snively was reelected into command of the expedition and he led his men back into Texas, where the remaining force was disbanded at Bird's Fort on the Trinity River. The Snively Expedition, like the Mier Expedition, was yet another example of poorly organized men trying desperately to strike a blow against Mexican forces.[25]

★ ★ ★ ★ ★

Tawakoni Creek and Bird's Fort Treaties

Sam Houston continued to aggressively push his peace efforts with the Texas Indians during early 1843. The U.S. government tried to help by sending former South Carolina governor Pierce Mason Butler—a 45-year old who had shown great leadership in the first Seminole war—to Texas as a Cherokee Indian agent in the west. Butler arrived at the council grounds along Tawakoni Creek, just south of the old Waco village, in mid-February.[26]

Butler found twenty Delaware and Shawnee families present, all relatives of mixed-blood Indian agents Delaware Jim and Jim Shaw. These Indians asked to settle in the Brazos River valley. Sam Houston granted them land at a heavily wooded spot on the Bosque River, a Brazos tributary, which was untouched by Anglo settlement. Jim Shaw, Delaware Jim, Louis Sanchez and Jesse Chisholm then began organizing diplomatic trading parties to visit the western tribes.[27]

George W. Terrell was appointed by Houston as the new commissioner of Indian affairs in Texas. When Terrell arrived at Tawakoni Creek, he was discouraged with what he found. "There is great distrust on the part of all the Indians towards our people," he wrote to Houston on March 13. The Comanches, for one, sent word in early 1843 of their distrust in negotiating with Texan officials because "the bones of their brothers that had been massacred at San Antonio had appeared on the Road and obstructed their passage." Terrell was ordered to negotiate with whoever appeared and his efforts were supported with money that had been appropriated by the Texas Congress for defense. Starting in the spring of 1843, nearly half a dozen councils followed, lasting into the spring of 1844.[28]

The first such council took place at the Tawakoni Creek council house that had been built near the old Waco town. Terrell negotiated with about 30 Delaware and Shawnee interpreters and their relatives, who signed the Treaty of Tawakoni Creek on

March 28, 1843. The other tribes represented were the Caddos, Ionis, Anadarkos, Tawakonis, Wacos, Wichitas and Kichais. Terrell, John S. Black and Thomas I. Smith represented Texas with Pierce Butler present as the United States commissioner. The agenda discussed a line being created to separate the Anglo-Texans from the Indian tribes but poor turnout prevented this from reaching fruition. Chief Linney signed for the Shawnees, who were encouraged to return to Texas in peace. Anadarko Chief José Mariá signed as a representative of the western Caddos.[29]

Following the Treaty of Tawakoni Creek, some of the Indians followed Terrell back to the republic's temporary capital at Washington, Texas. They reached the area about April 9 and camped a mile south of town. President Houston waited several days before riding out to greet them in his general's uniform. The former San Jacinto leader spent days treating with the Indians, offering Caddo Chief Red Bear a fine percussion rifle as a showing of good will. When Red Bear at first rejected the rifle, Houston belittled the Indian leader before his peers until Red Bear finally embraced the peace efforts.[30]

Pierce Butler, concluding that the United States should exercise control over the Plains tribes, began planning another council which he hoped would be more effective. He began courting the same Delaware, Shawnee, Cherokee and Caddo leaders who had met at Tawakoni Creek.[31]

Butler soon found that his efforts were met with resistance. Waco leader Acaquash—the only Waco who had attended the March discussion—feared that "the tomahawk, if buried, would soon be ploughed up again." The Wichitas and Comanches had no intention of negotiating with the Anglos. Sam Houston appointed Joseph C. Eldridge to act as a superintendent under Terrell to talk with Delawares and Shawnees living near the old Waco town.[32]

Eldridge and Indian agent Thomas Torrey moved north to meet with Chief José Mariá, who had moved his Anadarko village to a spot on the upper Trinity River, just west of the old Bird's Fort. The two Texans then moved west on June 3 to visit the Wichita and Comanche villages. When they arrived at the Wichita village, Chief Kechikaroqua formed his men in war formation on their horses. This unnerving "greeting" was found to be merely a demonstration of how the Wichitas could have handled the white negotiators.[33]

In council with Eldridge and Torrey, Chief Kechikaroqua expressed pleasure over learning that Sam Houston wanted his tribe to move back to Texas. The Indian negotiators next left for the Comanche villages on July 5, passing more Wichita and Kichai towns along the Cache Creek of Red River. Eldridge and Torrey had tense council sessions with Comanche Chief Pahayuco, whose tribe wanted to kill the negotiators based on the belief that the white men of Texas had knowingly spread smallpox to the Indians. In a showing of good faith, Eldridge returned two Comanche children who had been captured by John Henry Moore's expedition in 1840. The Comanches and the agents finally smoked a sacred peace pipe and Pahayuco agreed to take Eldridge's words to other Penateka Comanche leaders.[34]

Eldridge, Torrey and their Indian guides returned to Bird's Fort, where they found a dozen more Indian agents who wished to sign peace agreements with Texas. Terrell could only offer modest gifts to these leaders but he promised to deliver more goods to them in the spring. A dividing line between the whites and Indians was discussed but its location would not be decided until the Comanches were present. The Caddo and Wichita leaders did sign the peace document with Eldridge on September 29, 1843. The Texas peace commissioners returned to President Houston with news that they had accomplished spreading some good will. This belief was supported by the fact that Indian raids declined noticeably during early 1844.

★ ★ ★ ★ ★

Captain Hays' 1843 Actions

By the time Snively's forces had turned for Texas, Captain Jack Hays was the only military force in Texas. Unfortunately for history, several of his action reports for 1843 have not survived. To document the actions of his ranger company in 1843, there is but one report written by Hays plus newspaper accounts, his muster rolls, and the memoirs of those who served with him.

With the exception of the Snively Expedition during the early part of 1843, the year was free of major campaigns and major Indian battles. The rest of the action in Texas was left to any volunteer forces which were hastily assembled for short periods of time and the continual operation of Hays' rangers.

Capt. Hays' Spy Company: June 1–September 30, 1843

Captain:
John Coffee Hays

Privates:
John Adams [1]
James M. Alexander
Joseph Baker
Alfred Berry
Michael H. Chevallie [2]
R. Clark [3]
E. Davis [4]
James Dunn [4]
Andrew A. Erskine [4]
John P. Erskine [2]
Manuel Eschalara (guide)
Robert Addison Gillespie
Thomas Green [5]
Lewis Haas
Eli S. Hankins [2]
Ben F. Hill [6]
George Thomas Howard [6]
John C. Howard [2]
John Hudgons [4, 5]
John James
James Matthew Jett
William Glenn Jett
Thomas Lyons [1]
Green McCoy [4]
Benjamin McCulloch [4, 5]
Thomas McKennon [7]
J. T. Mintor [8]
William Nabors
William Perry
John Rahm
James B. Roberts [9]
John Schnooks [10]
Guy S. Stokes
Pitkin Taylor [11]
Joshua Threadgill [2]
Joseph Weeks [7]
Joseph Williams [12]
Francis Yoast [7]
John Young

1 Enrolled September 27, 1843.
2 Served June 1–July 15 and Oct. 1–Nov. 10, 1843.
3 Served through July 10, 1843.
4 Served through June 30, 1843.
5 Served Sept. 10–Oct. 20, 1843.
6 Served through July 30, 1843.
7 Enrolled July 18, 1843.
8 Served June 20–September 10, 1843.
9 Served June 20–August 21, 1843.
10 Served June 1–November 1, 1843.
11 Served June 1–July 31, 1843.
12 Served June 17–July 22, 1843.

Source: Muster and pay rolls, Texas State Archives.

By March 1, 1843, Hays had 15 rangers under his command, including Tejano Manuel Eschalara as his guide. Brothers Matt and William Jett, Ad Gillespie, Frank Paschal, William Small, Sam Luckie and Rufus Perry had already served with Hays for various lengths of time since 1841. Among those who had joined him more recently were Guy Stokes and Shap Woolfolk, who had served as rangers under Captain George Erath in 1840 and 1841. Stokes signed up with Hays on April 3, 1842, and Woolfolk had fought at Salado Creek.

Hays company reenlisted during April. Little is known of the action of these rangers during March, but they did set out in

April to make their first major scouting expedition of the year. Their target was the Mexican bandit Agatón Quiñones, who was their chief antagonist and had faced Hays' horsemen at Hondo Creek in 1842. His marauders attacked traders on the Laredo and San Antonio road and near the settlement of Corpus Christi. In late April, Agatón had a force estimated at between 100 and 300 Mexican soldiers. Hays rode out with 15 men and one month of provisions, taking a course along the Nueces before moving to the Rio Grande.

Shapley Ross had loaned his black horse to Giles O. Sullivan for the Mier Expedition and his horse had been lost when Sullivan and his comrades were taken prisoner. In early 1843, Ross sold some cattle to pay for a new horse in order to join Jack Hays' ranging unit. Another of Hays' rangers, Rufus Perry, later offered details of this scouting expedition.[35]

> We went out to near the Rio Grande. There I got after a Mexican and caught him and from him learned that there was no Mexican force on this side of the river. When the poor devil found out that I was not going to kill him, he was the proudest Mexican I ever saw. He waited on me like I was somebody.

They rode to a point opposite from Matamoros without encountering Agatón. Hays did manage to capture two Frenchmen who had entered Texas illegally. From them, he learned that a platoon of 400 Mexican soldiers was garrisoned at Matamoros.[36]

Spies in San Antonio reported the departure of Captain Hays' company to Agatón, who rode out with a 70-man detachment to intercept the noted Texas Ranger. They found the rangers camped on the Nueces with a herd of horses and mules that Hays' men had captured from Mexicans near the border. Agatón's men caught Hays along the Nueces but hesitated on attacking, hiding in the river bottoms. During the night, the Mexicans stampeded the rangers' captured horses. Hays had wisely hidden his men's horses elsewhere. Taking to their own mounts, the rangers were on the move the next day when they encountered Agatón's men. Rufus Perry later related the skirmish.[37]

> There was a party of Mexicans [that] overtook us near the Nueces. Ross and Woolfolk was riding behind Hays, Luckie [and] myself was next. Hays told me for us to get ahead and rally the boys and started back to my assistance. I saw by looking back that there was but ten Mexicans and they were bound to catch Ross.
>
> Woolfolk and I went back until I met them. I then threw my horse across the road and presenting my gun, they all stopped and commenced to fire on me. I held them there until Hays and the boys got nearly back to where I was when the Mexicans sounded a retreat. We ran them some distance when we saw about one hundred trying to cut between us and the timber.
>
> We then made tracks to beat them to the timber which we did. We got across the Nueces into old San Patricio, when we got them between us and them old adobe walls. You bet they let us alone while I had them at bay. You bet it was a hot time for a little while. They shot about fifty shots at me, but we took out. There was not over thirty steps from me. I killed one horse and shot the rider through the thigh. I must say I hit others.

During the wild ride to escape the Mexican horsemen, Shap Woolfolk, Ad Gillespie, Shap Ross and Guy Stokes lost their hats. Ross later related that his new horse had been run off by his opponents, reducing him to riding a Mexican pony. Without his hat, he was now reduced to riding home on the pony with his head wrapped in a turban made from an old calico shirt to protect himself from the scorching sun.[38]

Captain Hays' men started on to the Guadalupe River the next day to reach the nearest settlement. During the course of their flight, his men apparently lost some of their provisions. "We killed an old mustang to eat as we was nearly starved," related Perry. "I tell you it was the hardest meal to swallow I ever tried." When the rangers struck the settlement on the Guadalupe at Andy Lockhart's home, Perry was sent ahead to greet the family. He met with Matilda Lockhart, who had been captured by the Comanches in 1838 and returned in 1840 at the bloody San Antonio Council House Fight. Perry found 18-year-old Matilda to be a very hospitable hostess.[39]

"Captain Hays and Company." This painting by famed Texan artist Jack Terry depicts the Texas Ranger company of Jack Hays riding in front of the Alamo in San Antonio de Béxar. Hays' company operated from San Antonio throughout 1841–1845 and was the only ranging company in operation during 1843. It should be noted that the familiar tympanum (or hump) seen in this image was not built onto the Alamo until several years later. *Painting used with permission of Jack Terry.*

When I told her that we had not eat anything for three days, she said that she knew what it was to do without eating. She had just cooked a pot of beans and bacon and [a] large oven of corn bread, which she gave to me with a bucket of milk, which stayed our appetite until old Andy came out of the field. When he did, the first thing was to kill a beef and by the time it was skinned, his gal had us all the bread we wanted.

We stayed all day with the old man. We had a fine time. He was with me on the Moore expedition in '39. His daughter was with the Indians that we had the fight with. She told me that she could have come to us but she thought that we was other Indians.

After a brief stay at Andy Lockhart's home, Hays' rangers split up during the return ride to San Antonio. Many rode on back into town while some headed off to check on their homes in other counties. In San Antonio, Hays soon made plans in early May to make another trip toward the Rio Grande. In the meantime, Ben McCulloch had raised a party of volunteers for a raid on the Rio Grande settlements, and a Captain Wall of Victoria was gathering men to take action on bandits near Corpus Christi.[40]

On April 27, 1843, President Houston proclaimed martial law in the region from the Nueces and Frio rivers to the Rio Grande. Hays' company was duly ordered to arrest anyone in this region found without authority from the Texas government. The *Telegraph* reported in its May 17, 1843, issue that other bandits raided a Mexican settlement near Matamoros and returned with 100 horses. Another raiding party intercepted Mexican smugglers and took $4,000 in specie from them.[41]

The June 14 issue of the *Telegraph* reported that a party of 31 loaded wagons was waiting to leave the Rio Grande for Béxar, and equal numbers waited to go south. Agatón was their chief concern for the sake of their goods. The paper also reported that a band of Comanches had raided to Aransas Bay, capturing two families before moving to Camargo. During this period, President Houston was trying to work out peace treaties with the Indians. Commissioners had met with Indians at the Waco village, using Delaware scouts to assist them. None of the Comanches came in to sign treaties and the commissioners had a rough time.[42]

The peace talks appear to have eased tensions with Indians on the Texas frontiers, but Agatón's party and other bandits continued to attack traders. Hays made a scout west of the Nueces during May but failed to find Agatón.

Hays' 16-man company was increased by successful recruiting during May. His spy company was joined by such frontier veterans as Mike Chevallie, James Dunn, Green McCoy, James Roberts, Ben McCulloch and George Thomas Howard, who had been a major with the First Regiment of Infantry during 1840. Jack Hays had 36 privates during June and July. Frank Paschal left the company to successfully campaign for the Texas Congress later in the year.[43]

As with 1842, detailed reports on the scouting expeditions of Captain Hays' rangers do not exist for 1843. Several anecdotes of life as a ranger have been related which paint a picture of this period. On one scouting trip, Jack Hays and "Alligator" Davis—a large man who had once wrestled an alligator on the Medina River—came upon two little bear cubs about 30 miles from San Antonio. They ran the little cubs up a black jack oak and Davis offered to try and tie one up to take back to town to Mrs. William B. Jaques—"an elegant lady who was much admired by the Rangers, and who was fond of pets."[44]

Hays shook the oak until one of the cubs dropped into Davis' arms. A furious wrestling match ensued between Davis and the frightened bear cub while Hays howled with laughter. The pair soon managed to tie the cub to Davis' horse but did not secure his mouth. The cub bit into the horse, which caused Davis to be thrown and the horse to race away with the cub on its back.[45]

Jack Hays' company continued to crack down on Mexican bandits during the summer of 1843. During early June, his rangers captured three Mexicans who were armed with rifles and pistols. The papers found on these spies indicated that they were scouting for Agatón Quiñones' bandit gang. One of the three captured spies was Cristobal Rubio, a bandit who was wanted for various crimes around Seguin and San Antonio dating back to 1842.[46]

Captain Hays proceeded to interrogate Rubio and his two companions. The June 15, 1843, edition of Texas' *Clarksville Northern Standard* related:[47]

> Rubio acknowledged that he and his party had, for a long time, been committing murders and stealing horses along the Colorado, the Guadalupe, and other western streams, and that he killed [a Texan] upon the expectation of getting his horse, which was a fine one. After hearing these disclosures, Capt. Hays immediately ordered the prisoners to be executed and they were shot forthwith.
>
> A few such actions of retribution like this, will tend more to give peace and security to the frontier than all the "letters" and proclamations the President can write during his term of office.

The July 12, 1843, edition of the *Telegraph and Texas Register* affirmed this story of Captain Hays executing Rubio and the other two Mexican spies. During mid-July the rangers moved their camp to Leon Creek west of San Antonio in order to avoid the attention of Mexican spies who were constantly on the watch in San Antonio. Bles Herera provided beef to Captain Hays' rangers on July 20 in San Antonio.[48]

Hays' company also went out in the summer in response to an Indian band which road into the outskirts of San Antonio and killed a farmer working near the Alamo ruins. Townspeople suspected the Lipans, since Flacco had been killed, but Hays was convinced it was Comanches since their trail led north. His men followed the trail for about 120 miles in July but did not catch up with these Indians.[49]

The rangers rode into town in early August, where Hays was immediately alerted to the fact that a group of spies under Manuel Perez, an understudy of Agatón, had gathered on the Medina River. Townspeople told Hays that Perez had 100 men who were plotting to make raids on the San Antonio area.[50]

Hays took out 15 rangers, probably all that he had with him from camp when he rode into town. They scouted the outlaw camp on a small stream west of the river during late August. Mexicans spotted the rangers and began shooting. The Texans returned fire and the bandits broke camp and moved downstream. Hays cautiously followed due to his small unit size, conducting a running fight as the bandits headed out onto an open prairie. The Mexicans torched the prairie grass and forced the rangers to halt due to dense smoke. Hays took up a defensive position, expecting the Mexicans to attack him under cover of the fire. When the smoke cleared, Perez's men had fled the area.[51]

Hays returned to San Antonio in late September. A likely timeframe for his return would be about September 27, on which date John Adams enrolled in Hays' company. He was a replacement for J. W. Mintor, who resigned on September 10. Newspaper accounts show that his men scouted the Nueces-Rio Grande country during late 1843. During late September, traders reported seeing the rangers from Nueces down to San Patricio, indicating that Hays' spies were constantly on the move. Trading had slowed down between the Rio Grande and Béxar by early November, as merchants were afraid of their goods being seized upon entering Mexico. The once flourishing town of Victoria was partially deserted due to the conditions against trade.[52]

During September, President Houston took steps to pacify the Mexican government. He issued a proclamation freeing all Mexican prisoners captured by Texan forces. They were to report to Captain Hays in San Antonio by October 10, 1843, where they would be given an escort to Woll's military headquarters.[53]

Hays returned from his last scout of the year on November 1. His rangers had run into a Mexican party which included Leandro Garza, who was one of the two primary Mexican spies (along with Antonio Perez) most wanted by Texas. Garza was wounded in this fight, knocked from his horse by a rifle ball, but slipped away in the brush. The rangers also encountered a number of Mexican scouts along the Nueces who promised to help Hays recover stolen property. They informed the rangers that the Mexican government was disbanding its scouting companies along the Rio Grande, and that less support was being given to the bandits. The Mexican scouts felt that trade would improve in the coming months. Traders managed to kill Agatón in late November, certainly a welcome development for trade.[54]

Captain Hays' only surviving 1843 report is dated November 12, 1843, to Secretary of War and Marine George Washington Hill. In it, Hays gave further details of the scouting mission from which he and his rangers had just returned.[55]

> I learned that a party of the enemy's forces were stationed on the Leona, a river about thirty miles east of the Nueces, and proceeded with my company to ascertain their object[ive] in entering our territory.
>
> On my arrival on the Leona, I found that they had been there for some time, and had left about three days previous to my arrival. I succeeded in capturing some Mexicans who had belonged to the party, who informed me that they had been recalled a short time since by the General in command for the purpose of disbanding them.
>
> I have since received information from the traders and others from the Mexican frontier that all the ranging companies (cortados) have been disbanded or furloughed for six months. Three hundred and fifty of the regular troops with two pieces of artillery have also been removed to the interior, leaving the forces now in service on the frontier much less than it has been for eighteen months.
>
> I have also the pleasure to report that the western settlements have for several months past enjoyed, so far as I have been able to ascertain, almost an entire immunity

> from the incursions of the Indians. The only source from which danger is now apprehended is the robbing parties of Mexicans which may be expected to increase since the disbanding of the ranging companies which have until recently been employed by the Mexican government upon the frontier and which were chiefly composed of men destitute of principle and without the resources to enable them to obtain an honest livelihood, many of whom it is thought will be ready to engage in any enterprise, however disrespectful or hazardous, which may promise to afford them the means of subsistence.

Hays had returned to San Antonio on November 1 and had been forced to furlough the remaining 20-odd men still under his command. He informed Hill on November 12 that he had been forced to disband his spy company due to "the means furnished me not being adequate to meet the expenses necessarily incurred in keeping up the company." Hays had maintained his men's service even after his funds had run out and he had personally incurred $400 of debt in par funds. He intended to reorganize his rangers at "such time as their services may be again demanded."

Captain Hays also stated that there were a number of Mexicans living in Texas since the Woll invasion who had no other means to support themselves except robbing the settlements. Hays recommended that a small force of mounted men could "keep these in check" at only a small expense to the Texas government. He also asked Secretary Hill for directions on how to handle Tejanos who had returned their loyalty to Mexico during 1842. The returning Tejanos had now returned to San Antonio, where Hays felt they "no doubt will be ever ready to do the country what injury the advantage of living amongst us may give them."

Only $500 had been set aside to maintain his spies for 1843, although other funds must have been issued to him during the year to pay his men. At one point in the year, President Houston had directed a transfer of $520.29 to pay Hays' men for a specific voucher. Hays's August-September 1843 payroll alone had been $1,236, amounting to less than one dollar a day per man.[56]

Obviously, local merchants depended upon Jack Hays and trusted him enough to help supply his rangers. Quartermaster papers for 1843 show that James Goodman did $36 worth of horseshoing and arms repair for Hays' company. During October, William Small, who served under Hays during early 1843, presented a bill for $34.50 for additional shoeing. These bills were eventually paid a year later on December 28, 1844. During May and June 1843, William Elliott was due $11.37 for supplying the company with medical and general supplies—rope, chain, soap, chloride of lime, quinine and other pills. He was also paid on December 28, 1844, when Hays acquired funds to do so. Another San Antonio merchant, Nathaniel Lewis, supplied Hays with gunpowder and coffee during October 1843, and Lewis was finally paid six months later.[57]

Secretary Hill wrote to President Houston on November 25, stating that Hays had been active in service through the 12th of that month. "This force, though small, has been active, vigilant and efficient," he praised. "The ranging companies of the enemy on and near the Rio Grande have been disbanded and the principal portion of their regular troops withdrawn to the interior."[58]

A November 28 article in the *Telegraph* stated that Hays had left Seguin and was bound for Washington-on-the-Brazos. Hays visited with the Calvert family in Seguin during the holidays and apparently visited Susan Calvert, a young woman whom he had met earlier in San Antonio. The attractive young girl with dark hair and brown eyes was the daughter of Judge Jeremiah H. Calvert, who had recently moved his family to Texas from Alabama. It was the beginning of a courtship that would last several years.

CHAPTER 8

The Deadly Colts on Walker's Creek

January–June, 1844

The key Indian agent in Texas from the U.S., Pierce Butler, had more resources and thus more negotiating power than Sam Houston's appointed agents. He found the Indians receptive when he called for a meeting of all Plains Indians to be held at Cache Creek of the Red River in December 1843. Butler arrived with an escort of 30 U.S. dragoons and a large store of gifts.[1]

Butler spent 18 days with the Comanches and their associate tribes speaking of peace. He advised his superiors that the Indians would eventually need help in surviving as game became more scarce for hunting and the better farmlands were taken over by the Anglo Texas settlers. Butler took great interest in documenting the demographics of the Indian tribes he met with. In his report of January 31, 1844, Butler counted 1,500 people in the two main Wichita towns on the upper Trinity River. He found that another 500 or 600 lived in two Wichita communities near the Wichita mountains. Chief Jose Maria's Caddos had largely moved to the upper Trinity River, while some remained on the Brazos. Butler estimated the total population of southern Comanche tribes at 15,000 people, spread widely from Texas to the plains.[2]

The efforts of the Texas commissioners continued into the spring of 1844. Sam Houston built a permanent peace council house on Tawakoni Creek—complete with an apartment for his visits—and stocked it with corn. The most significant council occurred in April 1844, when some 500 Indians appeared at

Tawakoni Creek's council house. The group consisted primarily of Delawares, Shawnees, Wichitas and Caddos. Texas commissioners James C. Neill, Leonard H. Williams, Benjamin Sloat and Thomas G. Western distributed goods and spoke of peace with the two prominent Indian speakers, St. Louis of the Delawares and Caddo Chief Bintah.[3]

Caddo chiefs Red Bear and Jose Maria made speeches, as did Chief Kechikaroqua, who spoke for the upper Trinity River Tawakoni Wichitas. The key point of discussion during April and May was the creation of a boundary line to run from the old Waco town north to the Red River, splitting the upper and lower Cross Timbers. The proposed line would pass just west of Bird's Fort, the westernmost Texas settlement. Chief Kechikaroqua insisted that President Houston should be present for the negotiations before he would agree to any such measure. The Caddos accused the Wichitas of stealing and raiding, further breaking down negotiations during late May.[4]

Sam Houston sent John Connor and Louis Sanchez to the Penateka camp on the upper Colorado River in May 1844, to discuss the proposed boundary line. In spite of talks that promised hope of an agreement, Connor and Sanchez's efforts stalled when dangerous news arrived in June. Captain Jack Hays' rangers had fought a battle with Comanches and the uneasiness in the wake of this fight would cause peace talks to halt until the fall.[5]

★ ★ ★ ★ ★

Jack Hays' 1844 Ranging Company

The newly seated Eighth Congress of the Republic of Texas passed a joint resolution on December 19, 1843, to cover the wages and "liabilities that have been created for the support" of Captain Hays' rangers during the year. The sum of $6,450 was dispensed to Hays for distribution to the men and the merchants who had supplied his company.[6]

When Jack Hays left Seguin on New Year's Eve 1843, he rode on horseback for the temporary Texas capital at Washington-on-the-Brazos. He was accompanied by congressman Frank Paschal, congressman George Howard, William Cooke and Antonio Menchaca. This party arrived on January 4 and was invited to chat with President Houston.[7]

Hays informed Houston that four companies of Cherokees from the United States had visited General Woll at San Ferndando, across the Rio Grande. He had received the intelligence from Mexican traders, who indicated that Manuel Flores may have instigated the action.[8]

Sam Houston listened to the veteran Texas Rangers' ideas on how to maintain order on the southwestern prairies and pledged to work on legislation with his Congress. The friendship of the Texas president with Hays' father no doubt continued to work in his favor, as the Eighth Texas Congress passed an act for the protection of the southwestern and western frontiers on January 23, 1844. John C. Hays was authorized to raise a "company of mounted gunmen," and he was specifically designated as its commander. He was allowed a lieutenant and 40 privates. Hays was to be paid $75 per month, his lieutenant $50, and his privates $30 per month.

Hays' rangers were to be organized by February 1, 1844, or as soon thereafter as possible. Their original enlistment was to be for a period of four months, with payments to them made every two months. President Houston reserved the right to extend the service period of Hays' company in an emergency. Each ranger was to furnish his own arms, horse and equipment. As captain, Jack Hays was paid $75 a month. Lieutenant Ben McCulloch was paid $50 a month and each ranger was paid $30 a month. Their company was directed to "range on the western and southwestern frontier, from the county of Béxar to the county of Refugio, and westward, as the public interest may require."[9]

Captain Hays was not able to muster in his new company by February 1, but by February 25, he had 20 men. He was compelled to leave San Antonio during the month to scout between Gonzales and La Grange, sometime around February 20. He was accompanied by three trusted friends—William Cooke, George Howard and Frank Paschal. They encountered four or five Mexican marauders along a stream called Peach Creek. They managed to capture a horse but lost the bandits in the creek bottom. The *Telegraph and Texas Register* also reveals that Captain Ben McCulloch was out after Mexicans in the same area with a volunteer company from Gonzales.

Hays and company returned to San Antonio a few days later, where he organized his new ranging company. Ben McCulloch

Capt. Hays' Ranger Company: February 25–June 26, 1844

Captain:
John Coffee Hays
First Lieutenant:
Benjamin McCulloch

Privates:
John Adams
Fielding Alston
Christopher Black Acklin [1]
Alfred Berry
Robert S. Barnes [2]
Pasqual Leo Buquer [3]
Michael H. Chevallie
John H. Carolin
Alexander Coleman [4]
James Dunn
John P. Erskine
Peter Fohr [5]
Robert Addison Gillespie
Lewis Haas
James P. Hudson [6]
James Matthew Jett
William Glenn Jett
Madison G. Jacobs [7]
Elisha James [8]
John James [9]
Isham G. Jones [10]
Griffith H. Jones [6]
James B. Lee [11]
John Lowe [11]
Thomas Lyons [11]
Green Marshall [12]
Wiley Marshall [12]
T. W. Minter
T. A. Nethery [13]
Franklin L. Paschal
Cicero Rufus Perry
Henry Perry
John Rahm
O. C. Resig [14]
Joshua Threadgill
James Taylor [15]
Josiah Taylor [12]
Pitkin Taylor [12]
Rufus Taylor [15]
Joseph A. Tivey [2]
Samuel Hamilton Walker
Alford H. Wood
Robert Shapley Woolfolk [13]

1 Enrolled April 26, 1844.
2 Enrolled April 7, 1844.
3 Served through May 26, 1844.
4 Enrolled May 10, 1844.
5 Served March 10–June 11, 1844.
6 Enrolled March 8, 1844.
7 Enrolled March 10, 1844.
8 Enrolled February 29, 1844.
9 Enrolled May 26, 1844.
10 Enrolled March 3, 1844.
11 Enrolled February 26, 1844.
12 Enrolled March 1, 1844.
13 Enrolled March 15, 1844.
14 Served March 10–April 25, 1844.
15 Served March 1–April 25, 1844.

Source: Muster and pay rolls, Texas State Archives.

was elected his lieutenant and 25 privates were on board by that time. During March and April, other rangers would join his company and finally bring his strength up to the designated 40 privates. Among those enlisting for service were congressman Frank Paschal and Sam Walker, who had only recently escaped from a Mexican prison. Walker, who had arrived in Texas in early

Pasqual Leo Buquor (1817–1901) served in Captain Jack Hays' rangers in 1841 and 1844. During the Civil War he also served as the mayor of San Antonio.
Portrait courtesy of Buquor's great-great granddaughter, Sylvia Villarreal Bisnar.

1842, had first served under Captain Jesse Billingsley during the Woll campaign and subsequently under Jack Hays. Walker stayed with the Mier Expedition after Captain Hays departed in December 1842, and was captured. Walker remained a prisoner through July 1843, when he managed to escape to the coast with others and secure passage on a ship back to New Orleans. He departed Louisiana in January 1844, and soon reached San Antonio as Captain Hays was forming a new ranger company. After his rough treatment in Mexico, Sam Walker had little desire to take any prisoners when he fought.

Other notable veterans whom Hays enlisted during March and April include Kit Acklin, Pasqual Buquor, Mike Chevallie, James Dunn, Matt Jett, William Jett, Griff Jones, Rufus Perry, Joe Tivey, Josiah Taylor and Rufus Taylor.

Hays made another trip to Houston to visit with President Houston around the first days of March 1844. Texas Revolution veteran John W. Lockhart was present at the hotel when Hays checked in and signed the register book. Lockhart was surprised that the "small, boyish-looking youngster, with not a particle of beard on his face," could be the famed Texas Ranger who was so often written about in the weekly newspapers. To his surprise, he found that the youthful-appearing frontiersman was indeed "the 'Captain Jack'" he had heard about and Lockhart noted that Hays stayed in town only long enough to conduct his visit with the government before departing quickly for San Antonio.[10]

Hays' company left San Antonio again by mid-March to pursue a group of Texas outlaws who had raided ranches near San Antonio and headed north towards the Colorado River with nearly 2,000 head of cattle. A new rumor that General Woll was marching on San Antonio again almost started a panic, but spies soon put down the rumor and calm returned. News that Hays was forming a new ranging company compelled some Mexican-born San Antonians to leave for the Rio Grande.[11]

Jack Hays rode out with his men to gain intelligence on the Woll rumor but soon found it to be of no concern. San Antonio merchant John Twohig was among the citizens joining Hays for this quick ride, but he accidentally shot himself in the process.[12]

> In 1844 it was reported that the Mexican Army was again approaching San Antonio. One night while saddling my horse to go out, quietly and without creating any excitement with Col. Jack Hays and others to ascertain if the enemy was approaching, I received a severe wound in the right leg caused by the discharge of my own pistol while putting it in the holster which was then hanging on the pummel of my saddle. I was standing by the side of my horse. This wound was for a while considered fatal and I suffered much from it for over a year.

Twohig's wound would prevent him from riding with the rangers again in 1844, but Hays was able to assemble the most able company ever under his charge during this period. His men were armed with the five-shot Colt revolvers. Although Colts had been used by Hays, Sam Walker, and several others on occasion on the Texas frontiers, 1844 was the first year that the rangers were fully equipped with Colts. Ranger Sam Walker wrote to the Colt factory on November 30, 1846, saying, "The pistols which you made for the Texas Navy have been in use by the Rangers for three years." Walker by that point had been in enough combat with the rangers to say that the rangers' "confidence in them is unbounded, so much so that they are willing to engage four times their number." Another account by Texas Navy commander Edwin Ward Moore agrees that Colt revolvers reached the hands of the rangers from the Navy around the early part of 1844.[13]

Around June 1, 1844, Captain Hays and 15 rangers left

camp near San Antonio and rode north to the area between the Pedernales and the Llano rivers. In a report written to Secretary of War George W. Hill two weeks later, Captain Hays said that his rangers were attempting to "ascertain what tribe of Indians was committing so many depredations."[14]

After scouring the northern country between the Pedernales and Llano, Hays turned for San Antonio. He wished to go no further "on account of the negotiations that were going on." Although he had seen "sufficient signs of Indians to have induced me to proceed farther up the country," Hays had orders to go no further and he prudently turned for home.[15]

His rangers recrossed the Pedernales River and made camp on June 8 at a stream later identified by Hays as Walker's Creek. This place was said to be four miles east of the Pinto Trace—the old Indian trail from Nacogdoches to the southwest—at a point equidistant from Austin, Gonzales and San Antonio. Modern maps show five creeks known as Walker, and accounts of this Hays expedition differ widely as to the location of this body of water. In his report, Jack Hays wrote that his men made camp "about fifty miles above Seguin." John Caperton, who prepared a biography of Jack Hays in 1879, wrote that this encounter with Comanches occurred "within about 35 or 40 miles of San Antonio, at a place called Cista's [Sisters] Creek." One source puts the ranger camp at a point on Sisters Creek, two miles above where it empties into the Guadalupe.[16]

The rangers dismounted their horses, unsaddling or loosening the cinches. Hays had a four-man patrol, well back protecting the rear, which soon galloped in to alert him that they were being followed. Two men, Kit Acklin and Alexander Coleman, had been collecting honey from a bee tree when Coleman spotted approaching Comanches from his elevated vantage point. "I immediately ordered my men to saddle, and prepare to fight," wrote Hays, "for I could have no doubt but that their intentions were hostile."[17]

His veteran rangers each carried a rifle and two of the new Colt five-shooters. They rode cautiously and soon spotted the Comanches who had been trailing their rear guard. Later evidence would show that this force of about 60 Indians included Yamparika Comanches, Kiowas and a few Shoshones.[18]

These Comanches only turned and rode away at a slow pace, indicating that they were not scared by the presence of the 16

Benjamin McCulloch (1811–1862) was second-in-command of Captain Jack Hays' rangers at the time of the famous Walker's Creek battle of June 8, 1844.
Texas State Library & Archives Commission, 1983/112-R-485-1.

rangers. They drifted back toward some woods, where Hays presumed many Comanches might be waiting. Experience taught the rangers not to charge them. "Hays was too old an 'Indian fighter' to be caught by such traps and made no efforts at pursuit," the Clarksville *Northern Standard* reported on July 24.[19]

The Comanches slowly circled, trying to draw the rangers into charging upon them, as they edged closer to the woods. Hays wrote that the Comanches used "every art and strategy to throw me off my guard, and induce me to give chase to them. They, however, did not succeed in their design." The Indians shouted insults at the Texans in Spanish and Hays reportedly shouted his own insults at Yellow Wolf, one of the Comanche leaders.[20]

Hays kept his men at a walk and moved up the side of the stream. Their ploy having failed, the Comanches galloped into the woods and vanished, but soon a considerable body of them was seen to be forming along the crest of a slight hill. The rangers halted, counting 60 to 70 Comanches riding back and forth waving their lances and shields and shouting challenges, dashing down the slope a few paces before wheeling back into line.[21]

This game went on for a time as the Indians tried to goad the rangers into firing at long range for which their padded shields

Samuel Hamilton Walker (1817–1847) arrived in Texas in 1842 and participated in the battle of Salado against General Woll. A survivor of the Mier Expedition, Walker had only recently escaped from a Mexican prison when Jack Hays formed his 1844 ranger company. Walker later praised the performance of the Colt five-shooter pistol he and other rangers used with great effect at Walker's Creek. Photo by Mathew Brady, circa 1847, taken shortly before Sam Walker's death in the Mexican War. *Author's collection.*

would stop the balls. Once the rangers fired, the Comanches thought they could rush down the slope, showering them with arrows and engaging them at close range with their lances. Hays wisely held his ground and kept his men riding at a walk towards the hill.[22]

The rangers were visible to the Indians as they rode forward up the gentle slope, but as they came to the steeper base of the hill they were out of sight of the Comanches for a few critical moments. A few curious Indians rode down the hill to see where the Texans had gone. In that moment, Hays had led his men in a gallop around the hill for a charge up the slope to attack the surprised Comanches on their flank. The rangers fired their rifles into the massed Indians, killing a number of them. Rufe Perry stated that the rangers "went around to the other side of the brush and come in on them. About sixty of the red devils come out of the brush onto the prairie when we opened fire on them."[23]

The melee moved down the slope onto the level ground, and in a matter of minutes the Comanches rallied into formation and turned to charge the heavily outnumbered rangers. Jack Hays, knowing that his men had fired the last of their loaded rifles, shouted as the Indians closed in, "Drop your rifles, men."[24]

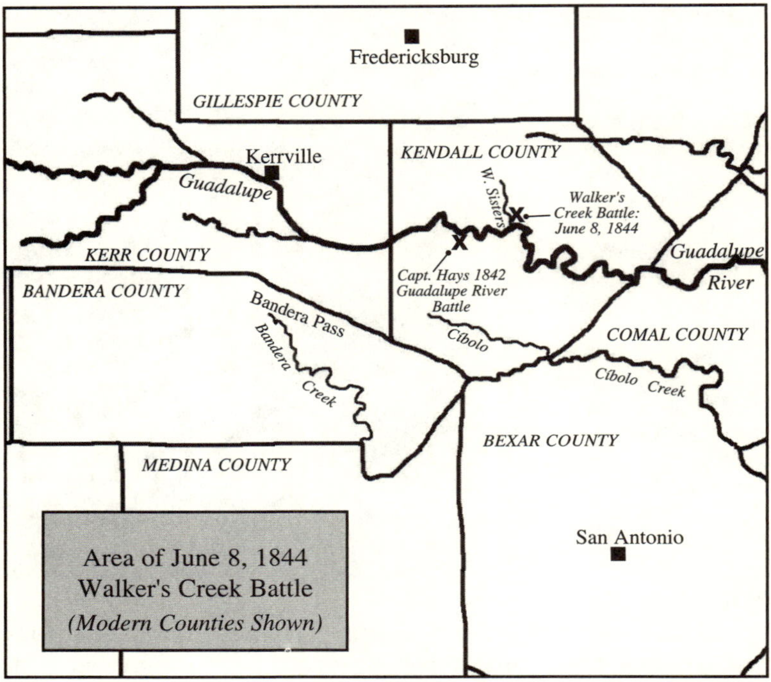

Area of June 8, 1844
Walker's Creek Battle
(Modern Counties Shown)

Hays and his small company of rangers were unwittingly changing the course of frontier fighting this day, trusting in their little-used five-shooter Colts. The Comanches had maneuvered the rangers out into the open and caused them to empty their rifles. Outnumbering the Texans some four to one, they must have felt some security against only the little pistols and knives carried by the rangers. Suddenly, however, Hays' men opened fire with their Colts and continued firing round after round. Comanches tumbled from their saddles. Hays wrote that the "five-shooting pistols did good execution. Had it not been for them, I doubt what the consequences would have been. I cannot recommend these arms too highly."[25]

Although the Comanches fled after the first severe round of Colt fire, the rangers pursued them and created several more close-action encounters. The fight was a moving one which was "desperate[ly] contested by both parties," according to Hays. In between moments of close action, the rangers were able to change cylinders on their pistols. Hays related that is was not until "after the third round from the five-shooters" that the Comanches gave way and fled. Even after that point, when the rangers' pursuit came too close to them, the Indians turned and made "desperate charges and efforts to defeat me."[26]

During these counter-charges, the Colt pistols took their toll on the Comanches. The rangers, however, suffered their own casualties in the counterattacks. During one Comanche assault, Sam Walker and Ad Gillespie were caught ahead of the other rangers. Walker shot an Indian who was riding in to spear him but as his back was turned another Comanche drove a lance into the Ranger. As the Indian jerked his lance out of Walker, John Carlin shot him through the head and assisted Walker into a thicket. In the wild action of the Comanches that suddenly surrounded them, the Texans fought bravely. Ad Gillespie was shot through with an arrow that knocked him from his horse.[27]

Captain Hays and his other men drove their attackers back while his wounded men were helped away. During this intense action, James Lee was also severely wounded by arrows and Andrew Erskine was less severely wounded in the thigh with an arrow. Another ranger, Peter Fohr, was killed outright. Despite his wound, Gillespie even managed to reload his rifle.[28]

Hays considered that his men had fought "with a courage that is rarely displayed" during this close contact portion of the fight when his rangers charged into the ranks of their opponents. In addition to Comanches, this force was found by Hays to contain a few Waco Indians and some Mexicans. By the time the fight had stretched out over three miles, there were still at least 20 Comanches able to fight, double the number of effective rangers. Hays could see a chief yelling at his warriors, trying to garner their courage for a final attack. Doubting that his rangers could survive another serious charge, he asked if anyone had a charged rifle. Gillespie nodded, dismounted and rested his Yager rifle on a large boulder. "Shoot that damned chief!" Hays cried. Gillespie's rifle blasted and a distance away the Comanche chief was knocked from his saddle in mid war cry.[29]

This was enough for the surviving Comanches. The rest of them broke away, each trying to escape without an attempt to haul off their own dead and wounded. Any injured Indians who escaped this day did so on their own. The rangers had one dead, many wounded, and many horses killed or wounded. They were too tired to pursue. Hays felt his men had killed "twenty on the ground, and wounding, to the lowest estimate, twenty or thirty more" with their .36 caliber Colt pistols.[30]

Hays camped on the field while preparing his injured men and horses for the ride back to San Antonio. The second day after the battle four Comanches rode up, almost stumbling into the rangers' camp. They were apparently trying to locate some of their own wounded men, thinking the Texans had long cleared the scene. "I immediately ordered six men to give chase to them," wrote Hays, "thinking at the same time that they had embodied, and presumed to give me another fight." This time it was not a trap and the rangers pursued the four Comanches for a mile. They managed to kill three of them and the fourth escaped.[31]

In two days of fighting with their new Colt pistols, Hays' rangers had killed 23 Indians and Mexicans and had seriously wounded another 30. Their own 16-man force had suffered four rangers wounded and one killed.

The rangers returned to San Antonio, taking care of their own wounded, and arrived about June 15, 1844. Peter Fohr, the ranger killed in battle the previous week, left a will which he had created in San Antonio on September 2, 1843. It was presented for probate on June 15 by his attorney, Thomas Addicks.[32]

One day after reaching San Antonio, Captain Hays wrote a report of the Walker's Creek engagement on June 16. He ran into Mary Maverick on June 20 and told her about the big fight with the Comanches. He credited the escape of his men to Ad Gillespie killing the Comanche chief. "We were right glad they fled," Hays stated. "We were nearly used up with the fatigue of a long day's march that day and the exertious on the battlefield, and we were almost out of ammunition. The Indians made a magnificent fight under the circumstances."[33]

A new colonizer who reached San Antonio in early July and heard of Hays' fight wrote, "This great victory was greatly due to the use of Colt's revolvers that the Texians used for the first time in this engagement, to the great astonishment of the Indians, who fought bravely."[34]

Among the names given as participating in the Walker's Creek fight are: Captain Hays, Sam Walker, Kit Acklin, Alexander Coleman, Rufe Perry, John Carlin, James Lee, Peter Fohr, Andrew Erskine, Ad Gillespie, Pitkin Taylor, Josiah Taylor, James Dunn and Mike Chevallie. Other names listed by early

When the Colt's Patent Arms company produced its new .44 caliber, six-shot revolver in early 1847, Samuel Colt named it the Walker Colt in honor of Texas Ranger Samuel Walker. Walker, who had visited the Colt factory, received a pair of the new Colt pistols shortly before his death in the Mexican War.
Courtesy of the Texas Ranger Hall of Fame and Museum, Waco, TX.

Indian wars historian A. J. Sowell as being present for Walker's Creek were his uncle Tom Galbreath, Creed Taylor, Sam Luckie, George Jackson, George Neill, None of these men appear to have served with Hays during this time, as they do not appear on any of his muster rolls. The accounts given by Sowell mix details of earlier Jack Hays Indian fights with the 1844 Walker's Creek battle, thus explaining his confusion over which rangers fought in which battle.[35]

Hays' fight at Walker's Creek was also known to some as the "Pedernales Fight" or "Hays' Big Fight." Sources differ as to the precise location of the fight. Hays may very well have dubbed the creek Walker's Creek, a name that might not have stayed with the stream. The battle did receive public notice. The *Houston Morning Star* ran a long account in its June 29, 1844, issue. Most of the writers of that period, however, failed to see the significance the five-shooter Colt pistol had played in Hays' rangers taking on such a superior frontier force with such success.

In time, however, historians would realize that in the 15 minutes of most intense gun action involving Hays' rangers and their Colt pistols the history of the West had been forever changed.

"Up to this time, these daring Indians had always supposed themselves superior to us, man to man, on horse," ranger Sam Walker later wrote. "The result of this engagement was such as to intimidate them and enable us to treat with them."[36]

The Walker's Creek Comanche battle fought by Hays, Walker and company was even later depicted as an engraving on the cylinder of about 100 presentation model pistols produced by Samuel Colt's company in 1847. Colt called his new .44 caliber, six-shot revolver the Walker Colt in honor of Sam Walker, who had met with Colt in New York to help improve designs on his new pistol. Colt had suggested to Walker in a letter dated November 27, 1846, that Walker and Jack Hays should look to Colt's Patent Arms as their supplier for repeating pistols. Walker quickly wrote back, confirming his confidence in the Colt brand: "The pistols which you made for the Texas Navy have been in use by the Rangers for three years, and I can say with confidence that it is the only good improvement that I have seen. The Texans who have learned their value by practical experience, their confidence in them in unbounded, so much so that they are willing to engage four times their number."[37]

Using Walker's suggestions, Colt would create the new 4.5-pound Walker Colt with a heavy nine-inch barrel to improve the accuracy over his earlier Colt Paterson five-shooter model which the Texas Rangers had used. Sam Walker had received a pair of the new Walker Colts by October 5, 1847. Four days later, he died in combat during the Mexican War at the pueblo of Humantla, still clutching one of the new Walker Colts in his hand.[38]

The 100 presentation models of the Walker Colt which depicted the 1844 Texas Ranger victory over the Comanches at Walker's Creek became collector's items. Sam Colt sent one pair to General Zachary Taylor and another pair to Jack Hays.

★ ★ ★ ★ ★

Other 1844 Frontier Fights

Hays' Walker's Creek fight was the most noteworthy battle with Texas Indians of 1844 but other settlers challenged Native Americans in lesser publicized frontier encounters during the year. One such fight was known as the Manchaca Fight. In the spring of 1844, a party of Indians came down from the Colorado

River hills and followed the river until they reach Hill's Prairie, located about 4 miles south of Bastrop. They rounded up a large number of horses and headed back for the hill country. The Indians left an easy trail to follow as they moved their stolen horses up a divide between the Colorado River and one of its tributaries.[39]

A pursuit party of sixteen men was organized under Captain Abraham Wiley Hill, who had settled in Bastrop County in 1835. Hill's volunteers rode swiftly in pursuit and soon found the Indians encamped for the night near a watering hole known as Manchaca springs where they believed they were beyond the Texans' reach. Captain Hill's men attacked them just after dawn, firing with such intensity that the Indians soon fled in every direction. Efforts to pursue them through the rough hill country were given up after the Indians were found to be thoroughly scattered. Hill's men returned to the Manchaca springs camp and collected the stolen horses and camp equipage of the Indians.[40]

Texas merchants were equally troubled with periodic raids by the Indians. The little town of Webberville east of Austin was originally a settlement known as Webber's Prairie, where Joseph Manor and Frank Nash formed a mercantile business during 1844. Nash and Manor confronted three Indians one night who were attempting to steal a mule that Manor had staked near his home. The Indians shot and killed the mule and Manor in turn killed one of the thieves with his rifle. The other two Indians seized their fallen comrade and carried him off into the night before the Texans could organize a pursuit party.[41]

Two Milam County residents were killed in another Indian battle which occurred during 1844. A party of seven or eight Indians were spotted on Cedar Creek in Milam County and they were pursued by a group of citizens. The Indians soon found that they would be overtaken and they halted in a strong position to prepare for battle. The Texan settlers decided that their numbered were too few to successfully engage the Indians in their fortified position and one rider was sent to gather reinforcements.[42]

William Oldham, a veteran frontiersman who had held the rank of major as paymaster on Colonel James Cook's Mier Expedition, raised about thirty men and advanced to assist the other settlers. The Indians had moved out in the meantime. One of Oldham's spies reported them to be about 12 miles north of

Caldwell in Burleson County. The combined Texan forces overtook the Indians at their campground that evening and prepared to attack. The Indians discovered them, however, and fled into the Cedar Creek bottomlands. The Texans had brought several dogs and they were sent forward to sniff out the Indians' trail.[43]

The Indians attempted to throw off the dogs by wading through the creek but the dogs continued to follow them after they had left the creek and taken up a position near Cedar Creek. The dogs trailed the Indians to a raised piece of ground in a hardwood thicket, where they stopped and howled furiously. Two Texans, Reed and Bingham, advanced to where the dogs were baying and found that the Indians had dug holes in the sand to protect themselves from the guns of the Texans. Reed spotted an Indian and raised his gun to fire.[44]

The Indian fired at the same instant as Reed and both men were wounded. Reed's chest wound would prove to be fatal. William Oldham's volunteers quickly arrived and a battle ensued to drive the Indians from their Cedar Creek position. Bingham was also killed in the fight before Oldham decided that the heavily entrenched Indians could not be driven out without more loss of lives. The following day, Alexander Thomson and other citizens returned to the battlefield to recover the bodies of Bingham and Reed. They were given a proper burial in Yellow Prairie in Burleson County.[45]

CHAPTER 9

"I Laid Down to Die"

Summer–Fall 1844

Captain Hays' rangers remained in San Antonio through the latter days of June to let his men recover from their wounds received in the Walker's Creek fight. They were still in town on June 27, when his company completed new muster rolls.

Another Texas frontier force was in action during the summer of 1844. Rancher Henry Kinney established a ranging company to protect his own interests and those of the citizens living near him in the Corpus Christi area. During June, his volunteer company fought a battle with Comanches who had raided their area. More than a dozen Texans were killed or wounded, including Captain Kinney, who was slightly wounded by a Comanche spear while trying to save his company clerk, Juan Ruiz. At least six Comanches were killed or badly wounded in the brief encounter. The Texas secretary of war would authorize Kinney on August 5, 1844, to operate a regular ranging company with a strength of up to 56 men "for the protection of Corpus Christi." The Ninth Congress later passed a resolution for the appropriation of $2,349 to pay for the expenses and disbursements of Kinney's ranging company. Extant republic records do not indicate who commanded Kinney's rangers during the summer of 1844 but muster rolls show that Captain Henry Clay Davis was in command of this company by November.[1]

Jack Hays' men acquired another area to patrol that summer when Henry Castro began settling a large colony of mostly new immigrants west of the Medina River. The project had the support of the Texas government. Hays wrote to Anson Jones on July 21, 1844, from Béxar, concerning Castro's work to establish a new colony. As the ranger commander, Hays pledged to "do everything in my power to enable him to effect his object as soon as possible."[2]

Captain Hays informed Jones that his small ranging unit would not be able to properly "afford the colonists much protection in their new settlement. I think, however, if my force was increased to 15 or 20 in addition to my present numbers, they could proceed to the lands and commence their operations in safety." Hays stated that Castro was in San Antonio but had been detained a short time while Hays recovered from "a severe spell of sickness," from which he had finally recovered.[3]

When Castro did finally depart Béxar on July 25, he went in company with five of Hays' rangers, the captain possibly not being in full health. In addition to the rangers, Castro had six other citizens with him, including former ranger John James, all of whom were "well armed."[4]

Castro's surveyors camped on Medio Creek, 12 miles west of San Antonio, the first night. The diary kept by Castro shows their food sources while on expedition.[5]

> July 26th.—John James, who accompanied us, killed three bears on the Potranco Creek; saw many wild horses. James Dunn, one of the rangers, ran them and killed a fine stallion. Cross the Medina River and killed two deer and one alligator and caught some trout; camped on the Medina.

Castro's land grant started four miles west of the Medina. One of the rangers reported seeing some mounted men on July 27, causing an alarm in the expedition. Six of the men set out to reconnoiter while the other half dozen men covered the camp. No encounters were made and Castro's party continued on, reaching Hondo Creek on July 29. Castro found the land bountiful with fish, deer, persimmons and honey. The surveyors returned to San Antonio on July 31, with two of Hays' rangers sick with fever.[6]

When Castro returned to town, he found that Prince Friedrich Wilhelm Carl Ludwig Georg Alfred Alexander, the 30-year-old

Capt. Hays' Ranger Company: June 27–October 28, 1844

Captain:
John Coffee Hays
First Lieutenant:
Benjamin McCulloch

Privates:
Christopher Black Acklin [3]
John Adams [1]
William Adams [2]
Fielding Alston
Richard Anderson [4]
Edward Brookfield [4]
Michael H. Chevallie
John H. Carolin
Alexander Coleman
James Dunn
John P. Erskine
Robert Addison Gillespie
Lewis Haas [5]
Thomas Hancock
James P. Hudson [5]
Madison G. Jacobs
James Matthew Jett
William Glenn Jett
Elisha Jones
Griffith H. Jones
Isham Jones
John Johnson [6]
John Lamon
James B. Lee
John Lowe
Thomas Lyons
Graviel Martinez [6]
Travisa Melchor [4]
T. W. Minter
Daniel Murchison [4]
George Jefferson Neill [4]
T. S. Nethery
William Sanders Oury [7]
Cicero Rufus Perry [3]
Henry Perry
William F. Powell [8]
John Rahm
Guy S. Stokes [8]
James Taylor [7]
Josiah Taylor
Pitkin Taylor [6]
Rufus Taylor
Joshua Threadgill
Joseph A. Tivey
Samuel Hamilton Walker
Roland Whit [9]
Robert Shapley Woolfolk
H. Young [6]
John Young

1 Discharged August 27, 1844.
2 Enrolled July 10, 1844.
3 Wounded on duty August 12, 1844.
4 Enrolled September 10, 1844.
5 Discharged on August 27 "on account of indisposition."
6 Enrolled August 28, 1844.
7 Enrolled July 20, 1844.
8 Enrolled July 15, 1844.
9 Enrolled July 1, 1844.

Source: Muster and pay rolls, Texas State Archives.

prince of Solms-Braunfels from Prussia, and his elaborately adorned companions had arrived in San Antonio with hopes of starting their own settlement. Prince Carl had traveled extensively through Texas and had been appointed commissioner-general for a colony of German settlers that wished to establish residence in Texas. His scouting efforts and land purchases would soon lead to the establishment of a settlement called New Braunfels on a well-watered land tract on the Guadalupe and Comal rivers.[7]

Henry Castro wrote that John Rahm, "a desperate character who belonged to Captain Hays' company of rangers," was attempting to talk some of his new colonists into leaving Castro and instead joining Prince Carl of Solms-Braunfels' new German settlements northwest of San Antonio.[8]

In the meantime, Hays had written to Secretary of War George Hill on July 21, about a new threat of Mexican invasion. He said that "a secret spy in my employ arrived in town" around July 11 with information that a Mexican force was assembling with plans to invade San Antonio. The Mexican troops numbered 600 and were reportedly mounted on good horses, prepared to divide into three divisions. If the first force was repulsed, it was to retreat, followed by the second, and then the third to maintain a constant annoyance to the Texas settlers. Hays' spy returned on July 19 with further information, saying that the Mexicans had already purchased 400 horses and were planning to commence their raid "during the month of August."[9]

These rumors never materialized, although smaller raids would continue to bother settlers during the late years of the Republic. The Comanches continued to attack traders during early August. One of Henry Castro's settlers, a European named Rhin, was killed and his cart was burned. Rhin's American driver escaped and hid in the woods until riders found him. "One of the hands of poor Rhin was found nailed to a tree," noted Castro.[10]

★ ★ ★ ★ ★

Ambush of Hays' Rangers

During early August, Captain Hays sent out small scouting parties from San Antonio to check on the frontier. Joseph Tivey, an 1841 minuteman who had fought with Hays at Walker's Creek, suffered a leg wound when his weapon accidentally discharged into his thigh. When he was carried back into San Antonio, the doctor wanted him restrained during surgery. "No, we cannot do it," his fellow rangers exclaimed. "He is a free Texan." The doctor therefore probed Tivey's wound to find the bullet without anesthesia and Tivey recovered sufficiently to remain in the ranging service.[11]

Another four-ranger scouting party was sent to check the area south of the Nueces River on Turkey Creek. They reached the three forks of the Nueces on August 12. This force included Rufus Perry, John Carolin, James Dunn and Kit Acklin. Rufus Perry later related this scout.[12]

> Hays heard that there were some Mexican cavalry recruiting their horses between the Nueces and the Rio Grande. He sent me with three other men, Acklin, Dunn, Carlin [*sic*], to stampede their horses. We got as far as the Nueces. Just on this side I saw the trail of a horse. I followed it until I was satisfied that there was a man on it.
>
> I told the boys to camp up on a bluff, but they camped close to some thickets. I told them when I come to camp that an Indian would not have camped there and I thought the Indians [were] not far off. I went up on a hill in order to look out but saw nothing. I had a presentiment that there was something wrong.
>
> About after eating our dinner, James Dunn and John Carlin went to the river to go in bathing. They had just got off their clothes when Acklin and myself was attacked in camp by about 25 Indians. We both jump[ed] to our feet. I told Kit to hold his fire until we could get to our horses but he fired his gun, killing one in his tracks, then left me.

Perry raised his rifle to fire at another Comanche but was shot through his left shoulder with an arrow. In spite of his painful wound, he downed another Indian. "They were not over 30 steps from me," he related. "I had one of Colt's first 5-shooters. I shot that 4 times and I am satisfied that I did not miss a shot."

Perry was then shot again, this time through the belly. A third bullet glanced off his temple and caused blood to flow heavily from his forehead. The young ranger fainted from blood loss. When he regained consciousness, he made his way to where Dunn and Carolin were at the river. The trio was soon joined by Kit Acklin, who managed to pull the arrow out of Perry's shoulder. The spike of the arrowhead remained lodged in the ranger's shoulder and would not be cut out for another two years.

The Comanches were not finished with them, as Perry continues.

Cicero Rufus Perry (1822–1898) and three other of Jack Hays' rangers were attacked by Comanches on August 12, 1844. Although badly wounded, Perry managed to crawl back to San Antonio, where he spent two years recovering from his near-fatal wounds. *Author's collection.*

> I caught hold of one of the horses' tails and went across, but I fainted again. Carlin took my gun and pistol to load them when the Indians made a second charge on us. They run off and left Acklin and me, taking my gun pistol with them. They had their horses. About that time, I came to and ran to a dense thicket where I lay down with the wound in my face down in the dust and little sticks. It stopped the blood.

After Rufe Perry had been lying in the dirt for some time, he began to hear the Indians moving through the brush around him. "I could hear them talk and knock on the brush," he recalled. "They stayed but a short time, then went away. I remained until dark, when I started to the water about 200 yards away. I had to crawl on my hands and knees for I lost so much blood that I would faint and fall to the ground. It took me from dark until daylight to get to the water."

Carlin and Dunn had fled, leaving Perry and Acklin to fend for themselves. Perry was badly dehydrated and he drank heavily from the river. He washed the dried blood from his face and then filled one of his boots with water. He then crawled into the hole left by a large fallen tree and stayed hidden all throughout the day to avoid being found by the Indians again.

After dark, he set out on foot for San Antonio. "I did not go over three miles before I laid down to die, as I thought I could not go any further." After lying for a while, however, Perry got up again and started on his way. It took him all night and part of the next day to reach the Leona, "about 10 miles from where I started. I traveled then whenever I was able to go day or night without anything to eat but three prickly pear apples."

Perry finally reached San Antonio on August 18, a week after being shot, where he was met by a Mexican boy. "He ran ahead of me and by the time I got to the square, I met a great many for I was like one risen from the dead." Dunn and Carlin had already reported that Perry had been killed and that Acklin would soon perish. The first two rangers had returned naked and sunburned from their flight from their river bath. Hays chastised these two for leaving their men.

Prince Carl of Solms-Braunfels noted in his diary of ranger Rufe Perry: "Traveled 120 miles on foot; six and a half days without food. Has three arrow wounds." Three days later, the prince updated his diary on Perry: "He has five wounds. In the evening, the Dr. cut the arrow from his jaw bone."[13]

Kit Acklin survived on beans and pears and eventually made his way back to San Antonio one day after Perry. "I was taken to Nat Lewis' store where I remained for a month," said Perry. "Then I was taken to another place where I stayed two months longer before I was able to ride. Then George Neill was detailed to take me home, which he did." Perry felt that he looked more like a ghost than a man, so much so that "my own mother did not know me." His painful wounds slowly healed with the help of several women who treated him for many months.

Frank Paschal was paid to stay with Perry through October, effectively taking both rangers out of service. Ben McCulloch was also sick for ten days at this time and was treated by Paschal. It would be nearly two years before veteran ranger Rufe Perry was able to go out again on the Texas frontier to fight.[14]

Comanches came within the edge of San Antonio on August 26 and captured eleven mules which were grazing nearby. An alarm was sounded throughout town and Hays' rangers pursued the thieves without recapturing any of the mules.[15]

During the late summer and early fall, Captain Hays' rangers performed special tasks. Ben McCulloch earned extra pay for carrying dispatches to Washington-on-the-Brazos in late August. The Texas government was in Washington, following the flight from Austin after the Mexican invasion of 1842. The rangers

Capt. Hays' Ranger Company: October 29–December 29, 1844

Captain:
John Coffee Hays
First Lieutenant:
Benjamin McCulloch

Privates:
Christopher Black Acklin
William Adams [1]
Fielding Alston [2]
Richard Anderson [6]
Edward Brookfield [6]
John H. Carolin
Alexander Coleman [1]
Robert Addison Gillespie
Thomas Hancock
Madison G. Jacobs [3]
James Matthew Jett
William Glenn Jett
Elisha Jones
John Richard Johnson
John Lamon [4]
James B. Lee
Thomas Lyons
Green Marshall [1]
Graviel Martinez [1]
T. W. Minter [5]
Daniel Murchison
George Jefferson Neill
T. S. Nethery [4]
William Sanders Oury
Henry Perry [1]
William F. Powell
John Rahm [1]
James Taylor
Josiah Taylor
Pitkin B. Taylor [1]
Joseph A. Tivey
Samuel Hamilton Walker
Roland Whit [4]
Robert Shapley Woolfolk
John Young

1 Furloughed November 29, 1844.
2 Furloughed December 23, 1844.
3 Furloughed November 14, 1844.
4 Furloughed November 19, 1844.
5 Furloughed November 24, 1844.
6 Furloughed December 17, 1844.
7 Enrolled July 20, 1844.
8 Enrolled July 15, 1844.
9 Enrolled July 1, 1844.

Source: Muster and pay rolls, Texas State Archives.

were the only safe way to transmit official dispatches to and from the temporary capital. McCulloch submitted another voucher in December for travel to and from Washington "on business for the company."[16]

Henry Castro's colonists set out from San Antonio early on the morning of September 1 and proceeded to work on his new settlement across from the Medina River. On September 9, a colonist found a fresh trail of 50 Comanches. "Information sent to Captain Hays and precautions taken against a surprise from the Indians," Castro wrote in his diary. "Built a guard house." Jack Hays and Mike Chevallie arrived at the new settlement of Castroville on September 10, but they departed the next day when they perceived no immediate danger from the Indians.[17]

In October, ranger Tom Lyons and Alfred Berry were paid when money became available to cover an official trip that they had made in June 1844, to Corpus Christi and back to San Antonio.[18]

Many stories have been handed down about the adventures of Captain Hays' rangers during the Republic years. One such story involves a friendly contest among the Comanches, rangers and Mexican *rancheros* of San Antonio. At some unspecified date in late 1844, a band of Comanches appeared near town to seek a peace treaty with the Texans. Jack Hays suggested to these chiefs that the men hold a joint rodeo for all citizens to enjoy as a showing of the friendly nature between the two parties. Fifty Comanches rode into town with about an equal number of Mexican *rancheros*. One of the *rancheros*, Chief Buffalo Hump of the Comanches and Captain Hays were selected to act as masters of ceremony for the event.[19]

John C. Duval, a survivor of the 1836 Goliad Massacre, was on hand for the event. He later described "rangers mounted on their horses, and dressed in buckskin hunting shirts, leggins and slouched hats, and with pistols and bowie knives stuck in their belts" who galloped among the crowd. He related that the rangers drank "mescal" and "scorch gullet" during the early preliminaries. Duval watched as a Mexican *ranchero* placed a spear on the ground. One of the Comanches raced by on horseback and swerved down from his saddle to snatch up the spear without dismounting. "The same feat was then performed by every warrior, Ranger and caballero on the ground, without a single failure," wrote Duval.[20]

The Comanche, ranger and caballero riders then substituted a glove in place of the spear which was similarly picked up from the ground as riders passed at full speed. The contest next progressed to a shooting match in which the riders fired arrows or pistols at a bull's eye board as they approached it on horseback at full speed. According to Duval, none of the Indians failed "to strike the board with one or two arrows as they went by."[21]

Duval later described that all parties were festively adorned with their own particular garb for the event. Prizes for the contest included pistols and Bowie knives. For best horsemanship, the judges selected ranger John McMullen, with second prize going to Comanche rider Long Quiet, and third to the well-known ranger-trader Henry Kinney. Fourth place went to a Rio Grande-area *ranchero* named Don Rafael. At the end of the friendly sporting event, various presents of goods were offered to the Comanches.[22]

Some among the crowd tried to persuade their judges to display some of their own riding finesse. Hays and Chief Buffalo Hump politely declined the opportunity to show off and the day ended with the rangers and Comanches parting on good terms.[23]

John Caperton, who later became good friends with Captain Hays, wrote that this friendly contest occurred "shortly before annexation." Hays told him that the rangers "showed themselves in every way to be as good horsemen as the Indians. For their excellent training, courage, skill, aptitude and success in this perilous service, they were largely indebted to their leader, a man of rare qualities and a natural commander."[24]

During the fall months, Hays divided his company into small platoons in order to more effectively cover the wide expanse of the southwestern frontier. Jack Hays was paid on October 28 for a number of old vouchers. He started a new muster roll for his company on October 29, but financial problems caused him to begin cutting his numbers. He furloughed ranger Madison Jacobs on November 14 and let three more go on November 19. Ten days later, he cut eight men and reduced his number by another three during December. His company had dropped from 37 men to 22 by late 1844.[25]

The Austin-area residents were still plagued with occasional Indian raids. One such event occurred on November 3, 1844, when Indians made an approach to Austin and captured two children some 400 yards from the home of widow Nancy Simpson. She had sent daughter Jane Simpson, 14, and son William Simpson, 12, to bring in the cows. A party of Indians believed to be Wacos seized the children and rode off. Mrs. Simpson raced through town, pleading for men to go after her children.[26]

A small group was formed which included Joseph Lee, Thomas Wooldridge and Columbus Browning. The rescuers reached the scene of the kidnapping and found that a small number of Indians were on foot. As they trailed the Indians, they found pieces of Jane Simpson's dress in the timber. The Indians had entered a ravine south of Mount Bonnell and the Texans pursuing them lost the trail. The Indians divided up for a time and young William Simpson later saw the bloody scalp of his sister hanging from one of the Indians. Superintendent of Indian Affairs Thomas G. Western would receive news in January 1845 from Delaware Indians that the Simpson children were seen with a band of Wacos near Brushy Creek. The remains of Jane Simpson were later found near the residence of George Davis. William Simpson was later restored to his mother after being purchased from Indians by a trader at Taos, New Mexico.[27]

★ ★ ★ ★ ★

The Regulator-Moderator War

The eastern settlements of Texas had settled into a relative peace with the small groups of Indians who remained in their counties. The only raid of consequence that has been recorded was a minor event in 1843 in an area of Burnet County which later became Anderson County. Near the settlement of Mound Prairie, a band of Indians stole some horses and butchered a fat ox belonging to David Roberts.

Lewis M. Russell organized a pursuit party and followed them to where they crossed the Trinity River. The Texans sighted them about 2 miles west of the river, where the Indians had stopped to barbecue their stolen ox. Their encampment was at the head of a ravine which led to the river. The ravine was "completely enveloped with a thick jungle of brush, briars and vines," related William R. Russell, son of the scouting party leader. "The scouts charged on them, but the Indians made good their escape down the ravine. The scouts captured all their horses and returned home without firing again."[28]

Another disturbance compelled Sam Houston to call up mounted volunteers in northeast Texas during the summer of 1844. The so-called Regular-Moderator War was actually a land feud which began in 1839 and continued through 1844 in Harrison and Shelby counties in the Redlands of East Texas. The roots of the conflict lay in the land swindling and other frauds that had been perpetrated in the neutral grounds between the U.S. and Mexican borders. During one such dispute involving Joseph Goodbread and Sheriff Alfred George, Goodbread was shot in 1840 in Shelbyville by one of the sheriff's assistants, Charles W. Jackson.[29]

Jackson and Charles W. Moorman then organized a party called the Regulators to prevent "cattle rustling." Principal leaders Edward Merchant, John M. Bradley and Deputy Sheriff James J. Cravens in turn formed the Moderators to moderate the Regulators. The groups turned violent when Jackson's trial commenced on July 12, 1841, before a judge who was a friend of the Moderators and of Goodbread. The Regulators burned homes and so intimidated the court that it could not proceed. President Sam Houston reportedly remarked, "I think it advisable to declare Shelby County, Tenaha, and Terrapin Neck free and independent governments, and let them fight it out."[30]

Jackson and another Regulator were ambushed and killed by the Moderators. The guilty Moderators were captured 25 miles north of Crockett by the Regulators, tried in Shelbyville in October 1841, and several were hanged. The fighting continued sporadically over the next three years. An ex-Regulator named Hall was accused of hog theft and was shot dead by a Moderator in Shelbyville. Hall's killer, a man named Stanfield, managed to escape from the Shelbyville jail, only to be pursued and ambushed by the Hall family. Stanfield's killers were taken to court, where Regulator judge John Ingram dismissed the charges against them. A short time later, revenge was again exacted when James Hall was killed while plowing in his field.[31]

In the summer of 1844, the Moderators met and renamed themselves the Reformers, electing James J. Cravens as their leader. The Reformers and Regulators did agree to a truce on July 24, 1844, but their peace was short-lived. Their struggles resumed in August shortly after another murder. Some 225 Moderators attacked 62 Regulators near Shelbyville. Reinforcements arrived to bolster the Regulators, who lost one man in the fighting. An indecisive battle known as the Church Hill Battle was waged against the Moderators (Reformers), who had taken shelter in an old log meeting house. President Houston was finally compelled to call up the Texas Militia to put the feuding to an end.[32]

On August 15, 1844, Houston ordered Travis G. Broocks and Alexander Horton to take the militia and make peace in East Texas. Horton and Broocks began organizing a mounted company to put down the violence. Captain Leonard H. Mabbitt, former commander of rangers in East Texas during 1838–39, was appointed captain of a mounted company by order of Houston on

Capt. Mabbitt's Shelby Co. Mounted Volunteers: Aug. 26–Nov. 13, 1844

Captain:
Leonard H. Mabbitt
First Lieutenant:
Bird L. Hanks [1]
Second Lieutenant:
George W. Haynes [2]
Orderly Sergeant:
Thomas F. Smith [2]
Second Sergeant:
Amos J. Roark [3]
Third Sergeant:
Jesse A. Mitchell [4]
Fourth Sergeant:
Eldridge H. Vaughan [2]
First Corporal:
Martin H. Gunter [3]
Second Corporal:
Stephen Mayfield [3]
Third Corporal:
K. Alexander Sandlin [2]
Fourth Corporal:
James Wilson [4]
Surgeon:
S. A. Stockton [3]
Farrier:
E. D. Williams [4]
Sadler:
William Scott [5]
Trumpeter:
Martin Chaddick [4]

Privates:
John C. Anderson [6]
Benedict Beacham [5]
J. T. Bean [3]
Thomas Benton [7]
Matthew G. Carrico [8]
Alexander Chumney [9]
William Colwell [10]
Asa W. Dorsett [2]
John C. Dorsett [11]
Joseph East [3]
Thomas R. Foster [4]
Demetrius Hays [12]
A. Wallace Kirkpatrick [2]
E. M. Kolier [5]
J. T. Lakey [13]
D. A. Lindsey [5]
R. E. Lindsey [5]
J. M. Miller [3]
John Peoples [14]
James W. Robertson [8]
Martin Shaddock [4]
William B. Templeton [2]
William Windle [2]

1 Enrolled Aug. 28, 1844.
2 Enrolled Sept. 5, 1844.
3 Enrolled Sept. 10, 1844.
4 Enrolled Sept. 7, 1844.
5 Enrolled Sept. 8, 1844.
6 Enrolled Sept. 28, 1844.
7 Enrolled Sept. 12, 1844.
8 Enrolled Oct. 11, 1844.
9 Enrolled Sept. 18, 1844.
10 Enrolled Sept. 14, 1844.
11 Enrolled Oct. 1, 1844.
12 Enrolled Sept. 9, 1844.
13 Enrolled Sept. 15, 1844.
14 Enrolled Oct. 2, 1844.

Source: DRT, *Muster Rolls of the Texas Revolution,* 233–34.

August 26, 1844. By early September, he had enlisted 34 volunteers and he added four more men during early October.[33]

Captain Mabbitt's Shelby County company arrested ten of the leaders from both sides and brought them to San Augustine. Militia organizer Broocks was arrested by the Moderators but was soon released. An agreement to disband both sides was finally drafted by a committee consisting of Judge William B. Ochiltree, Isaac Van Zandt, and Senator David S. Kaufman, among others. Leaders for both the Moderators (Reformers) and Regulators accepted the terms.[34]

Leonard Mabbitt's Shelby County mounted company was then disbanded in mid-November by orders of President Houston. Ironically, members of both the Regulators and Moderators would join together two years later to serve in Captain Mabbitt's company during the Mexican War—to the relief of Houston and reportedly to the ire of General Zachary Taylor.[35]

★ ★ ★ ★ ★

Peace Talks Renew at Tawakoni Creek

Sam Houston quietly expressed concern over Jack Hays' June battle with the Comanches at Walker's Creek. He felt that this would disrupt the peace process he had been trying so desperately to achieve for 18 months. Despite this battle, Comanche leaders did agree to attend another council session at Tawakoni Creek in the fall of 1844. They insisted, however, that President Houston must attend.[36]

Chief Mopechucope, one of the elders of the Hois division of the Comanches, sent a messenger to Houston. Old Owl explained that any treaty must include a boundary line from the Cross Timbers to the confluence of the Colorado and San Saba rivers down to the Rio Grande. Although Texas law did not recognize land titles to Indians, Houston responded to the Comanches that he would be willing to discuss their proposed line.[37]

Sam Houston did travel to the council house on Tawakoni Creek for the council at the falls of the Brazos on October 7, 1844. Present for this meeting were representatives from the Comanches, Delawares, Shawnees, Caddos, Wacos and Lipans. In his opening address, he blamed other "bad men" on murdering the Comanche chiefs at the San Antonio Council House in 1840. He told his listeners that he wanted to put an end to the fighting that President Lamar had stirred up. "He made war, too, on the Cherokees and drove them from the country," Houston stated. "Now this has to be mended. War can do us no good."[38]

Chief Buffalo Hump—the Hois war leader whose given name Potsanaquahip literally meant "Long Time Erect Penis" in native tongue—was the most prominent of those who spoke on behalf of the Indian delegates. In two days of meetings, Houston proposed that the Indians stay west of a line drawn from Comanche Peak, above the Waco town on the Brazos, to just below the mouth of the San Saba, then running south through the hills west of San Antonio. Buffalo Hump then stood and angrily proposed a line much farther east that would include Austin in Comanche lands. When Houston pushed for a trading house, Buffalo Hump announced, "We do not want it."[39]

Potsanaquahip insisted that his people needed most of Texas for their bison and wild horses. "I want my friends, these other Indians, to settle on the line and raise corn and I can often come down among them," he said. In the end, Houston talked the Comanches and their allies into signing a treaty of 22 articles on October 9 in which he conceded to not restrict these Indians on their movements. The boundary line was not specified but the two parties did agree that a string of Indian trading houses at the Comanche Peak and on the middle Brazos and lower San Saba rivers would be considered a demarcation line separating the two nations.Chief Buffalo Hump in turn agreed that if they found bad men encroaching on their hunting grounds, the Comanches would deliver them unharmed to the Texas government.[40]

The Texans agreed to issue passports to prominent warriors if they had the need to approach San Antonio while en route to Mexico. The move of Potsanaquahip to make peace with Sam Houston left Chief Pia Kusa as the only prominent Hois leader who refused to make peace during 1844. His band of Comanches would continue to conduct plundering raids into Mexican territory during the fall months.[41]

September 2, 1844, was election day in Texas, although ten days would pass before the results were known. Frontiersman Ned Burleson lost his campaign for president to Dr. Anson Jones, the secretary of state and a fellow San Jacinto veteran. Burleson won two more counties than Jones, but the official congressional canvass of the votes tallied 6,993 for Jones and 5,694 for Burleson. This election proved to be the closest presidential race of the Republic of Texas period.[42]

Sam Houston made his last address to the Texas Congress on December 4 before President Jones assumed office. He took pride in announcing the fact that Texas had been free from Mexican incursions during his last two years in office and that a relative peace had been made with the Indians. He acknowledged that there remained a certain number of unlawful Indians among the tribes residing within Texas. He stated that "it is unjust to attribute to a tribe or body of men disposed to obey laws, what is properly chargeable to a few renegades and desperadoes."[43]

Houston's valedictory was delivered five days later at Washington-on-the-Brazos. He spoke of the impending annexation of his country into the United States, acknowledging that some still maintained a desire for "separate and independent national existence." On the other hand, the United States were inviting Texans "to a full participancy in all its privileges, and to a full community of laws and interests."[44]

The former hero of San Jacinto would return to his home in Liberty County on the Trinity River on December 19 to reunite with his wife Margaret and son Sam Houston Jr. There, he opened a law office and continued his land speculation.[45]

The Republic of Texas would enter the new year of 1845 still an independent nation strapped with financial troubles and a frontier still troubled by roaming bandits and occasional Indian depredations. The Texas Militia had been used only sparingly in 1844 to help quell the long-standing Regulator-Moderator War. The rangers of Corpus Christi had maintained peace in their area with only Captain Hays' San Antonio-based rangers seeing any action with Comanches and cattle rustlers. These two companies marked the only Texas Rangers presence in Texas during 1843 and 1844, but the fabled frontier service would see a new rise in membership during 1845.

CHAPTER 10

The 1845 County Ranging Companies

1845

Newly seated President Anson Jones quickly took steps to reimburse the senior ranger commander for the expenses he had incurred while keeping Mexican bandits and Comanches in check throughout 1844. Jones recommended after his December inauguration that the Ninth Congress should pass legislation to settle the various accounts that Captain Hays had made on behalf of his rangers.[1]

The Ninth Congress would ultimately prove to be the last in service for the Republic of Texas era. It would also be the last legislature to meet in the old river town capital of Washington-on-the-Brazos. One of the more heavily contested resolutions which passed on December 20 was that of moving the capital back to Austin. The location of the Texas government continued to be a hotbed even after the so-called Archives War.

Nine members of the House of Representatives, led by former ranger leaders John "Rip" Ford and William Turner Sadler, argued that the location of Austin, "liable at any moment to hostile incursions from the Indian and Mexican foe, renders that point at all times an insecure repository for the Archives of the nation." Their arguments were ultimately overturned and Washington-on-the-Brazos would cease to be the Texas capital after the close of the Ninth Congress.[2]

On New Years' Day 1845, Captain Jack Hays had only a small group of ten rangers in service, including himself. They

Lt. Davis' Corpus Christi Rangers: Nov. 28, 1844–Feb. 28, 1845

Captain:
Henry Clay Davis
Lieutenant:
Mayberry B. Gray

Privates:
J. H. Aaron
John Brannon [1]
Robert H. Clements
Michael Dugan
George W. Fletcher
John N. Gainer
John Hoffer [2]
Jacob Jackson Humphreys [3]
Charles Johnson
George Lord [3]
Peter Mahoney
Patrick McEvoy
John Mills [3]
Lawson F. Mills [3]
Daniel Murphy
James P. Ownby
Philip C. Paul
Ary Peratt
William B. Phew
Basil Pyant
William Richards
John Ross
Riviero Ruocindo
William Y. Scott
Pomicina Villareal
Andrew Walker
Harrison Wood

1 Served Jan. 2—Feb. 28, 1845.
2 Served Dec. 6, 1844—Feb. 28, 1845.
3 Served Dec. 2, 1844—Feb. 28, 1845.
4 Served Nov. 28, 1844—Jan. 28, 1845.

Source: Source: Muster and pay rolls, Texas State Archives.

were John Carlin, Tom Hancock, Tom Lyons, Francis McKay, Daniel Murchison, William Powell, Shap Woolfolk, William "Bigfoot" Wallace and John Young. Wallace had only received his freedom from Mexican prisons on September 16, 1844, and made his way back to Texas. Hays added three more of his long-time rangers back to his muster roll on January 10, 1845: William Adams, William Jett and William Oury, the latter also freshly freed from his Mexican imprisonment.[3]

Captain Henry Clay Davis was operating a company of Corpus Christi Rangers from November 1844 through February 1845. Henry Kinney offered to employ a group of volunteer rangers "to act as soldiers for the protection of the citizens of Corpus Christi." The men were allowed to elect their own commander. Kinney would furnish ammunition and supplies, including sugar, coffee, bread and meat. Private soldiers were to be paid $20 per month, the company lieutenant $40 per month and the captain $60 per month. The men elected Henry Clay Davis as the company's captain. Davis had previously served as a cavalryman

Henry Lawrence Kinney (1814–1862), operator of a trading post near Brownsville and senator of the Ninth Congress of Texas, funded a ranging company in Corpus Christi during 1844–45 to protect his region of coastal Texas. *Author's collection.*

under Colonel Lysander Wells at the 1840 Council House Fight, and took command of the company on November 28, 1844.

Kinney reserved the right at the end of each month to discharge "one or all of the company by paying the amount due up to the time of discharge." Kinney's second in command was Lieutenant Mayberry B. Gray, who had served in the Texas Army during 1836 and fought at the battle of San Jacinto. Davis and Gray originally enrolled 21 other men when the company went into service on November 28. Five more men joined Captain Davis' company in early December and January, making the company's size 28 total men during February 1845.

Clay Davis' men had varying degrees of experience. Many had never served in any official military status. Basil Pyant and William Y. Scott had served two years in the First Regiment of Infantry from 1839–1841. Michael Duggan, Patrick McEvoy, John Mills and Lawson F. Mills had all served in the San Patricio Rangers during 1841. Jacob Humphreys, a veteran of the 1840 Plum Creek Comanche battle, had served under Jack Hays during 1841. Finally, James Ownby had commanded rangers during the 1839 Cherokee War crisis and also the San Patricio Rangers during 1841.

In return for supplies and payment, the rangers were bound to furnish their own horses and sufficient arms. Kinney's means of maintaining order in Davis' company was specified on their muster roll: "Any soldiers disobeying an order of his officer shall have the privilege of trial by court martial, or be discharged by said Kinney without being paid for his services—the court martial foresaid to consist of one officer and two privates."

True to his word, Kinney made payments to his Corpus Christi Rangers on January 28, 1845. By keeping his word and offering

Captain Peter Hansborough Bell (1812–1898) took command of the Corpus Christi Rangers on February 28, 1845. Bell, a San Jacinto veteran, had served in Captain Hays' rangers in 1840 and was adjutant general of the Texas Militia in 1841. He was later elected the third Governor of Texas in 1849. *Texas State Library & Archives Commission, 1981/57-6.*

true payment—which many Texas Rangers did not receive during their service period during the Republic years—Kinney was able to keep all but one of his rangers in service after the first two months. Davis resigned after serving three months as captain and was replaced on February 28 by Captain Peter Hansborough Bell, who had served in Jack Hays' ranging company in 1840. Bell's Corpus Christi company would continue to serve through December of 1845.

Texas and the United States were both under new leaders in 1845 as talks progressed of adding Texas to the Union. President James Knox Polk had taken office in Washington while President Anson Jones was shaping his cabinet in Washington-on-the-Brazos. The U.S. Congress passed a resolution for Texas to become a state and the offer was open for acceptance until the end of 1845. Annexation talks and work on drafting a new state constitution would consume the year.

A new act to provide for the Texas frontier was approved by Congress on February 1, 1845. Jack Hays was once again called on to command a company for Béxar County, but he was also assigned to "organize and command" four additional ranging companies "for the protection of the frontier." Robertson and

Capt. Hays' Ranger Company: February 12–Sept. 28, 1845

Captain:
John Coffee Hays
First Lieutenant:
Robert Addison Gillespie

Privates:
John Adams
William Adams [1]
Jefferson Bonds
John M. Carolin
Michael H. Chevallie
Richard Clute [2]
James Coghill [3]
James B. Cox [4]
William G. Crump [2]
David J. Davis [5]
John Crittenden Duvall [2]
Manuel Eschalara [6]
John P. Erskine [1]
Matthew Fairchild [4]
Joseph M. Forqhar [7]
William Gibson [8]
James Goucher [3]
Thomas Hancock [7]
William J. Herbert
Richard Hillburn
William Holman
William Glenn Jett
John Richard Johnson [9]
Elisha Jones [1]
William Laughlin [6]
Harold Leander [10]
Thomas Lyons
Nathaniel R. Mallon
James K. Markey [8]
Graviel Martinez [2]
Rafael Martinez [5]
Francis McKay [7]
John McMullen
T. W. Mintor [1]
Daniel Murchison [7]
Dr. A. Myers [2]
Governeur H. Nelson
P. R. Oliver [11]
William Sanders Oury
O. R. Powell [6]
William F. Powell
Charles L. Pyron [6]
Gideon Scallorn [10]
William Small [5]
Francis G. Spain [8]
Josiah Taylor [1]
Joshua Threadgill [1]
Joseph A. Tivey
Calvin S. Turner [2]
Samuel Hamilton Walker
William A. A. Wallace
Roland Whit [3]
James Wilkinson [2]
Robert Shapley Woolfolk
John Young

1 Served through May 11, 1845.
2 Joined August 12, 1845.
3 Joined September 13, 1845.
4 Joined September 16, 1845.
5 Served May 12–August 11, 1845.
6 Joined May 12, 1845.
7 Served through August 11, 1845.
8 Joined September 23, 1845.
9 Served 2/12–5/11, 9/23–28/1845.
10 Joined September 19, 1845.
11 Joined September 1, 1845.

Source: Muster and pay rolls, Texas State Archives.

Milam counties were to organize ten-man ranger units, each commanded by a lieutenant. Travis County was authorized to have 15 rangers and a lieutenant, while Refugio and Goliad counties were

Lt. Smith's Robertson Co. Rangers: Feb. 16–April 16, 1845

Lieutenant:
Thomas Ingles Smith

Privates:
James F. Bartlett
Thomas Bell
William Bolton
Robert S. Hulmes
Samuel W. Marlin *
Robert Matthews
Thomas Sutherland Menefee
James W. Sanford
Charles Sevier
George W. Sevier

* "Not accepted" on muster roll.

Source: Muster and pay rolls, Texas State Archives.

to share another 15 men and a lieutenant. Captain Hays was to act as commander of the Béxar County Rangers and could operate a larger company of 30 men. Hays, as a captain, was to be paid $75 per month. Pay for the lieutenants was dropped to $30 per month and $20 per private per month, a move indicative of the poor condition of the Texas treasury.[4]

This new frontier act of February 1 did allow up to $10 per month per ranger for ammunition, subsistence, horse-shoeing and medicines. The five new ranging companies were ordered to "scour the frontiers of their respective counties, protect them from incursions, and when concentrated in emergencies, to be under the command of Captain Hays." The sum of $30,000 was appropriated to provide for the new ranger battalion.

The Ninth Congress in its February 1 act also acknowledged the Corpus Christi Rangers funded by Henry Kinney. He was formally authorized to raise a company of 40 rangers, an increase over the 28-man-company already operating under Captain Henry Clay Davis. The sum of $15,000 was appropriated to cover the expenses of Davis and Kinney's Corpus Christi Rangers.[5]

On February 12, 1845, Hays mustered in his new company of 30 rangers in San Antonio. Ad Gillespie became his lieutenant. In addition to Bigfoot Wallace and William Oury, four more of his rangers were liberated ex-prisoners of war from the Mier Expedition: John McMullen, Jack Johnson, William Gibson and Sam Walker.

In all, six county ranging companies—all approved by the February 1 frontier protection act—would be in service by March. Hays' long-standing Béxar rangers had been the first to organize a new unit. They were followed on February 16 by a

Lt. Coleman/Cady's Travis Co. Rangers: Feb. 20–Aug. 20, 1845

Lieutenant:
Alexander Coleman [1]

Privates:
William W. Allen
John Brothers
C. C. Browning [2]
John Burleson
David C. Cady [3]
Thomas C. Collins [4]
D. Crawford Edmondson
James E. Edmondson
William Gibson [2]
Pleasant Green
Anderson Harrell [5]
John Harrell
Josephus Hornsby [2]
Reuben Hornsby Jr.
John Matthews [5]
David Scott [5]
Joseph Scott [6]
William Simmons [2]
Harvey Smith
William Snoddy [5]
Edward Turner [6]
Jonas Wells [2]
Thomas Wooldridge [5]
Francis Yoast [6]

1 Served through June 20, 1842.
2 Served through May 20, 1842.
3 Became lieutenant commanding on June 20, 1842.
4 Enrolled July 1, 1842.
5 Enrolled May 20, 1842.
6 Enrolled July 4, 1842.

Source: Muster and pay rolls, Texas State Archives.

small company of Robertson County rangers under Lt. Thomas Ingles Smith on February 16, 1845. Smith had first served as a ranger under Captain George Erath in 1840 and fought as a volunteer with Captain Eli Chandler's Robertson County Minutemen against Indians in May 1841. Smith had also served in Colonel Clark Owen's volunteer regiment during the spring of 1842 and was later wounded at Salado Creek. He also served for a time in Captain Bogart's spy company during the Somervell Expedition but was among those who returned home prior to the ill-fated battle of Mier. During 1843, Thomas Smith had played a key role in the Archives War and in 1844 he had led a scouting party into the Wichita Mountains in search of hostile Indians.[6]

It should be noted that many republic papers list Lt. Smith as "Thomas J. Smith" versus Thomas I. Smith. Lieutenant Smith's ranger unit remained in service for two months and was disbanded on April 16, 1845. Smith would later receive $170 in payment for his frontier services as "Lt., Robertson County Rangers."[7]

Travis County would become home to the Texas capital once again as the seat of government moved from its temporary home at Washington-on-the-Brazos to Austin. The third approved coun-

Lt. Teal's Milam County Rangers: March 1–Dec. 5, 1845

Lieutenant:	Ross Morris [2]
Richard S. Teal [1]	Jesse Mumford [1]
	Thomas Oldham [2]
Privates:	G. Shirley [1]
John Anderson [1]	A. Price Standifer [3]
John A. Angel [1]	H. Standifer [2]
Edward Bailey [2]	Daniel Sullivan [1]
John Barron [2]	R. Switchfield [2]
Thomas Barron [2]	John Thompson [2]
James Boren [2]	William Thompson [2]
William Boren [2]	_____ Tilley [2]
William Boswell [2]	Ezra Webb [2]
Benjamin Bryant [2]	____ White [2]
William Chalk [3]	
William Eichelberger [2]	
Robert Flack [2]	
Jared Groce [1]	
Robert Harvey [2]	
Buat Hitchcock [2]	
Daniel McKay [1]	
William McKinney [1]	
Lewis Moore [2]	
Robert Moore [2]	

[1] Served March 1–Dec. 5, 1845.
[2] Served Sept. 5–Dec. 5, 1845.
[3] Served March 1–Sept. 1, 1845.

Note: Price's rangers remained on duty throughout 1845.

Source: Muster and pay rolls, Texas State Archives.

ty ranging company mustered into service was under Lieutenant Alexander Coleman, who had served more than six months as a Jack Hays ranger in 1844 and had been in the Walker's Creek fight. Lieutenant Coleman mustered in 16 privates on February 20, 1845, including 21-year-old Reuben Hornsby Jr. and John Burleson, brother of the Texan vice president.

Coleman served three months before turning over command of his company on May 20 to Lieutenant David C. Cady, who had made Ned Burleson's Indian expedition of 1842 and had served the first three months in the Travis County company under Coleman. Cady's Travis Rangers added several men in early July, bringing the company complement up to twenty men. His company would serve into the fall months and later be incorporated into the service of the United States.[8]

Milam County—one of the frontier counties which had been authorized in February to raise rangers—did organize a small

Lt. Price's Goliad/Refugio Co. Rangers: March 14–June 14, 1845

Lieutenant:
John T. Price [1]

Privates:
Alfred Berry [2]
Joseph Bratton
Albert Ewers
John Lacey
John Lamon
William P. Miller
Elisha Pennington
John Reed
John W. Rich
Peter Rouche
Hugh S. Stapp
John Trimmier
Archibald White Templeton
William H. Watts
James Wright

[1] Entered service on March 6, 1842.
[2] Enrolled on March 21 at Goliad.

Note: Price's rangers remained on duty throughout 1845.

Source: Muster and pay rolls, Texas State Archives.

company under Lieutenant Richard S. Teal, a veteran of Captain George Erath's 1841 Milam County Minutemen. Teal organized his men in Milam, originally enrolling ten privates in addition to himself on March 1, 1845. Two men, William Chalk and A. P. Standifer, would serve six months with the Milam Rangers while the other eight would continue to serve under Lieutenant Teal into early December. Three of Teal's original company members—Daniel McKay, John Anderson and Daniel Sullivan—had previously served as Milam County Minutemen under Captain George Erath in 1841. Teal went to the Texas Congress in Washington on June 2, 1845, and drew $510 "on requisition for frontier protection." Three more former Erath rangers—Benjamin Bryant, Ross Morris and William G. Thompson—and former ranger captain Thomas Barron would later join Teal's rangers on September 5, 1845.[9]

The Goliad and Refugio counties ranger company was mustered into service in Victoria on March 14, 1845, under Lt. John T. Price. Price was paid $30 per month as "Lieutenant commanding Goliad and Refugio mounted rangers." By March 21, his company was in Goliad and numbered 16 total men including William H. Watts, whose brother had been killed by Comanches during their great raid on Linnville in August 1840. His company remained in service through August 28. His men made trips between Goliad, Corpus Christi and Victoria during their service period. Although no muster roll remains, further records indicate that Lt. Price's rangers remained on duty in Goliad from September through March 25, 1846. Price certified that his expenses for paying and providing for his rangers during their first three months of service had amounted to $990.[10]

As Captain Jack Hays was organizing his own company during February, he received reports that several hundred Indians were assembling on the Rio Grande. They were believed to be preparing for an attack on the Mexican frontier villages. An Indian chief named Santa Anna, leading 50 Comanches, passed through Corpus Christi during early March. Hays took his men on a scout to that area and concluded that these Comanches were hostile.[11]

The Texas auditor certified on March 25, 1845, that Captain Hays was entitled to a credit of $5,412.05 out of the frontier defense appropriation, an allowance that was approved by the republic's comptroller.[12]

During the spring of 1845, the Comanches complained that other Indians from outside of Texas were coming in and taking so many buffalo that they were in turn forced to encroach upon Mexican settlements to aid their own survival. Hays discussed the Republic's policy with Secretary of War William Cooke and then held a meeting with Buffalo Hump and other Comanche chiefs to urge them not to wage war on either Texas or Mexico.[13]

Little has been recorded on the specific scouting actions of Hays' rangers during the spring of 1845, but quartermaster papers show that they were indeed active. One blacksmith presented a note for $136.50 for shoeing the horses of these rangers and repairing two coffee mills between February and July. San Antonio merchant Nat Lewis supplied Hays' men with food, spices, medicines, powder, lead, and buckshot during this period.[14]

After serving three months, six of Hays' rangers elected to retire from the ranging service on May 11, 1845. Six new men enlisted under Hays, keeping his company size at 30 men.

★★★★★

The First Rangers of Dallas

A sixth new company of rangers was formed on June 1, 1845, in an area which is now part of the present Dallas metroplex. John

Lt. McGarrah's Fannin Co. Rangers: June 1–Sept. 30, 1845

Captain:
John McGarrah

Privates:
Rufus Anderson
Frederick Ballard
Alexander Boutwell
William W. Brotherton
James Caldwell
Thomas Cousins
King S. Custer
Joseph N. Dalton
Tola Dunn
John Fitzhugh
William Garnett
James Herendon
Jackson Hewitt
Matthew House
John M. Kinkaid
Abraham B. (Abram) Lucas
George F. Lucas
Peter F. Lucas
Thomas J. McDonald
George McGarrah
George McPherson
John Mounts
Thomas Mounts
Paschal Rice
William Rice
Christopher Searcy
Gallatin Searcy
T. B. Searcy
Samuel Shelby
John Stephenson
Isaac P. Thomas
A. J. Tucker
Samuel Tucker
William B. Tucker
Hiram Vail
Henry Vernon
George Wilcox
Pleasant Witt

Source: Author's search of audited Republic of Texas claims, including Peter M. Maxwell PD, R 171, F 50–147.

Neely Bryan, a 31-year-old who had attended the Fayetteville, Tennessee, Military Academy and later became a lawyer, was the first permanent settler of the settlement which became Dallas. He established his home in late 1841, shortly after the Indians around the present Arlington area had been driven out by ranger and militia expeditions that year. Bryan would serve as postmaster, ferry operator on the Trinity River and as a store owner in the area of present downtown Dallas. His home would also later double as the settlement's new courthouse. In 1844, he would help survey and plat the new town.

Shortly after the arrival of John Neely Bryan, John McGarrah and his family settled in an area of present Collin County which was then within the boundaries of massive Fannin County. They moved from Arkansas to claim a headright of 640 acres. McGarrah established his homestead in November 1842 and his fortified home became known as Fort Buckner in honor of his hometown of Buckner, Arkansas. In February 1843, an early settler named Dr. Calder was killed and scalped by Comanches within sight of Fort Buckner. The armed men within the little fort were able to scare off the Indians when they attempted to approach Buckner.[15]

In the summer of 1843, Tarlton Cunius opened a blacksmith shop at the Buckner settlement and Jack McGarrah opened a trading post, the only one available for early Dallas-area settlers within 40 miles. As the leading settler of the area and owner of Fort Buckner, McGarrah was elected as lieutenant in command when a local ranging company was organized on June 1, 1845.

Lieutenant McGarrah's company numbered about 40 men from the area surrounding his settlement and included his son-in-law Tola Dunn. His men operated in the traditional ranger method, providing their own supplies. McGarrah affirmed that men such as George McPherson and Jackson Hewitt "did furnish his own horse, gun, ammunition, medicine and provisions." Some of these Dallas-area rangers called on their buddies to help with the necessary equipage. James Hernendon, for example, furnished Rufus Anderson "the gun he used in the company, his clothing and other outfits, and some money, besides boarding"—in all amounting to some $65 or $70.[16]

Jack McGarrah was paid for "services as Lt. of Fannin Rangers" for four months for the period spanning June 1—September 30, 1845. Although ranger Frederick Ballard only served for three of these months, the balance of McGarrah's Fannin County Rangers were not dismissed from service until August 25. Years later, a group of eleven of McGarrah's rangers applied for payment which was still due for their services. While there is no indication that this company clashed with any Indian tribes during this time, the men indicated that they had successfully patrolled the northern Texas frontiers between Red River and the Dallas-area Trinity river for four months.[17]

The county ranging companies fulfilled their intent of keeping the peace within their respective counties. The few Indian depredations which occurred during 1845 were isolated events where individuals were attacked by small bands of Indians. One such loss occurred on June 7, 1845, near Hornsby's Bend in the Austin area. Daniel Hornsby—whose brothers Josephus and Reuben Hornsby Jr. were currently serving in Lieutenant Coleman's

Former Texas Ranger Daniel Hornsby was killed by Comanches on June 6, 1845, on the Colorado River. The Former Texas Rangers Association held a ceremony on October 25, 2008, at Hornsby's Bend to honor all 16 men of Reuben Hornsby's extended family who served as rangers during the early years of Texas. The Ranger cross in the foreground of this photo is placed before the grave of Daniel Hornsby. In the background is another Ranger cross before Reuben Hornsby's grave. *Author's photo.*

Travis County ranging company—fell victim to a small band of Comanches. Eighteen-year-old Daniel and companion William Atkinson, brother of the Reverend A. J. Atkinson of Austin, had gone out from Hornsby's Bend to fish on the Colorado River.[18]

Atkinson and Hornsby had left the Reuben Hornsby home and headed up the Colorado to find a good fishing hole. While they were engaged in their sport, a small group of Comanches slipped up close behind them. Both young men were run through their backs with spears before they had any apprehension of trouble. As Daniel Hornsby pitched forward into the river, he was shot with several arrows which fatally wounded him.

Hornsby's body sank into the river but Atkinson, in spite of the horrible spear wound through his back, attempted to swim the stream. He did make it across the Colorado and he crawled about ten paces up onto the bank. The men who eventually found him guessed from his wounds "that one of the Indians has swam along by his side and jagged him in the side with an arrow." The Indians who overtook Atkinson on the opposite bank finished killing him, removed his scalp and dumped his body in the river.[19]

The men living at Hornsby's Bend gathered that evening when Daniel Hornsby and William Atkinson failed to return from their fishing trip. Hornsby's body was found about a mile and a half from where he had been murdered. The body of Atkinson was also found near the spot on the river bank where he had perished. Two sets of Indian tracks led from the river to the spot where Atkinson died.

The Comanches fled the area without receiving any retaliation from the pursuit party. They moved along the Colorado River, leaving a victorious symbol for their fellow Indians to discover. The Comanches formed two representations of coffins in the river sand with an arrow stuck in each one. This was believed to serve as sign for some of the Comanches' roving companions to indicate how many Texans had been slain by them.[20]

★ ★ ★ ★ ★

During mid-May 1845, Hays' spies along the Rio Grande reported that reinforcements had arrived for the Mexican troops on the river. Hays wrote to the government that he would drive back any Mexican force he found east of the Rio Grande. A confidential agent of the United States who was operating in Texas, C. A. Wickliffe, wrote to U.S. President Polk that he was planning to urge Hays' rangers to drive the Mexicans from the region west of the Nueces.[21]

President Anson Jones favored Texas to remain independent rather than becoming annexed by the United States. Tensions with Mexico compelled President Polk to instruct General Zachary

Dr. Anson Jones (1798–1857) was head surgeon of the Texas Army's Second Regiment during the battle of San Jacinto. As the final president of the Republic of Texas, Jones would direct the activities of the Texas Rangers in 1845 as they were pressed into federal service. *H.A. McArdle San Jacinto Notebook, Texas State Library and Archives Commission.*

Taylor to concentrate U.S. troops at Corpus Christi. By May 1845, President Polk had ordered 4,000 troops into Texas from Louisiana. These men marched toward Austin and San Antonio as ships carrying infantry and supplies reached the Corpus Christi area on July 26, 1845.[22]

Although Jones proclaimed a cessation of all hostilities between Texas and Mexico in June 1845, some of the Texas Indians sensed otherwise. Comanche leaders and other Allied Indian chiefs visited San Antonio during the summer to talk about peace.[23]

Chief Pia Kusa of the Hois division of the Comanches—known to Captain Hays and other Texans as "Chief Santa Anna"—called upon Hays during June. Pia Kusa was described during this period as being "portly looking" and weighing more than two hundred pounds "with a countenance expressive of both good humor and good nature." During 1844, Pia Kusa had refused to accept Sam Houston's peace treaties and his reputation was that of one of the Comanches' "fiercest and most relentless warriors."[24]

Hays asked Santa Anna (Pia Kusa) to return to San Antonio and then informed Secretary of War Cooke of his intentions to continue treating with this war chief. Weeks later, during late July, Chief Buffalo Hump (Potsanaquahip) told Indian agent Benjamin Sloat that he planned to lead a war party of Comanches to the Mexican border. When Buffalo Hump's Comanches encamped near San Antonio during early August, he rode in to see Jack Hays with agent Sloat in his company. Hays tried to talk the Indian chief out of taking his men to the Rio Grande, but to no avail.[25]

The Comanches became more troublesome in the late summer, at a time when Texas was working to approve annexation terms with the United States. A band of about 150 Comanches killed a Mexican trader and captured five others on the San Pedro River in August. Hays' rangers were able to peacefully treat with these Comanches and secure the release of the hostages and many stolen livestock. Hays communicated to the secretary of war in early September that the Comanches felt that they had a right to kill Mexicans since the Mexicans west of the Rio Grande were at war with Texas.[26]

CHAPTER 11

Rangers in Federal Service

1845

Major Hays' Ranger Battalion

U.S. President James Polk did not want war but Mexico's hostile nature had compelled him to move U.S. regular army troops into Texas after the Ninth Congress had voted overwhelmingly in favor of annexation. The impending movement of Texas under control of the United States had brought about discussion of the Texas Rangers in Austin.

The Texas Congress realized that the U.S. would soon assume the principal responsibility for protecting Texas. Captain Jack Hays and some of his county ranging units remained in service during late summer 1845 as Secretary of War William Cooke reviewed his republic's mounted service. The time and political process required for Texas to formally become part of the United States insured that rangers would remain on the frontier.

General Zachary Taylor knew that the presence of so many United States troops in Texas during 1845 had already been considered by Mexico to be an act of war. Taylor had been given authorization by President Polk to accept additional volunteers from Texas, Alabama, Kentucky, Louisiana, Mississippi and Tennessee during the buildup period. General Taylor wrote to President Jones on August 16 that he recommended the rangers should continue defending the frontier for the time being.[1]

Anson Jones wrote to General Taylor on August 23, from Austin, giving his intentions of the use of Texas Rangers:[2]

Executive Department
City of Austin Augt 23rd 1845

Sir,

I have the honor to acknowledge the receipt of your letter of the 16th Inst which was delivered me last evening. I have recieved [*sic*] no definite information in regard to a commencement of hostilities on the part of Mexico against the United States but have rather inclined to the opinion that She would not adopt that course. The troops which She is moving towards Matamoros I thought probable might be intended only for the defence of that point & that the collection of them there was induced by the fact that the U.S. were moving troops to Corpus Christi & that the intention of the Govt of Mexico was to act only defensively at present[.] This view however may not be correct & it is certainly best to be fully prepared for the opposite alternative & a due regard to the general welfare may make it necessary & quite proper that the whole of your force Should be concentrated at Corpus Christi for the defence of that point.

In this situation of affairs I concur in your recommendation that the different points on our frontier now occupied by any troops in the Service of Texas Should continue to recieve [*sic*] adequate protection in the manner you propose against any outbreaks of Indians which might occur as well as against our Mexican enemies. I would therefore designate as you request the following companies to be mustered into the Service of the U.S. in the manner you propose viz: One full company of Rangers (mounted gunmen) under the command of Captn P. Hansborough Bell at Corpus Christi[.] One full company of Rangers as above under the command of Captn John T. Price at or near Goliad this company to be continued in position near Goliad or to be transfered [*sic*] to Corpus Christi as you may think proper to direct. One full company of Rangers at Béxar under the command of Major J.C. Hays[.] One full company of Rangers at the city of Austin under the command of Capt. D.C. Cady[.] One full company of

Lt. Smith's Robertson Co. Rangers: Sept. 15–Dec. 15, 1845

First Lieutenant:
Thomas Ingles Smith
First Sergeant:
Robert S. Hulme
Second Sergeant:
Thomas Bell
First Corporal:
Patrick Calloway
Second Corporal:
Elkana Capp

Privates:
Charles Barclay
James B. Barrie
Thomson Coker
John A. Covington
John Covington
William Cox
Andrew Eaves
William R. Howe
Thomas Johnson
Melchesiace Killian
William J. Lewis
Shadrick Manus
Robert Matthews
James McDaniel
John Menefee
Thomas Sutherland Menefee
Edward Miles
John Morrow
Bird S. Pullen
James R. Pullen
James W. Sanford
Charles Sevier
George W. Sevier
Thomas Shelton
John Thomas
Jacob Wycoff

Source: Muster and pay rolls, Texas State Archives.

Artillery at Austin under the command of an officer to be selected & appointed by me[.] One company of Rangers of thirty men at Caldwell Milam Co. under the command of Lt. R.S. Teal[.] One company of rangers of thirty men at T.I. Smiths in Robertson Co. under the command of Lt. Thomas I. Smith. One company of rangers of thirty men at Dallas in Fannin County, under the command of Lt. John McGarrah.

These Several companies will it is believed afford adequate protection under present circumstances to the several points indicated on our frontier and Serve as nuclei around which to rally a volunteer or militia force in the event of any Sudden outbreaks of the Indians, or an irruption [*sic*] on the part of the Mexicans[.] Send by the bearer of this to Col. Clark L. Owen of Texana a Commission as Col. in the volunteer infantry of Texas with instructions from the Secty of War & Marine to enroll and have in readiness a force not exceeding One thousand men & to muster them into Service & place himself under your

> command & cooperate with you in the event of an actual invasion by Mexico or upon your request. The number of men you may wish called into Service, under Col. Owen not exceeding the above number you will please make known to him & they will be mustered accordingly[.]
>
> Each man will be expected to furnish himself with a rifle & fifty rounds of ammunition, & to conform strictly to the orders of the officer in command.

Anson Jones sent a second letter on August 23 to Clark Owen, restating his orders as previously expressed to General Taylor. He informed Owen that Captain Bell was authorized to enroll 60 men and Captain Price was to form a second company of the same size. Both were to be mustered "into the service of the U.S. to act as spies or rangers."[3]

President Jones further detailed that General Taylor was expecting an attack by Mexican troops on his position. Therefore, Taylor "does not think it prudent to detach any portion of his forces at this time for the defense of our frontier." Jones had been authorized by Taylor to muster into U.S. service "any companies I may think proper to designate for the protection of the said frontier." The president informed Colonel Owen that he had therefore one ranger company under Major Hays to be stationed at Béxar, one ranger company under Captain Cady to defend the Austin area "and probably one other company of artillery."

Lieutenant Richard Teal was to maintain 30 rangers in Milam County while another 30 men under Lieutenant Thomas Smith would range Milam County and Lieutenant Jack McGarrah's 30 rangers would protect Fannin County. The balance of Anson Jones' instructions to Owen gave him command of Texian infantrymen and the president's thoughts on the state of the frontier.[4]

> Gen. Taylor's forces with Capt's Bell and Price, companies of Rangers and the other several ennumerated [*sic*] corps will I think afford the necessary temporary protection in almost any event which may occur and will form so many nuclei around which to rally any volunteer or militia force which it may become necessary in case of invasion or Indian disturbances to call into the service of the country.

> The Indians on our frontier with the exception of one or two very small bands continue to manifest a very pacific disposition and I anticipate no outbreak on their part. I can scarcely believe that Mexico will have the foolish temerity to invade Texas and wage war against us and the U.S. But it is my duty to be prepared for the worst event which may happen and to be ready to cooperate with Gen. Taylor with all the force necessary to give them a proper reception should they come.
>
> For this purpose I have caused to be forwarded you by the Secretary of War and Marine a commission as Colonel of Infantry in the volunteer service of Texas, which I hope it will suit your feelings and convenience to accept. Instructions are furnished with the Commission. Should you conclude to accept and discharge the duties of this appointment I leave the manner of carrying out your instructions to your sound discretion. You are much nearer the scene for action than we are here, and will be governed by circumstances. I do not wish any movement made unless upon the most reliable proof that there is an actual invasion of the country made or about to be made or upon a request from Gen. Taylor. In either of the above events you will act promptly—but not otherwise. In the mean time there need be neither alarm nor excitement among the people. I should wish strict discipline enforced and none enrolled except those who are willing to be subordinate in all respects to the officers in command...I think you will find an efficient coadjutor in Col. B. McCulloch of Gonzales, and I should be much pleased to see him placed second in command to yourself if agreeable to you.

The correspondence of General Taylor shows the confidence he had found in the small bands of Texas Rangers. In response to a letter from Jack Hays in San Antonio, Taylor wrote on September 1, "The commander of the rangers at San Antonio, Major Hays, has a reputation as a partisan, and to him I have especially intrusted the duty of keeping me advised of any movements on the Rio Grande in the neighborhood of Laredo."[5]

Major Hays was therefore given authority to command four ranger companies—as many as 300 men. His rangers would be formally mustered into federal service for at least six months under orders of General Taylor while the regular army was organized. Captain W. W. Bliss, Taylor's adjutant and son-in-law, wrote to Hays on September 12 to advise him that his company would serve in conformity with U.S. Militia regulations. His company would continue to serve as rangers, with Hays acting as their major.[6]

Bliss directed Major Hays that his company "will be particularly charged with the duty of procuring intelligence of the movements of the Mexicans and protecting the Frontier against Indian Depredations, and the General desires me to say that he places great confidence in your known activity and experience in Frontier Service." Bliss noted to Hays that the U.S. War Department's instructions forbade him from disturbing any Mexican forces near the Rio Grande "or commit any overt act calculated to provoke hostilities."[7]

Major Hays' new ranger battalion was to primarily scout and report for the U.S. Army during its organization and to keep Indian resistance in check. By the time Hays received his orders from adjutant Bliss, another ranger company had been revamped which would fall under his direction. Captain Peter Bell had led Henry Kinney's Corpus Christi Rangers since assuming command from Henry Clay Davis on February 28. His company had been keeping the peace along the coast and had monitored the arrival of the first U.S. troops and supplies which had arrived via ships in late July.

Bell's new muster roll of September 10, 1845, shows him to be in charge of a 77-man unit, double the size he had been authorized to maintain earlier in the year. The Corpus rangers would officially be designated as part of Major Hays' Texas Mounted Volunteers. Hays and some of his rangers escorted Secretary of War and Marine William Cooke to Corpus Christi and back during late September—no doubt to visit with General Taylor and to check on Captain Bell's new ranging company.

Major Hays was back in San Antonio by September 26, on which date he filled out a travel voucher which Secretary Cooke signed the following day. Jack Hays was officially listed on his muster rolls as captain of his San Antonio Rangers until September 28. On that date, 42 men under Hays and Lieutenant Ad Gillespie formally completed their service.[8]

Battalion of Texas Mounted Rangers
Major John Coffee Hays, Commanding

Captain Gillespie's San Antonio Mounted Rangers
September 28, 1845—March 28, 1846

Captain:
Robert Addison Gillespie
First Lieutenant:
Michael H. Chevallie
Second Lieutenant:
John Adams
Surgeon:
Francis McKay
First Sergeant:
William A. A. Wallace
Second Sergeant:
John Carolin
Third Sergeant:
Richard Hillburn
Fourth Sergeant:
William F. Powell
First Corporal:
Roland Whit [1]
Second Corporal:
William Laughlin
Third Corporal:
Calvin S. Turner [2]
Fourth Corporal:
J. Stoutenburgh
First Bugler:
Francis A. Bettinger

Privates:
Christopher Black Acklin
Wade Alsobrook
Fielding Alston
Delaware Beaver
Jefferson Bonds
James R. Calhoun
George Carroll
James Lawrence Cherry
Samuel G. Cherry
Francis Cludt
James E. Coghill
James B. Cox
Chesney Crownover
William G. Crump
Edward Davis
Martius Deis
Charles Donoho
James Dunn
William Duval
John C. Duvall
Henry Earl
Matthew Fairchild
Gustavus Feldt
Thomas Galbreath
Peter Gallagher
William Gibson
James Goucher
Peter Guillendo
Robert H. Hall
Thomas Hancock
John A. Harmon
Joseph Harper
O. P. Harrison
William Harrison
Leander Harrold
James Hays
William J. Herbert
William Holman
A. M. Holmes
G. H. Hudson
Elisha Irons
William Irons
John R. Johnson
Eli Jones
Elisha Jones
John Lamon
K. B. Lockhart
Franklin Lowe
Jacob Lucksing
J. Lycet
Thomas Lyons
Nathaniel R. Mallon
James K. Markey
Graviel Martinez
Benjamin McCulloch
M. K. McDermott
John McMullen
Samuel Mitchell
John Moore
Governeur H. Nelson
Andrew J. Nicholson
P. R. Oliver
William Sanders Oury
Otis Peck
Joseph A. Pivey
O. R. Powell
Charles L. Pyron
James Reddish
James Roberts
Joseph Robinson
Gideon Scallorn
Francis G. Spain
James H. Spence
Washington Stephens
James Taylor
Josiah Taylor
Rufus Taylor
Joseph A. Tivey
Samuel Hamilton Walker
James A. Wilkinson
Joseph Williams
Robert Shapley Woolfolk
John Young
James Youngblood

1 William Chism substituted on December 28, 1845.
2 Thomas E. Cherry substituted Feb. 28, 1846.

Source: Charles D. Spurlin, *Texas Volunteers in the Mexican War,* 247–49.

Battalion of Texas Mounted Rangers
Major John Coffee Hays, Commanding

Captain Bell's Corpus Christi Mounted Rangers
September 10, 1845—July 6, 1846

Captain:
Peter Hansborough Bell

First Lieutenant:
Maberry B. Gray

Second Lieutenant:
Dewitt C. Lyons

First Sergeant:
John T. White

Privates:
James H. Aaron
William Adams
Daniel Allen
Hiram A. Allen [1]
Alfred Berry
Alonzo Blair [1]
James Francis Blair [1]
Charles Bradley [1]
John Bradley [1]
John Brannon
Edward Brookfield
Edwin K. Brown
John Callahan
Jacob Castleman
John Castleman
Solomon Cleveland [1]
Jackson Criswell
Joseph E. Criswell
Dennis Divier
Daniel Doughty
William J. Downing
Albert Ewers
Patrick Faddin
William Ferrel
Jacob Fifer [1]
Alfred L. Friar [1]
Henry Hall [1]
H. A. Hart
Michael Hely [1]
William Hickman
James Holster
James Howard [1]
Jacob J. Humphreys
John James
William Jordan
Austin D. Looke
James M. Manning
James Marrs [1]
John McGloin
John McPeters [2]
Thomas McPeters
William L. Millican
Henry Miller
John E. Mills
Lawson F. Mills
Thomas Murphy
John O'Meary
William S. Osborne
Philip C. Paul
George Petigrew
Thomas Pough
Patrick Quinn
L. J. B. Rhine
William Richards
John Ross
Montrevell Roundtree
Matthew Ryen
Thomas Simons
John St. Luke
David H. Sutherland
Moffett E. Trimble [1]
Miles Turner [1]
Andrew Walker
John White
Peter White
Samuel C. Whiting
Benjamin F. Whitson
Francis Whitson [1]
John Wood [1]
Spencer Wood [1]
Samuel Yates
Albert Yowes [3]

1 Discharged on March 10, 1846.
2 Discharged March 10, 1846; rejoined company on April 1, 1846.
3 Discharged March 10, 1846; rejoined company on May 1, 1846.

Source: Charles D. Spurlin, *Texas Volunteers in the Mexican War,* 242–43.

Battalion of Texas Mounted Rangers
Major John Coffee Hays, Commanding

Captain Price's Victoria and Goliad Counties Rangers
September 25, 1845—June 25, 1846

Captain:
John T. Price
First Lieutenant:
A. White Templeton
Second Lieutenant:
George W. Guthrie
First Sergeant:
Charles Blackwell
Second Sergeant:
Alancius Holdridge
Third Sergeant:
Jacob A. Miller
Fourth Sergeant:
Willard Post
First Corporal:
Joseph Bratton
Second Corporal:
John T. Campbell
Third Corporal:
William Dial
Fourth Corporal:
John Lamar
Bugler:
Augustus Walters

Privates:
Henry Bachman
Ezekiel Ballard
John Ballard
Martin Boatwright [1]
William Boothe
A. Bowyer
John C. Brightman
David Castlebury
James Castlebury
Andrew Criar
Wiley C. Cummins
James Doane
Augustus Ensworth
Francis H. Fisk
James Fowler
Felix W. Goff
James M. Goff
Edward Hardy
John Hepperman [2]
Jacob Hoodle
Nicholas Izard
John T. Jameson
Charles T. S. Jordt
Boswell Kent
John D. Kirby
John Lacy
Gustavous Lane
Milton T. H. Love [2]
Epson Luter
James H. Manning [2]
Allen Marshall
Green Marshall
Wiley Marshall
Ezra Maxon
Ephraim D. McDowell
Stephen McLaughlin [3]
Joseph Miller [3]
Cullen Mimms
Thomas J. Mimms [3]
William Mimms
William Morris [3]
E. D. Muster
Henry Noble
J. Thomas Noble
William Noble
Enoch W. Orcutt
William Parkinson
Alexander Pendarris
Armistead R. Peyton
William Pickett
Eugene Puchalsky
Thomas J. Pughe
John Reed [3]
Louis Reed
Corano Rios
Hugh S. Stapp
Isaac Phillip Stem
Frederic Theil
William Watts
Samuel Wilkinson
Augustus Williams
James Wilson
Augustus Wolfkroner
Josiah Yates

[1] Discharged on March 20, 1846.
[2] Discharged on December 25, 1845.
[3] Discharged on March 25, 1846.

Source: Charles D. Spurlin, *Texas Volunteers in the Mexican War,* 255–56.

Battalion of Texas Mounted Rangers
Major John Coffee Hays, Commanding

Captain Cady's Mounted Rangers (Travis County)
October 1—December 31, 1845

Captain:
David C. Cady
First Lieutenant:
Pleasant Green
Second Lieutenant:
Alfred W. Luckett
First Sergeant:
Thomas C. Collins
Second Sergeant:
William D. Haily
Third Sergeant:
William Bryant
Fourth Sergeant:
Francis Yoast
First Corporal:
Thomas Barker
Second Corporal:
Caton Echart
Third Corporal:
George W. Ricks
Fourth Corporal:
Elisha Prewitt

Privates:
Thomas Beacon
Everett Bleakley
Alfred Bonner
John Brothers
John Brown
C. C. Browning
Oliver Buckman
James Casner
Richard Corn
Jacob Ferrout
David Fisher
Luther Flint
Robert Foster
Robert Germany
Alexander Hamilton
James Hamilton
Abel Harness
John Harrell
Turner Highsmith
William Right Hobbs
Joel W. Hudgins
Samuel Jennings
Elias Jones
August Lambreth
Bryant Lane
George Lane
James Latty
Benjamin Levitt
Leroy Murphy
Jonathan Nix
Bird Owens
Nelson Owens
William Owens
James Patton
Asa Perry
Jonathan Rogers
David Scott
Jonathan Scott
William Simmons
James Simpson
Anthony Smith
Taylor Smith
William Snoddy
Edward Stephens
William Steward
John Stone
John Talk
Joseph D. Thompson
Martin Thompson
Edward W. Turner
Richard Vaughan
Benjamin F. Warnock
Joseph Watkins
James Wells
John W. Wilbarger
Alexander Williams
Michael Young

Source: Charles D. Spurlin, *Texas Volunteers in the Mexican War,* 244–46. Captain Cady's rangers continued in service through July 4, 1846.

Captain Ad Gillespie immediately mustered the same men, with few exceptions, back into federal service that same day. He added a large number of men from around the San Antonio area and his Texas Mounted Rangers company originally numbered 99 men, plus Major Hays directing them. Mike Chevallie became his first lieutenant, John Adams the second lieutenant and Bigfoot Wallace the first sergeant. Among the veteran rangers who signed on this date as new hands were Kit Acklin, Tom Galbreath, Ben McCulloch, James Taylor and Rufus Taylor.

The third company under Major Hays' direction was that of Captain John T. Price, who had taken command of a 16-man county ranging unit in March per congressional orders. Like Bell, he recruited heavily to bolster his company size for federal service. Price mustered in the Texas Mounted Volunteers of Victoria and Goliad counties on September 25, 1845, with 76 men. His first lieutenant, Archibald White Templeton, had been with him for six months and his second lieutenant, George W. Guthrie, had previously served in Price's 1841 ranging company. Several of his other rangers were old-timers. Felix Goff had first served in Captain John Tumlinson's revolutionary rangers in early 1836. Isaac Stem and Ezekiel Ballard had served under Captain Price in early 1841. James H. Manning had served in Captain Joseph Chance's Washington Guards ranging company in 1836.

The fourth company of Texas Mounted Rangers was that of Captain David C. Cady, mustered into service on October 1, 1845, and consisting primarily of men recruited at Austin. His company originally consisted of 69 men—double the size of the Travis County Rangers which Cady had previously commanded. His first lieutenant, Pleasant Green, had been with the Travis County Rangers since their February organization. His new company was placed under the direction of Major Thomas J. Fauntleroy of the Second Dragoons. Cady's rangers made a number of scouting expeditions while attached to the Second Dragoons, although they did not have any noted Indian conflicts. Cady's company would remain in service into the Mexican war until disbanded on July 4, 1846.[9]

Toward the end of October, Major Hays sent Ben McCulloch with ten recruits from Gonzales on an expedition to Laredo. They found the citizens there eager to acknowledge the authority of Texas and ready for a company of rangers to be stationed in their area to check Indian depredations. During the latter weeks of 1845, Hays oversaw the scouting efforts of the companies of captains Gillespie and Cady. He rode in company with his men during late December and encamped opposite the Presidio de Rio Grande. The Comanches and bandits of the southwestern frontier were relatively quiet as the new year approached, so Major Hays took the opportunity to visit Austin in company with Secretary William Cooke. He stayed in town long enough to meet with President Jones on border defense and to attend the New Year's Eve festivities in the capitol.[10]

Hays, Cooke and the citizens of Austin lined Congress Avenue to watch a company of U.S. dragoons in full dress marching up the capital's main street. There was much celebrating in town that evening and one citizen noted that some of the friendly Tonkawa Indians on hand proceeded to get "gloriously drunk."[11]

During the early weeks of 1846, Hays maintained his headquarters in San Antonio. Captain Gillespie's rangers kept a camp nearby on the Medina River while portions of the battalion were out on scouting expeditions. On the night of January 13, 1846, a party of Waco and Kichai Indians raided San Antonio and drove off 35 horses. Captain Gillespie's Texas Rangers "closely pursued" these marauders, as reported by the January 21 *Texas Democrat*. Gillespie's rangers caught these Indians after a "hard and rapid march" of 70 miles. The rangers approached the Indian camp on the edge of a cedar brake but the Wacos and Kichais fled into the cover, leaving their stolen horses behind. Captain Gillespie's men returned to San Antonio on August 16 without injury, bringing back the stolen horses. The *Texas Democrat* gushed, "The Captain deserves great credit for the alacrity and energetic promptness of his movements. Such men are invaluable upon a frontier, and the people of San Antonio would doubtless dislike very much to be deprived of his services."[12]

The men found time to visit San Antonio and were able to relax at times. When German immigrant Dr. Ferdinand Roemer visited Béxar on February 10, 1846, he discovered Major Hays enjoying a local fandango. Roemer had expected to encounter a powerful, rugged man but he instead found Hays to be "a young slender-built man" with a "smooth, beardless face" who wore a black dress coat. Roemer could hardly have guessed the military importance of this man, whose piercing eyes alone held "traces of his hidden energy."[13]

★ ★ ★ ★ ★

"The Republic of Texas is No More"

Just one week after this little party in San Antonio, the Republic of Texas was living out its last days as an independent nation. The impending annexation of Texas into the United States did not sit well with Santa Anna and the Mexican government. Intelligence reports said that a Mexican army force was beginning to concentrate at Matamoros and General Taylor's U.S. troops were instructed to take position on the Rio Grande. Major Hays visited with Taylor and offered to help with the scouting duties that the army would need in Texas and Mexico. In short time, however, Taylor would find that his own cavalrymen were no match for the Texas Rangers and he would ask the governor of Texas for two mounted regiments.

The First Legislature of the State of Texas met in Austin on Monday, February 16 and Governor-elect James Pinckney Henderson reported his choice for inauguration day as Thursday. It was thus February 19, 1846, when outgoing President Anson Jones uttered his famous words, "The Republic of Texas is no more."

Seats were removed from the House and Senate chambers on this date and placed on the long gallery on the east side of the capitol, where the members of the legislature took their seats. Hundreds of Austin citizens also gathered to witness the flying of both the Lone Star flag and the Stars and Stripes of the United States. Judge Robert Baylor and Dr. Anson Jones delivered addresses to those gathered and celebrated the surrendering of Texan sovereignty and its incorporation into the United States.[14]

The elected officials of the First Legislature of the State of Texas included many men who had served with or led Texas Rangers and Frontier Regiment companies during the Republic years: William H. Bourland, Ned Burleson, William L. Cazneau, George Erath, James S. Gillet, Benjamin F. Gooch, Henry Kinney, Ben McCulloch, Samuel McFarland, Duncan Ogden, George A. Patillo, William Sadler, Arthur Swift, William "Buckskin" Williams and Robert "Three-Legged Willie" Williamson.

"The final act in the great drama is now performed," uttered Jones to the crowd. "The Republic of Texas is no more!"

Artillery boomed as the Lone Star flag was lowered and the Stars and Stripes were run to the top of the standard. Many a veteran frontiersmen was moved as his realization of past dreams symbolically played out before his eyes. All of their past skirmishes, Indian battles and revolutions as an independent republic were suddenly replaced by a new association with a powerful nation that would support Texas in its future conflicts.

The First Legislature of the State of Texas passed a resolution on March 14, 1846, which recognized the "chivalry and many gallant and daring deeds of Maj. John C. Hays, Capt. Benj. McCulloch and R. A. Gillespie." While only three leaders of the Texas Rangers had been named, the intent of the legislature was clear. The Republic of Texas had been well served by the ranging corps to fight Indians, repulse Mexican incursions, deal justice to bandits and cattle thieves, and help defend the outermost areas of Texas settlement.

The brainchild of Stephen Fuller Austin, the Texas Rangers of the Republic years had served nobly since Moses Morrison's first ten-man unit operated in 1823. Thousands of other Texans had taken to the field in the two decades which followed. The men were farmers, merchants, lawyers, legislators, old men and young boys who had secured able mounts, ammunition and whatever firearms they could muster before hitting the rough trails in pursuit of Indians, Mexican rebels, bandits and cattle rustlers. Their work was often thankless and they sometimes went years without being paid for their service. To most, what had mattered most was protecting their families and neighbors from imminent danger as the Republic of Texas struggled through war, financial troubles and various political turmoils.

Texas independence endured and admission into the Union ensured that the valiant traditions the earliest Texas Rangers had firmly established would be carried on by other rangers into the modern era.

Chapter 12

Afterword

The Republic of Texas was no more but the legendary Texas Rangers continued by necessity. John Coffee Hays would also continue to be the predominant figurehead of the ranging service even as it came under control of the U.S. military during the Mexican War.

During February 1846, Major Hays had gone to Corpus Christi to visit with General Taylor. While there, his rangers learned that some 600 Indians had raided the settlements southwest of San Antonio and were retiring northward with their stolen goods. Some secondhand accounts have it that Hays and about forty rangers cut off this war party in the vicinity of Bandera Pass and then tracked the Comanches back into the hill country near Enchanted Rock.[1]

Hays—as the story is told—rode with his rangers west from Enchanted Rock to a distinctive limestone formation on the Concho River called the Painted Rocks. The so-called "Paint Rocks" received their moniker from the hundreds of ancient Indian pictographs which adorn a high cliff overlooking the Concho. Hays' men arrived during the night ahead of the Comanches and took position. They attacked and killed some of the Comanches the next morning as they approached Paint Rock. The battle would last for two full days and nights as the Comanches attempted to flush the heavily entrenched rangers from their positions.[2]

During the first 48 hours of the engagement, Jack Hays' men reportedly suffered only one ranger wounded by an arrow while the Indians suffered heavy losses of lives. Once the Comanches recognized that their foe was once again Hays, they taunted "Devil Yack" during the second night. The battle of Paint Rock did not end until Major Hays personally shot and killed the leading Comanche chief on the third day. One of the rangers lassoed and retrieved the fallen chief's body. The remainder of the Comanches, low on ammunition and very much worn down, soon opted to retreat.[3]

The battle of Paint Rock is yet another of the controversial battles involving Jack Hays that simply may not have happened. Hays' so-called "Battle of Bandera Pass" (explained in Chapter 2 of this volume) was so named based on garbled accounts given second and third-hand many years later. The actual site of that battle was most likely not in Bandera Pass. The 1846 "Battle of Paint Rock" falls into the same gray area as Hays' famous Enchanted Rock solo battle of 1841.

Neither Paint Rock nor Enchanted Rock received coverage in contemporary Texas or national newspapers. Neither battle has a military report or a reliable first-hand account which has survived time. In the case of Enchanted Rock, this Hays episode was being told in print within years of its happening. The Paint Rock battle is more troubling due to the fact that it was completely ignored by late 1800s historians.

In addition to Hays, other Rangers mentioned in this fight are Mike Chevallie, Ad Gillespie, Ben McCulloch, Bigfoot Wallace, Emory Gibbons and E. M. Harrison. Captain Gillespie, of course, was the commander of the ranger company which was at that time under the supervision of Major Hays. At the time the battle reportedly took place—about March 1846 by historian Mike Cox's sleuthing—Chevallie, McCulloch and Wallace are indeed on the muster rolls for Gillespie's company. The ranger listed as having been wounded in the left arm was named as "Emory Gibbons" in the earliest account and as "Gibson" in a 1945 account of the battle. The only similar name on any 1846 Captain Gillespie muster roll is a "William Gibson."[4]

The first published account of the Paint Rock battle was a newspaper article written by Isaac Dunbar Affleck, apparently around 1910. The earliest printings of this story are no longer available, but it was reprinted by J. Marvin Hunter in the fourth edition of his magazine *Frontier Times* in January 1924. Affleck wrote that "no information on the subject has even been published" since the original report of the battle was destroyed when the state capitol burned in 1881. The recollections of the battle were given to Affleck by an E. M. Harrison (named as "F. M. Harrison" in a book published by J. M. Franks in 1924). This author failed to turn up an E. M. Harrison, an F. M. Harrison or an Emory Gibbons in a search of republic-era audited military claims, unpaid debts, and pension papers.[5]

Texas Ranger historians such as Walter Prescott Webb, Robert Utley, Mike Cox and Charles Robinson all apparently shared enough doubts as to the authenticity of the Paint Rock battle to give it little to no mention in their compilations. The earliest Ranger historians such as J. W. Wilbarger, John Henry Brown, James DeShields and A. J. Sowell—who interviewed many early Rangers—do not discuss a battle at Paint Rock.

Jack Hays was as much a folk hero as the Alamo's Davy Crockett and many men passed along stories of the fights he had reportedly fought. As with Bandera Pass, there is the possibility that the timing and events of the Paint Rock fight are confused with one of Hays' other earlier fights. Perhaps a more convincing document will one day surface which verifies the authenticity of the Paint Rock battle.

Captain Gillespie's San Antonio rangers were mustered back into federal service on March 28, 1846, for another three-month period. They served along with Captain Peter Bell's Corpus Christi rangers and Captain John Price's Victoria and Goliad counties rangers as the only such units in service. During April, General Taylor's army took position across the Rio Grande from Matamoros. Sam Walker—recently discharged from Gillespie's former company—persuaded Taylor to let him muster in a ranging company on April 21 at Point Isabel to scout and perform special missions beyond the capabilities of the U.S. regulars. Four days later, Mexican troops at Matamoros crossed the river and ambushed an American patrol. President Polk used this incident to secure a declaration of war on May 13. In the meantime, Taylor's 2,200-man army defeated 3,700 Mexicans under Gen. Mariano Arista on May 8 and May 9 in the battles of Palo Alto and Resaca de la Palma.

The call went out in May for mounted companies of Texans to join the effort on the Rio Grande. Governor James Henderson turned over his office to his lieutenant governor and was sworn into federal service as major general of Texas' mounted men. Companies of Texas Rangers were formed to aid the regulars and the First Regiment of Texas Mounted Riflemen was formed June 1846 under Colonel Jack Hays, Lieutenant Colonel Sam Walker and Major Mike Chevallie. Their ten companies were led by a few newcomers but primarily by men who had held key commands as Texas Rangers in the past: Ben McCulloch, Kit Acklin, Thomas Green, Ad Gillespie, Eli Chandler, Samuel L. S. Ballow, Claiborne C. Herbert, Frank S. Early, James Gillespie and James B. McCown.

General Taylor's army was nobly served by a long line of former Texas Rangers who now signed on to be paid regularly, for the first time for some of the men. They would be used to scout out Mexican forces, locate water sources, serve as advance guards and guerilla forces. They used rifles and Colt revolvers, riding the best horses available and operating without uniforms in sharp contrast to the regular army men.

The Second Regiment of Texas Mounted Volunteers was organized in July 1846 under Colonel George Tyler Wood, Lieutenant Colonel John E. Myrick and Major William R. Scurry. Its ten ranger captains included former Travis Guard Bird Holland, Houston County militia leader John L. Hall, San Jacinto cavalry veteran John Kemp Goodloe, and Cherokee War ranger veteran Alston Ferguson. The Third Regiment of Texas Mounted Volunteers was headed by Colonel William C. Young and Lieutenant Colonel James Bourland, both leaders of the 1841 Village Creek Expedition and battle. Their ten ranger company commanders included former Travis County Rangers leader David C. Cady, Henry McCulloch, former ranger battalion leader Daniel Montague and Samuel Highsmith, a veteran of the 1839 battle of Brushy Creek.

Taylor's force and the Texas Mounted Riflemen battalions moved into Mexico and seized Monterrey in September. Colonel Hays and Colonel Wood's rangers played a heavy role in the siege of this city and Captain Ad Gillespie was killed in the assault and capture of the city. The scouting efforts of Ben McCulloch were vital in revealing the best route of approach into Monterrey.[6]

Following this campaign, Hays returned to Texas to begin organizing a new ranger regiment that was expected to be called into service for 1847. His former subordinate Sam Walker became a captain of the U.S. Regiment of Mounted Riflemen and Walker went to Washington to lobby for better ordinance for the mounted troops. Walker's efforts with gunmaker Sam Colt soon produced the .44-caliber Walker Colt pistol, a six-shooter that would be used by the new rangers later in the Mexican War.

Ben McCulloch's rangers continued their scouting efforts for General Taylor's army during early 1847 as President Santa Anna gathered his army to crush General Taylor at the battle of Buena Vista. Major Mike Chevallie led a battalion of five ranger companies into Mexico to support Taylor in May after McCulloch's men had returned home. The rangers were criticized by some for being unruly and taking no exception to killing a Mexican when the opportunity presented itself for such vengeful killings.

When Colonel Jack Hays reorganized the First Regiment of Texas Mounted Volunteers in July 1847, his ranger captains included former San Jacinto company commander James Gillespie, veteran frontier fighter Benjamin Franklin Hill, Cherokee War veteran David Muckelroy, former First Regiment of Infantry Captain Martin Kingsley Snell and Samuel W. Sims, who had served as a colonel of mounted gunmen in 1839. Before leaving for the Mexican interior, Hays' regiment was armed with 394 of the Model 1847 Walker Colt six-shooter revolvers. Ironically, Sam Walker himself died in combat at the battle of Huamantla with two of his namesake pistols in hand.[7]

Hays' regiment reached Brigadier General Joseph Lane's headquarters at Puebla in mid-November 1847. General Winfield Scott had already led a successful attack on Mexico City in September and the war was winding down. The presence of more rangers was still something of note. General Ethan Allan Hitchcock wrote on December 6 that Hays' newly arrived rangers were without uniform but well mounted and heavily armed with rifles, pistols, Colt revolvers and swords. "The Mexicans are terribly afraid of them," he added.[8]

Lieutenant Colonel Peter Bell formed another regiment of Texas Mounted Volunteers in October 1847. His ranger company commanders included Samuel Highsmith, Henry McCulloch, former Texas president Mirabeau Lamar, former First Regiment of Infantry Captain James S. Sutton and former Jack Hays ranger Shapley P. Ross.

The Mexican War was finally ended with the February 2, 1848, signing of the Treaty of Guadalupe Hidalgo, although one final skirmish was fought three weeks later. The rangers left Mexico City on March 18 to proceed home and all were mustered out of service on April 29, 1848, with the exception of those under Jack Hays and Rip Ford. The rangers had ably served as the eyes and ears of Zach Taylor's army and those who helped defeat Santa Anna's army were viewed as heroes upon their return to their home state.

The Mexican War ultimately forced Mexico to recognize Texas as part of the United States, which additionally gained significant new territory—California, parts of Colorado and Utah, and most of Arizona, Nevada and New Mexico. Texas Rangers gained great attention in newspaper accounts, although some of the publicity centered on their grizzled appearance, unruly behavior and barbaric fighting techniques. Few reporters realized that some Texans used the battles of the Mexican War as a chance to settle old scores for friends and relatives slain during the republic years at Coleto Creek, Goliad, the Dawson massacre, or while in Mexican prisons following the Mier Expedition.

The first governor of Texas had taken command of Texian troops, including rangers, during his office. The next two men to lead Texas, George Wood and Peter Bell, had directly served as ranger commanders. Many of the seasoned rangers from the Mexican War would help control the frontiers of Texas through the 1850s and on into the Civil War. Their tactics may have been questioned by some but their ability to wage a hard-fought battle under tense conditions could not be denied.

The frontier spirit of those serving as rangers was something that could not be trained into the U.S. regulars. Stephen F. Austin's original vision in 1823 of an armed, mobile company of men ranging over the frontier to instill justice and peace against any foes who threatened Texas settlers had not died and in fact continues to this day.

Appendix

Texas Ranger Companies of the Republic of Texas

1835–1845

This compilation includes companies who were paid in the fashion of Texas Rangers or which were organized specifically as rangers, spies or county minutemen. Texas Militia companies which operated for short periods of time under supervision of regional militia leaders are not included. Militia battalions did, however, operate companies which ranged beyond immediate periods of crisis and these units are listed. Examples of brief militia expeditions not counted are those led by General Thomas J. Rusk and Edward H. Tarrant. Companies formed under Texas Milita direction to serve in a specific campaign—such as the 1839 Cherokee War or 1840 Battle of Plum Creek—are not listed unless a particular unit continued in frontier service after the immediate crisis period.

Each unit is listed under its original year of organization. Counties shown in parenthesis indicate where the unit was organized but not necessarily where it served.

1835 Texas Ranger Companies

Commander:	Company Service Dates/Notes:
Arrington, Capt. William W.	Appointed Ranger Captain on Nov. 28, 1835; No evidence company was ever mustered into service.
Barnett, Capt. George Washington	Robertson's Colony Rangers; July 20—Aug. 28, 1835
Burton, Capt. Isaac Watts	Regional Ranging Company; Dec. 19, 1835—June 24, 1836
Coe, Capt. Philip Haddox	Robertson's Colony Rangers; July 9—Aug. 31, 1835
Coleman, Capt. Robert Morris	Robertson's Colony Rangers; June 12—Aug. 28, 1835

Friar, Capt. Daniel Boone	Regional Ranging Company which served between Brazos and Colorado Rivers; Nov. 1, 1835—Feb. 1, 1836
Goheen, Capt. Michael R.	La Grange Rangers; Aug. 1—Sept. 13, 1835; Goheen assumed command from Capt. Moore at Parker's Fort
Hillhouse, Capt. Eli	Regional Ranging Company Which Served Between Brazos and Trinity Rivers; Based at Parker's Fort, Oct. 23—Dec. 24, 1835
Moore, Capt. John Henry	La Grange Rangers; July 25—Aug. 1, 1835; command passed to Capt. Goheen
Seale, Capt. Eli	Regional Ranging Company; Dec. 24, 1835—Jan. 25, 1836; Seale assumed command after death of Capt. Hillhouse
Williamson, Capt. Robert McAlpin	Robertson's Colony Rangers; July 25—Sept. 13, 1835

1836 Texas Ranger Companies

Commander:	Company Service Dates/Notes:
Allen, Capt. James C.	Buckeye Rangers; Mounted Cavalry/ Ranging Unit; July—Oct. 1836
Barron, Capt. Thomas Hudson	Robertson's Colony Rangers; Feb.—March 16, 1836; Also: Ranging Company of Col. Coleman's Battalion; August—Dec. 31, 1836
Billingsley, Capt. Jesse	First Division of Rangers under Col. Edward Burleson; July 1—Oct. 1, 1836
Boales, Capt. Calvin	First Division of Rangers under Col. Edward Burleson; Sept. 11—Nov. 14, 1836
Chance, Capt. Joseph Bell	Washington Guards Ranging Company; March 20—June 1, 1836
Clapp, Capt. Elisha	Ranging Company of Maj. James Smith's Battalion; Sept. 10—Dec. 10, 1836
Costley, Capt. Michael	Ranging Company of Maj. James Smith's Battalion; Sept. 11—Dec. 11, 1836
Franks, Capt. Louis B.	Robertson's Colony Rangers; Feb. 1—April 1, 1836
Gholson, Lt. Albert G.	March 16—May 7, 1836; Assumed the command from Capt. Barron
Haggard, Capt. Squire	Ranging Company of Maj. James Smith's Battalion; November 1836—March 19, 1837; Assumed command when Capt. Jewell was promoted to Major, Rangers.
Head, Capt. James A.	Regional Ranging Company; Based at Parker's Fort, Jan. 27—April 27, 1836

Hill, Capt. William Warner	First Division of Rangers under Col. Edward Burleson; July 3—Oct. 3, 1836
Jewell, Capt. George Washington	Ranging Company of Maj. James Smith's Battalion; Sept. 19—November, 1836
Kimbell, Lt. George C.	Gonzales Mounted Rangers; Feb. 23—March 6, 1836; Perished at Alamo.
Lockhart, Capt. Byrd B. Sr.	First Division of Rangers under Col. Edward Burleson; July 4—Aug. 16, 1836
McGehee, Capt. John Gilmore	Texas Revolution Scouting Unit organized by Col. Edward Burleson; Feb. 24—March 16, 1836
McGehee, Capt. John Gilmore	First Division of Rangers under Col. Edward Burleson; July 1—Nov. 20, 1836
Parker, Capt. James Wilson	Regional Ranging Company; Based at Parker's Fort, Jan. 1—May 19, 1836
Pierson, Capt. John G. Warren	Post Washington Mounted Company; June 30—Sept. 30, 1836
Putnam, Capt. Dickinson	Second Division of Rangers under Col. Jesse Benton; June 24—Nov. 1, 1836; Assumed command from Capt. Burton
Robbins, Capt. Thomas	Cavalry/Ranging Company; April 25—Aug. 13, 1836
Robertson, Capt. Sterling Clack	First Division of Rangers under Col. Edward Burleson; July 25—Sept. 11, 1836
Robertson, Capt. Sterling Clack	Robertson's Colony Rangers; Jan. 17—Feb. 1836
Robless, Lt. Alexander	Ranging Company of Col. Coleman's Battalion; Oct. 5—Dec. 31, 1836; Robless assumed command from Capt. Walden
Sadler, Capt. William Turner	Regional Ranging Company Which Served Between Trinity and Neches Rivers; Based at Fort Houston, Jan. 1—March 16, 1836
Scurlock, Capt. William	Regional Ranging Unit under General Rusk's Supervision; July 4—Aug. 12, 1836
Smith, Capt. James	Nacogdoches Mounted Volunteers; April 11—July 11, 1836
Smith, Lt. Samuel	Second Division of Rangers under Col. Jesse Benton; Aug. 6—Oct. 25, 1836
Thomas, Lt. Benjamin R.	Ranging Company of Col. Coleman's Battalion; Sept. 6—Dec. 31, 1836
Townsend, Capt. Stephen	Robertson's Colony Rangers; Feb. 1—May 12, 1836
Tumlinson, Capt. John Jackson Jr.	Bastrop County Area Rangers; Jan. 17—Aug. 16, 1836

Walden, Capt. Alfred P.	Ranging Company of Col. Coleman's Battalion; Aug. 15—Oct. 5, 1836
Wheelock, Capt. E. Louis Ripley	Second Division of Rangers under Col. Jesse Benton; May 8—Aug. 8, 1836
Wilson, Capt. William C.	Part of Colonel Benton's Ranger Regiment; March 1—June 1, 1836
York, Capt. John	First Division of Rangers under Col. Edward Burleson; July 1—Nov. 20, 1836

1837 Texas Ranger Companies

Commander:	Company Service Dates/Notes:
Andrews, Capt. Micah	Company C, Major William Henry Smith's Ranger Battalion; Jan. 1—August, 1837
Barron, Capt. Thomas Hudson	Company A, Major William Henry Smith's Ranger Battalion; Jan. 1—Nov. 27, 1837
Bowyer, Capt. John M.	Harrisburg Mounted Gunmen; June 18—Dec. 18, 1837; a detachment of company was led by Lt. A. B. Vanbenthuysen
Curtis, Lt. Charles	Company A, Major William Henry Smith's Ranger Battalion; Oct. 20–Nov. 28, 1837
Eastland, Capt. William Mosby	Company D, Major William Henry Smith's Ranger Battalion; Jan. 1, 1837—March 2, 1838
Lynch, Capt. John L.	Company A, Major William Henry Smith's Ranger Battalion; Nov. 28, 1837—Feb. 20, 1838
Mather, Lt. Joseph	Company E, Major William Henry Smith's Ranger Battalion; Sept. 17—Oct. 1, 1837
Monroe, Capt. Daniel	Company B, Major William Henry Smith's Ranger Battalion; Jan. 1—Dec. 14, 1837
Moore, Lt. William H.	Company B, Major William Henry Smith's Ranger Battalion; Dec. 14, 1837—April 30, 1838
Smith, Capt. Lee C.	Company E, Major William Henry Smith's Ranger Battalion; March 17—Sept. 17, 1837
Wren, Lt. Nicholas	Company C, Major William Henry Smith's Ranger Battalion; August—October, 1837

1838 Texas Ranger Companies

Commander:	Company Service Dates/Notes:
Augustine, Capt. Henry W.	Mounted Spy Company, Third Militia Brigade; Aug. 8—22, 1838
Blythe, Capt. Champion	Mounted Gunmen, Major Leonard H. Mabbitt's Ranger Battalion; Aug. 30—Sept. 22, 1838

Box, Capt. James Edward	Mounted Riflemen (Houston County); Oct. 14, 1838—Jan. 14, 1839
Bradshaw, Capt. James	Mounted Riflemen, Major Leonard H. Mabbitt's Ranger Battalion; Oct. 10—Dec. 1, 1838
Briscoe, Capt. George C.	Fannin County Rangers, Second Militia Brigade; Nov. 16, 1838—Jan. 10, 1839
Brookfield, Capt. William Charles	Mounted Rangers, Nacogdoches County; Oct. 12—24, 1838
Brown, Capt. Squire	Mounted Gunmen, Major Leonard H. Mabbitt's Ranger Battalion; Sept. 22—Dec. 28, 1838; assumed command from Captain Blythe
Chisum, Capt. Claiborne	Mounted Spy Company, Fourth Militia Brigade; June 9—Sept. 9, 1838
Daniels, Capt. Joseph	Milam Guards, Second Militia Brigade; Nov. 15, 1838—Feb. 14, 1839
Durst, Capt. James H.	Mounted Rangers (Mixed Anglo/Indian company), Gen. Kelsey Douglass' Ranger Battalion; Dec. 24, 1838—Jan. 25, 1839
Durst, Capt. John M.	Mounted Gunmen, Third Brigade, Texas Militia; Nov. 17–Dec. 16, 1838
English, Capt. George	Mounted Volunteers, Third Regiment, Third Militia Brigade; Oct. 10, 1838–Jan. 13, 1839
Ferguson, Capt. Joseph	Mounted Volunteers, Third Regiment, Third Militia Brigade; Dec. 8, 1838–March 8, 1839
Haley, Capt. Richard	Shelby County Mounted Volunteers, Third Regiment, Third Militia Brigade; Oct. 14, 1838–Jan. 10, 1839
Hart, Capt. John	Mounted Gunmen, Fourth Militia Brigade; Nov. 19, 1838—Jan. 1, 1839
Journey, Capt. Nathaniel T.	Fannin County Rangers; Sept. 13, 1838—March 13, 1839
Lyday, Capt. Isaac	Red River County Rangers; Sept. 1, 1838—Feb. 28, 1839
O'Neal, Capt. James R.	Fannin County Spies, Fourth Militia Brigade; April 8—Sept. 8, 1838
Panther, Capt.	Mounted Shawnee Rangers, Gen. Kelsey Douglass' Ranger Battalion; Nov. 25, 1838—Jan. 25, 1839
Renfro, Capt. David	Mounted Gunmen, Third Militia Brigade; Oct. 7—Nov. 9, 1838
Ross, Capt. Reuben	Houston Volunteer Guard, Medina River country ranging unit headquartered in San Antonio; Jan. 1–April 1, 1838

Sadler, Capt. William Turner	Mounted Rangers, Major Leonard H. Mabbitt's Ranger Battalion; September—Nov. 7, 1838
Sánchez, Capt. Lewis	Mounted Rangers (Nacogdoches County), Gen. Kelsey Douglass' Ranger Battalion; Sept. 7, 1838—Jan. 27, 1839
Simpson, Lt. John P.	Fannin County Mounted Gunmen, Fourth Militia Brigade; Dec. 1, 1838—Jan. 14, 1839
Sloan, Capt. Robert	Fannin County Rangers; Sept. 14, 1838—Jan. 14, 1839
Smith, Capt. James	Mounted Volunteers/Spies, Third Militia Brigade; Oct 7—Dec. 1, 1838
Snively, Capt. Jacob	Mounted Rangers, Major Leonard H. Mabbitt's Ranger Battalion; Sept. 14—Dec. 13, 1838
Stephens, Capt. Hiram B.	Nacogdoches County Mounted Rangers; Aug. 4—Sept. 15, 1838
Stiff, Capt. Jesse	Fannin County Mounted Gunmen, Fourth Militia Brigade; Dec. 1—29, 1838
Stout, Capt. William B.	Red River County Rangers; Nov. 20, 1838—May 26, 1839
Timmons, Capt. James F.	Mounted Gunmen, Gen. Kelsey Douglass' Ranger Battalion; Oct. 12, 1838—Feb. 6, 1839
Whitaker, Capt. Madison G.	Mounted Rangers, Third Brigade, Texas Militia; Oct. 30–Nov. 11, 1838
Wilson, Capt. Jason	Red River County Mounted Gunmen/Rangers, First Regiment, Fourth Militia Brigade; May 27–Aug. 27, 1838
Wortham, Capt. John	Houston County Rangers, Gen. Kelsey Douglass' Ranger Battalion; Nov. 9, 1838—Feb. 8, 1839
Wyche, Capt. William P.	Sabine County Mounted Volunteers, Third Regiment, Third Militia Brigade; Nov. 4, 1838–Feb. 4, 1839

1839 TEXAS RANGER COMPANIES

Commander:	Company Service Dates/Notes:
Adams, Capt. Solomon	Houston County Rangers; Feb. 8—Aug. 9, 1839; took command when Capt. Wortham was promoted to major.
Andrews, Capt. Micah	La Grange County Ranger Company; March 10—June 10, 1839
Bennett, Capt. Joseph L.	Mounted Gunmen, Houston and Robertson counties; July 28—Sept. 3, 1839

Billingsley, Capt. Jesse	Bastrop County Ranger Company; February—March 1839
Bird, Capt. John	"Austin Volunteers" Ranging Company; April 24—May 26, 1839
Black, Capt. George K.	Nacogdoches County Mounted Rangers; Oct. 22, 1839–Jan. 29, 1840
Box, Capt. James Edward	Mounted Rangers, Gen. Kelsey Douglass' Ranger Battalion; Jan. 15—Mar. 25, 1839; Houston County Rangers, March 26—Oct. 18, 1839
Brookshire, Capt. Nathaniel	"Austin Volunteers" Ranging Company; May 26—July 24, 1839; took command after the death of Capt. Bird
Burleson, Capt. Jacob	Mounted Volunteers (Ad hoc Rangers); Feb. 24–25, 1839
Caldwell, Capt. Mathew	Gonzales County Rangers; March 16—June 16, 1839; Caldwell later commanded a detachment of spies which operated with the First Regiment of Infantry during Dec. 1839—Jan. 1840
Carroll, Capt. Nathaniel H.	Mounted Gunmen, Co. C, Col. John Neill's Battalion; Sept. 15—Dec. 1, 1839
Castro, Capt. Cuelgas de	Mounted Lipan Apache Volunteer Rangers under Col. John H. Moore, Jan. 25—Feb. 25, 1839
Cleveland, Capt. James W.	Mounted Rangers, Gen. Kelsey Douglass' Ranger Battalion; Jan. 6—Feb. 5, 1839
Davis, Capt. Samuel	Mounted Gunmen, Co. D, Col. John Neill's Battalion; Sept. 10—Nov. 22, 1839
Doyle, Capt. Nimrod	Robertson County Rangers; March 8—June 10, 1839
Durst, Capt. Joseph	Mounted Rangers, Third Militia Brigade; Aug. 15—Sept. 27, 1839
Eastland, Capt. William Mosby	La Grange Volunteer Rangers under Col. John H. Moore; Jan. 21—Feb. 21, 1839
Edens, Capt. Balis	Ranger company under direction of Major Boley C. Walters; enrolled by Feb. 11, 1839; stationed at Brown's Fort in Houston County as of early March 1839.
Emberson, Capt. John	Red River and Fannin County Volunteer Rangers; March 16—Sept. 16, 1839
Erath, Capt. George Bernhard	Milam County Rangers; March 8—June 8, 1839
Evans, Lt. William G.	"Travis Spies" Ranging Company (Harris County); March 20—Sept. 20, 1839
Franks, Capt. Louis B.	Mounted Volunteers; Ad Hoc Rangers

	under Col. Henry W. Karnes, Ranger Battalion commander; June 6–23, 1839
Garrett, Capt. John	"Houston Yagers,"Volunteer Ranging Company, Col. Karnes Mounted Gunman/ Ranger Battalion; April 8—Aug. 8, 1839; Lt. John A. Creery acting commander from June 11–Aug. 8, 1839
Gill, Capt. John Porter	Mounted Gunmen, Co. B, Col. John Neill's Battalion; Sept. 14—Nov. 22, 1839
Gonzales, Capt. José María	San Antonio Mounted Volunteers, under Col. Henry W. Karnes; Sept. 8—Nov. 21, 1839
Hallum, Capt. William V. R.	Mounted Gunmen, Co. E, Col. John Neill's Battalion; Sept. 14—Nov. 22, 1839; company originally commanded by Capt. William Foster Young
Hamilton, Capt. Jacob E.	Mounted Rangers, San Augustine County; July 22—Aug. 10, 1839
Harrison, Capt. Greenberry Horace	Mounted Gunman Company, Col. Karnes Mounted Gunman/Ranger Battalion; June 28—Aug. 10, 1839
Jordan, Capt. Alexander	Nacogdoches County Mounted Rangers; June 21—Aug. 5, 1839
Lane, Capt. John William	Mounted Rangers, Fourth Militia Brigade; Aug. 15, 1839–Feb. 16, 1840
Lewis, Capt. Mark B.	Volunteer Ranging Company, Col. Karnes Mounted Gunman/Ranger Battalion; March 2—Sept. 9, 1839
Long, Capt. George W.	Mounted Gunmen, Co. F, Col. John Neill's Battalion; Sept. 9—Nov. 30, 1839
Mathews, Capt. James D.	Robertson County Rangers; March 8—June 8, 1839
McLean, Capt. Ephraim Walton	Galveston Mounted Gunmen, under Col. Henry Karnes; Nov. 19—Dec. 8, 1839; took command after departure of Capt. William Wilson
Merrill, Capt. Nelson	Bastrop County Rangers; June 10—Sept. 10, 1839
Middleton, Capt. John W.	Sabine County Rangers; July 15—Aug. 14, 1839
Neill, Capt. John C.	Volunteer Ranging Company, Col. Karnes Mounted Gunman/Ranger Battalion; June—August, 1839
Ownby, Capt. James P.	Volunteer Ranging Company, Col. Karnes Mounted Gunman/Ranger Battalion; March 2—Sept. 9, 1839

Plácido, Capt.	Mounted Tonkawa Volunteer Rangers under Col. John H. Moore; Jan. 25—Feb. 25, 1839
Reed, Capt. Henry	Mounted Gunmen, Co. G, Col. John Neill's Battalion; Oct. 3—Nov. 22, 1839
Roberts, Capt. Mark R.	Fannin County Mounted Rangers; Sept. 16, 1839–March 16, 1840
Rogers, Capt. James	Mounted Volunteers (Ad hoc Rangers); Feb. 24–26, 1839
Ross, Capt. Reuben	Volunteer Rangers (Harris County); July 1—Sept. 30, 1839; later joined Mexican Federalists on Sept. 30, 1839
Seguín, Capt. Juan N.	Mounted Volunteers; Ad Hoc Rangers under Col. Henry W. Karnes, Ranger Battalion commander; June 6–23, 1839
Sims, Capt. James W.	Mounted Riflemen, Red River County; Aug. 2—Nov. 2, 1839
Smith, Capt. Henry Madison	Nacogdoches County Rangers under Maj. Boley C. Walters Battalion; March 1—Sept. 1, 1839
Smithwick, Capt. Noah	Bastrop Rangers under Col. John H. Moore; Jan. 24—Feb. 25, 1839
Sowell, Capt. Joseph	Fannin County Rangers, Fourth Militia Brigade; Aug 1—31, 1839
Tumlinson, Capt. John Jackson Jr.	Spy Company, Col. John Neill's Mounted Gunmen Battalion; Oct. 13—Nov. 22, 1839
Williams, Capt. Samuel	Mounted Gunmen, Co. A, Col. John Neill's Battalion; Sept. 11—Dec. 2, 1839
Wilson, Capt. William F.	Galveston Mounted Gunmen, under Col. Henry Karnes; Sept. 8—Nov. 19, 1839

1840 TEXAS RANGER COMPANIES

Commander:	Company Service Dates/Notes:
Askins, Capt. Wesley	Red River County Mounted Gunmen; Oct. 1—Nov. 20, 1840
Barkley, Capt. Robert	Nacogdoches County Mounted Rangers under Major James H. Durst; July 4—Oct. 4, 1840; under acting command of Lt. Daniel Woodlan during latter weeks of company's service
Caldwell, Capt. Mathew	Gonzales County Rangers; Sept. 25—Nov. 16, 1840
Castro, Chief	Lipan Apache Scouting Company; Sept. 20—Nov. 7, 1840

Cocke, Capt. James Decatur	Border Guards (Harris County); June 18—Sept. 10, 1840
Cunningham, Capt. John R.	Béxar County Volunteer Rangers; Oct. 1–Nov. 11, 1840
Dawson, Capt. Nicholas Mosby	Colorado County Ranging Company (Ad hoc unit); Sept. 20—Nov. 7, 1840
Erath, Capt. George Bernhard	Milam County Spy Company; July 14—Sept. 20, 1840
Flores, Capt. Salvadore	Béxar County Volunteer Rangers; Oct. 1–Nov. 11, 1840
Greer, Capt. Thomas N. B.	Boggy and Trinity Rangers; Feb. 23—May 23, 1840
Jackson, Capt. Daniel R.	Fannin County Rangers; March 28—Sept. 28, 1840
Nichols, Capt. Ebenezer B.	Pitkin Guards ; Stationed in San Antonio; June 7—August 27, 1840
Pierce, Capt. Constantius	Pitkin Guards (Harris County); March 7—June 6, 1840; Sept. 25–Nov. 16, 1840
Rabb, Capt. Thomas J.	Fayette County Ranging Company (Ad hoc unit); Sept. 20—Nov. 7, 1840
Sterne, Capt. Adolphus	Nacogdoches County Mounted Rangers in Maj. James H. Durst's Battlion; July 8—Oct. 16, 1840
Stout, Capt. Henry	Red River County Rangers; June 11—Sept. 10, 1840
Stout, Capt. William B.	Red River County Rangers; May 2—Aug. 2, 1840
Wells, Lt. Moses	Travis County Ranging Company; April 9—July 9, 1840
Wilson, Capt. Jason	Red River and Fannin County Rangers; Oct. 24, 1840—Jan. 25, 1841
Woodhouse, Capt. Matthew P.	Travis Guards; March 1, 1840—March 2, 1841; originally commanded by Capt. M. H. Nicholson

1841 Texas Ranger Companies

Commander:	Service Dates/Notes:
Baker, Capt. John Reagan	Refugio County Minutemen; Oct. 25—Dec. 12, 1841; under acting command of Lt. Matthew W. Cody from Nov. 9
Becknell, Capt. William	Red River County Minutemen; June 25, 1841—June 25, 1842
Bourland, Capt. James	Mounted Volunteer Company which made expedition to present Dallas-Fort Worth area; Mid-April—May 30, 1841

Brookfield, Capt. William Charles	Houston County Minutemen; June 19—July 1, 1841
Burton, Capt. William M.	Mounted Riflemen, Nacogdoches County; July 10—Aug. 10, 1841
Cairnes, Capt. William J.	San Patricio County Minutemen; Aug. 29, 1841—Feb. 12, 1842
Callahan, Capt. James Hughes	Gonzales County Minutemen; May 7—Dec. 20, 1841
Chandler, Capt. Eli	Robertson County Minutemen; March 29—Nov. 5, 1841
Creaner, Capt. Charles N.	Victoria County Minutemen; July—August 1841
Crist, Capt. Daniel Murry	Burnet/Houston County Mounted Volunteers; July 10—Aug. 10, 1841
Daniels, Capt. Joseph	Travis Guards; Jan. 23—December, 1841
Dolson, Capt. George M.	Travis County Minutemen; March 28—Dec. 28, 1841; company led by Lt. James W. Newcomb after March 31.
Dunn, Capt. James	Victoria County Mounted Volunteers (Ad hoc); March 14—June 5, 1841
Emberson, Capt. John	Lamar County Mounted Gunmen, Fourth Militia Brigade, headquartered at Fort Inglish; August 7–29, 1841
Erath, Capt. George Bernhard	Milam County Spies, Jan. 1—March 2, 1841; Milam County Minutemen, March 9—Dec. 24, 1841
Flacco, Chief	Lipan Apache Scouting Company; March 20—June 4, 1841; July 12–Aug. 2, 1841
Gage, Capt. David	Nacodoches County Minutemen; April 12—Oct. 19, 1841
Green, Capt. Thomas	Fayette County Mounted Riflemen; March 20—June 4, 1841
Greer, Capt. Thomas N. B.	Montgomery County Minutemen; April 10—Oct. 7, 1841
Hall, Capt. John L.	Houston County Mounted Volunteers; July 10—Aug. 10, 1841
Hays, Capt. John Coffee	Rangers/Béxar County Minutemen; Jan. 10—May 10, 1841; June 1—Oct. 1, 1841
Killough, Capt. Samuel B.	Robertson County Rangers/Mounted Gunmen; Jan. 20—March 5, 1841
Lane, Capt. John William	Mounted Riflemen, Fourth Militia Brigade, stationed in Cross Timbers at Fort Inglish; July 5–Oct. 5, 1841
Lilly, Capt. Joseph D.	Paschal County Minutemen; June 12—Nov. 31, 1841

Matthews, Capt. Mansell Walter	Lamar County Minutemen; June 1—Sept. 27, 1841
McDaniel, Capt. John	Refugio County Minutemen; Dec. 16, 1841—Feb. 24, 1842
Miles, Capt. Alanson T.	San Patricio County Minutemen; May 14—Aug. 25, 1841
Ownby, Capt. James P.	San Patricio County Rangers; May 18—June 6, 1841
Pérez, Capt. Antonio	San Antonio Rangers; Jan. 20—May 20, 1841
Price, Capt. John T.	Victoria County Rangers; Jan. 3—May 2, 1841; also Company of Spies, June 20–July 2, 1841
Sowell, Capt. Joseph	Fannin County Minutemen; July 6—Sept. 26, 1841
Stout, Capt. Henry B.	Mounted Gunmen, Fourth Militia Brigade, stationed in Cross Timbers at Fort Inglish; July 15–Oct. 15, 1841
Webb, Capt. Alexander W.	Bird's Fort Rangers; Sept. 9, 1841—March 19, 1842
Zumwalt, Capt. Adam	Victoria County Minutemen; May—Dec., 1841

1842 Texas Ranger Companies

Commander:	Service Dates/Notes:
Bogart, Capt. Samuel	Washington County Scout Company; Sept. 25, 1842—Jan. 20, 1843
Burleson, Capt. Edward	Commandant of Volunteer Ranger Unit; Aug. 5—Sept. 20, 1842
Cameron, Capt. Ewen	Corpus Christi Mounted Gunmen; April 12—Sept. 1842
Gillespie, Capt. James H.	Bastrop Mounted Volunteers; March 10—April 22, 1842
Hays, Capt. John Coffee	Mounted Rangers, Bexar County; February 1842—Jan. 7, 1843
Menchaca, Capt. José Antonio	Bexar County Cavalry Company; July 1—Sept. 11, 1842
McLean, Capt. Ephraim Walton	Corpus Christi Spies/Ranger Company; April 9—Aug. 15, 1842
Stiff, Capt. Jesse	Fannin County "Guards" (Minutemen); April 22—May 19, 1842

1843 Texas Ranger Company

Commander:	Service Dates/Notes:
Hays, Capt. John Coffee	Spy Company, Bexar County; March 1—Nov. 12, 1843

1844 Texas Ranger Companies

Commander:	Service Dates/Notes:
Davis, Capt. Henry Clay	Corpus Christi Rangers; Nov. 14, 1844—Feb. 28, 1845
Hays, Capt. John Coffee	Ranger Company, Bexar County; Feb. 25—Dec. 31, 1844
Mabbitt, Capt. Leonard H.	Mounted Company of Volunteers, Shelby County; Aug. 26—Nov. 13, 1844

1845 Texas Ranger Companies

Commander:	Service Dates/Notes:
Bell, Capt. Peter Hansborough	Corpus Christi Ranging Company; Feb. 28, 1845—July 6, 1846; Part of Major Jack Hays' Texas Mounted Volunteers
Cady, Lt. David C.	Travis County Ranging Company ("Travis Guards"); June 30—Dec. 31, 1845; Cady replaced Lt. Coleman and later became captain of his company
Coleman, Lt. Alexander	Travis County Ranging Company ("Travis Guards"); Feb. 20—June 30, 1845
Gillespie, Capt. Robert Addison	San Antonio Mounted Rangers; Sept. 28, 1845—March 28, 1846; Major Jack Hays' Regiment
Hays, Capt. John Coffee	Ranger Company, Bexar County; Jan. 1—Sept. 28, 1845
McGarrah, Lt. John	Ranger Company, Fannin County; June 1—Sept. 30, 1845; operated from Fort Buckner in present Collin County
Price, Lt. John T.	Ranger Company, Goliad and Refugio counties; March 14—Sept. 24, 1845; Captain of Texas Mounted Volunteers, Victoria and Goliad counties, Major Jack Hays' Regiment; Sept. 25, 1845—June 25, 1846
Smith, Lt. Thomas Ingles	Ranger Company, Robertson County; Feb. 16—April 16, 1845
Teal, Lt. Richard S.	Ranger Company, Milam County; Sept. 5—Dec. 5, 1845

Chapter Notes
Volume IV

Abbreviations to the Republic Claims Papers, 1835–1846.
Texas State Library and Archives Commission, Austin.

AC Audited Claims are those military-related claims submitted to the Comptroller or Treasurer of the Republic of Texas that were audited, approved and paid by the Republic government.

PD Public Debt Claims are claims for services provided between 1835 and 1846 that could not be paid until after Texas' annexation in 1846. These were largely paid between 1848 and the early 1860s, mainly from the 1850 Boundary Compromise money Texas was paid for its lost territory.

PP Republic Pension Papers were generally filed from the 1870s to the early 1900s by veterans who served in the Texas Revolution and other Republic-era military units.

UC Unpaid Claims are those documents which do not fit in one of the above categories or those whose final payment disposition is unknown.

Chapter 1
The Vasquez Incursion

1. James Kimmins Greer, *Texas Ranger: Jack Hays in the Frontier Southwest* (College Station: Texas A&M University Press, 1993), 60–61. Originally published by E.P. Dutton and Company, Inc. as *Colonel Jack Hays: Texas Frontier Leader and California Builder* in 1952.

2. Gerald Swetnam Pierce, "The Army of the Republic of Texas, 1836-1845" (University of Mississippi, copyright 1964, on file in the Texas Room of the Houston Public Library), 233.

3. Ibid., 233–34.

4. Ibid., 234–35.

5. Ibid., 232–35.

6. (Karl) Hans Peter Marius Nielsen Gammell, *The Laws of Texas, 1822–1897,* vol. 2 (Austin, Tex: The Gammel Book Company, 1898), 770–71; Pierce, "The Army of the Republic of Texas," 235–36.

7. Gammell, *The Laws of Texas, 1822–1897*, vol. 2: 746.

8. Pierce, "The Army of the Republic of Texas," 237; *Telegraph and Texas Register*, March 9, 1842.

9. Pierce, "The Army of the Republic of Texas," 237–38.

10. Ibid., 238.

11. Jesús F. de la Teja, ed., *A Revolution Remembered: The Memoirs and Selected Correspondence of Juan N. Seguín* (Austin: State House Press, 1991), 43. Joseph Milton Nance, *Attack and Counter-Attack: The Texas-Mexican Frontier, 1842 (*Austin: University of Texas Press, 1964), 11.

12. Nance, *Attack and Counter-Attack*, 11–12.

13. Ibid., 14; John Henry Brown, *History of Texas, From 1685 to 1892* (St. Louis: Becktold & Co.), Vol. II: 211–12.

14. Nance, *Attack and Counter-Attack,* 15.

15. Pierce, "The Army of the Republic of Texas," 239.

16. Nance, *Attack and Counter-Attack,* 15–16.

17. Ibid., 16–17.

18. Greer, *Texas Ranger,* 63.

19. John R. King PD, R 166, F 400; Benjamin McCulloch PD, R 171, F 464–68.

20. Brown, *History of Texas,* II: 212.

21. Ibid., 212; Handbook of Texas Online, s.v. "Ogden, Duncan Campbell," http://www.tshaonline.org/handbook/online/articles/OO/fog1.html (accessed September 22, 2008).

22. Pierce, "The Army of the Republic of Texas," 239; *Telegraph and Texas Register*, March 4, 1842.

23. Pierce, "The Army of the Republic of Texas," 240–41.

24. Brown, *History of Texas,* II: 212–13.

25. Nance, *Attack and Counter-Attack,* 26–27.

26. Brown, *History of Texas,* II: 213.

27. Nance, *Attack and Counter-Attack,* 26–27; Brown, *History of Texas,* II: 213.

28. Nance, *Attack and Counter-Attack,* 28–29; Brown, *History of Texas,* II: 213.

29. Brown, *History of Texas,* II: 213–14.

30. John Holland Jenkins, *Recollections of Early Texas: The Memoirs of John Holland Jenkins,* ed. by John Holmes Jenkins III (1958; repr., Austin: University of Texas Press, 1995), 220. John Twohig PE, R 242, F 648.

31. Brown, *History of Texas,* II: 213; Nance, *Attack and Counter-Attack,* 30.

32. Ibid., 214.

33. Greer, *Texas Ranger,* 64; Frederick Wilkins, *The Legend Begins: The Texas Rangers, 1823–1845* (Austin, Tex: State House Press, 1996), 119.

34. Pierce, "The Army of the Republic of Texas," 242.

35. Z. N. Morrell, *Flowers and Fruits in the Wilderness* (St. Louis: Commercial Printing Company, 1872), 83.

36. Ibid., 78–80.

37. Ibid., 83.

38. Ibid., 83–84.

39. Pierce, "The Army of the Republic of Texas," 243.

40. Ibid., 244–45.

41. Ibid., 247–48.

42. John H. Jenkins and Kenneth Kesselus, *Edward Burleson: Texas Frontier Leader* (Austin, Tex: Jenkins Publishing Co., 1990), 302.

43. Jenkins, *Recollections of Early Texas,* 95; Everett Blakey PD, R 137, F. 719–24.

44. Jenkins, *Recollections of Early Texas,* 96.

45. Nance, *Attack and Counter-Attack,* 52; Wilkins, *The Legend Begins,* 119–20.

46. Greer, *Texas Ranger,* 64; Brown, *History of Texas,* II: 215.

47. de la Teja, *A Revolution Remembered,* 44–45; Nance, *Attack and Counter-Attack,* 52–54.

48. Malcolm D. McLean, *Papers Concerning Robertson's Colony in Texas,* vol. 18 (Arlington: University of Texas Press at Arlington, 1991), 377–78.

49. Ibid., 378.

50. Nance, *Attack and Counter-Attack,* 111–12.

Chapter 2
Spring and Summer Ranger Actions

1. Brown, *History of Texas,* II: 215–16.

2. Samuel Bogart PD, R 138, F 206–207; Nance, *Attack and Counter-Attack,* 114–16.

3. Nance, *Attack and Counter-Attack,* 222–23.

4. Ibid., 114–15; Jesse Stiff PD, R 188, F 548–73.

5. Ephraim McLean PD, R 172, F 539.

6. Wilkins, *The Legend Begins,* 121.

7. Wilkins, *The Legend Begins,* 122; John R. King PD, R 166, F 400; Benjamin McCulloch PD, R 171, F 464–68.

8. Gary Clayton Anderson, *The Conquest of Texas: Ethnic Cleansing in the Promised Land, 1820–1875* (Norman: University of Oklahoma Press, 2005), 199.

9. Ibid., 199.

10. Ibid., 199–200.

11. Ibid., 200–201.

12. James L. Haley, *Sam Houston* (Norman: University of Oklahoma Press, 2002), 256–58.

13. Eli Chandler PD, R 199, F 253.

14. Haley, *Sam Houston,* 258.

15. Anderson, *The Conquest of Texas,* 200–201.

16. James T. DeShields, *Border Wars of Texas (*1912, repr., Austin: State House Press, 1993), 360.

17. Gregory Michno and Susan Michno, *A Fate Worse Than Death: Indian Captives in the West, 1830–1885 (*Caldwell, ID: Caxton Press, 2007), 76; DeShields, *Border Wars of Texas,* 363.

18. Ibid., 76; DeShields, *Border Wars of Texas,* 360.

19. DeShields, *Border Wars of Texas,* 360.

20. Michno, *A Fate Worse Than Death,* 76; DeShields, *Border Wars of Texas,* 360.

21. DeShields, *Border Wars of Texas,* 360–61.

22. Michno, *A Fate Worse Than Death,* 77.

23. DeShields, *Border Wars of Texas,* 361; Michno, *A Fate Worse Than Death,* 77.

24. Michno, *A Fate Worse Than Death,* 78.

25. Stephen L. Moore, *Savage Frontier: Rangers, Riflemen and Indian Wars in Texas,* vol. III (Denton: University of North Texas Press, 2006), 274–78, 321–26.

26. Handbook of Texas Online, s.v. "Gustav Elley" http://www.tshaonline.org/handbook/online/articles/EE/fel18.html (accessed May 12, 2008).

27. Catherine W. McDowell, ed., *Now You Hear My Horn: The Journal of James Wilson Nichols, 1820-1887* (Austin: University of Texas Press, 1961), 76. It should be noted that Nichols' editor gives the year as "1843" although 1842 would be two years after the great Comanche raid of 1840.

28. Ibid., 76.

29. Ibid., 76.

30. Ibid., 77.

31. McDowell, *Now You Hear My Horn,* 76; Handbook of Texas Online, s.v. "Pinta Trail" http://www.tshaonline.org/handbook/online/articles/PP/ayp2.html (accessed June 10, 2008).

32. A. J. Sowell, *Texas Indian Fighters. Early Settlers and Indian Fighters of Southwest Texas* (1900, repr., Austin, Tex: State House Press, 1986), 20–23.

33. Sowell, *Early Settlers and Indian Fighters of Southwest Texas,* 22–23, 317–19, 809–10; Creed Taylor PE, R 241, F 174–76.

34. Creed Taylor, "Jack Hays Fight on the Guadalupe." Captain Creed Taylor Manuscript, James DeShields collection, Center for American History, The University of Texas at Austin.

35. Sowell, *Early Settlers and Indian Fighters of Southwest Texas,* 20–23, 317–19, 809–10. Peter Fohr was wounded at Walker's Creek in 1844. It is doubtful that he was involved in this Guadalupe fight. All known accounts of a battle at Bandera Pass stem from the early writings of Texas historian A. J. Sowell, who got his versions of this fight from

Galbreath, Highsmith, and Taylor. Highsmith and Taylor claim that this fight occurred in the spring or June of 1841. In Sowell's book, Taylor mentions that Andrew Erskine used a five-shooter Colt in the battle, a statement which points toward a weapon that was more likely used in 1844 versus in 1841, when few were available to any rangers. Hays biographer John Caperton does state that Sam Walker first served under Hays in 1842 "and distinguished himself greatly in their movements against the Indians and Mexicans along the frontier." Caperton, "Sketch of Colonel John C. Hays," 52–53.

36. Taylor, "Jacks Hays Fight on the Guadalupe."

37. McDowell, *Now You Hear My Horn,* 77.

38. Sowell, *Early Settlers and Indian Fighters of Southwest Texas,* 22.

39. Taylor, "Jacks Hays Fight on the Guadalupe."

40. McDowell, *Now You Hear My Horn,* 77–78.

41. Taylor, "Jacks Hays Fight on the Guadalupe."

42. Sowell, *Early Settlers and Indian Fighters of Southwest Texas,* 23, 317–19.

43. McDowell, *Now You Hear My Horn,* 78.

44. McDowell, *Now You Hear My Horn,* 78; Sowell, *Rangers and Pioneers*, 58.

45. Taylor, "Jacks Hays Fight on the Guadalupe."

46. Betty Dooley Awbrey and Claude Dooley, *Why Stop? A Guide to Texas Historical Roadside Markers* (Houston, Tex: Lone Star Books, Fourth Edition, 1999), 28–29.

47. Green, *Memoirs of Mary A. Maverick,* 63–64.

48. Wilkins, *The Legend Begins,* 122.

49. Greer, *Texas Ranger,* 67–68.

50. Ibid., 68–69.

51. McDowell, *Now You Hear My Horn,* 79–82.

52. Ibid., 123.

53. Nance, *Attack and Counter-Attack,* 116.

54. Ibid., 188.

55. John J. B. Hoxey PD, R 163, 158–64; William H. Hughes PD, R 163, F 351–54.

56. Nance, *Attack and Counter-Attack,* 206.

57. Ibid., 206–207.

58. Nance, *Attack and Counter-Attack,* 245–46; Wilkins, *The Legend Begins,* 122.

59. Nance, *Attack and Counter-Attack,* 246–47.

60. Author's research of audited military claims and pension papers of Texas, Texas State Archives. See also Brown, *History of Texas,* II: 217.

61. Nance, *Attack and Counter-Attack,* 247–49.

62. Ibid., 249–51.

63. Ibid., 253.

64. Nance, *Attack and Counter-Attack,* 275–77.

65. Ibid., 286–87.

66. Brown, *History of Texas,* II: 216.

67. Nance, *Attack and Counter-Attack,* 287.

68. Ibid., 280.

69. Ibid., 280, 592–98.

70. Ibid., 227–28.

71. Raúl A. Ramos, *Beyond the Alamo: Forging Mexican Ethnicity in San Antonio, 1821–1861* (Charlotte: University of North Carolina Press, 2008), 187–88.

72. Ibid., 188.

73. Ibid., 188; Cayetano Rivas PE, R 235, F 512–515.

74. Jenkins, *Edward Burleson: Texas Frontier Leader,* 313.

75. Bartlett Sims PD, R 186, F 113–18; Reuben Hornsby PD, R 160, F 430–32; George J. Durham PD, R 150, F 434–436.

76. Author's search of public debt and pension papers of the Republic of Texas, Texas State Archives.

77. Jenkins, *Edward Burleson: Texas Frontier Leader,* 314.

78. Ibid., 314.

79. Nance, *Attack and Counter-Attack,* 280, 291.

80. Wilkins, *The Legend Begins,* 124.

81. Antonio Menchaca AC, R 69, F 662–64.

82. Wilkins, *The Legend Begins,* 123.

83. Nance, *Attack and Counter-Attack,* 280–81.

84. Ibid., 295.

85. Wilkins, *The Legend Begins,* 123–24.

86. Nance, *Attack and Counter-Attack,* 281.

87. Brian DeLay, *War of a Thousand Deserts: Indian Raids and the U.S.–Mexican War* (New Haven: Yale University Press, 2008), 45.

88. Ibid., 20. See also Pekka Hämäläinen, *The Comanche Empire* (New Haven: Yale University Press, 2008), 196, 210.

89. DeLay, *War of a Thousand Deserts,* 48, 79–83.

90. Ibid., 98; Hämäläinen, *The Comanche Empire*, 216.

91. DeLay, *War of a Thousand Deserts*, 77, 99.

92. Ibid., 98.

93. Hämäläinen, *The Comanche Empire*, 179, 303.

94. DeLay, *War of a Thousand Deserts*, 216–217.

Chapter 3
Woll Seizes Béxar

1. Nance, *Attack and Counter-Attack,* 297–99.

2. Wilkins, *The Legend Begins,* 126–27.

3. Nance, *Attack and Counter-Attack,* 300–301.

4. Ibid., 301–302. Nance asserts that Rubio was one of the two spies who were captured and that he was executed. Newspaper accounts from 1843, however, give the capture and execution of Rubio himself as June 1843. See details in chapter 6.

5. Ibid., 302.

6. Ibid., 302–303.

7. Ibid., 303–304.

8. Sowell, *Early Settlers and Indian Fighters of Southwest Texas,* 58–59.

9. Nance, *Attack and Counter-Attack,* 304–305.

10. Ibid., 306–307.

11. José María Rodríquez, "Memoirs of Early Texas." Published in 1913. Accessed http://www.tamu.edu/ccbn/dewitt/rodmemoirs.htm on June 4, 2009.

12. Ibid., 306–307.

13. Wilkins, *The Legend Begins,* 128–29.

14. Ibid., 129; Nance, *Attack and Counter-Attack,* 318; Brazos [pseud.], *The Life of Robert Hall* (Austin: Ben C. Jones and Company, Printers, 1898), 70.

15. John C Caperton, "Sketch of Colonel John C. Hays, The Texas Rangers, Incidents in Texas and Mexico, Etc. from materials furnished by Col. Hays and Major John Caperton." Typescript version. Original prepared in 1879. A typescript copy of this 77-page manuscript was obtained from the University of California in 1922 and is part of the James T. DeShields Papers, Center for American History, University of Texas at Austin. See 24.

16. Jesus Hernandez PE, R 220, F 269.

17. Wilkins, *The Legend Begins,* 129.

18. Ibid., 130.

19. Ibid., 131; Nance, *Attack and Counter-Attack,* 337.

20. Morrell, *Flowers and Fruits in the Wilderness,* 84.

20. Ibid., 84–86.

21. Wilkins, *The Legend Begins,* 131.

Chapter 4

Salado Creek Battle: "Give Them Hell!"

1. Brazos, *Life of Robert Hall,* 71.

2. Morrell, *Flowers and Fruits in the Wilderness,* 86.

3. Ibid., 86; Wilkins, *The Legend Begins,* 131.

4. Morrell, *Flowers and Fruits in the Wilderness,* 86–87.

5. Ibid., 87.

6. Ibid., 87–88.

7. Nance, *Attack and Counter-Attack,* 336–337.

8. Wilkins, *The Legend Begins,* 125–26.

9. Ibid., 88.

10. Ibid., 88.

11. Nance, *Attack and Counter-Attack,* 347–48; Brown, *History of Texas,* II: 223.

12. *Early Days in Texas,* unpublished memoirs of Nathan Boone Burkett dictated to his son-in-law John T. Hogwood in early 1895. Center for American History; Wilkins, *The Legend Begins,* 132.

13. McDowell, *Now You Hear My Horn,* 96.

14. Nance, *Attack and Counter-Attack,* 348; Nichols, *Now You Hear My Horn,* 95.

15. Burkett, *Early Days in Texas.*

16. Morrell, *Flowers and Fruits in the Wilderness,* 88.

17. McDowell, *Now You Hear My Horn,* 95–96.

18. Morrell, *Flowers and Fruits in the Wilderness,* 88–89; Nance, *Attack and Counter-Attack,* 350–51.

19. Nance, *Attack and Counter-Attack,* 355.

20. Morrell, *Flowers and Fruits in the Wilderness,* 89.

21. Wilkins, *The Legend Begins,* 133.

22. Nance, *Attack and Counter-Attack,* 355; Brown, *History of Texas,* II: 224.

23. Sowell, *Rangers and Pioneers of Texas,* 810.

24. Morrell, *Flowers and Fruits in the Wilderness,* 89.

25. Wilkins, *The Legend Begins,* 134.

26. Morrell, *Flowers and Fruits in the Wilderness,* 89.

27. McDowell, *Now You Hear My Horn,* 96; Wilkins, *The Legend Begins,* 134–35.

28. de la Teja, *A Revolution Remembered,* 95–97.

29. Brazos, *Life of Robert Hall,* 71; Burkett, *Early Days in Texas.*

30. James Ramsay to Miles S. Bennett, September 20, 1882. Bennett Papers, Center for American History.

31. McDowell, *Now You Hear My Horn,* 97.

32. Miles S. Bennett account from April 21, 1900, Center for American History.

33. Ramsay to Bennett letter.

34. Morrell, *Flowers and Fruits in the Wilderness,* 89.

35. Ramsay to Bennett letter.

36. Ibid.

37. Morrell, *Flowers and Fruits in the Wilderness,* 89–90.

38. Wilkins, *The Legend Begins,* 135; McDowell, *Now You Hear My Horn,* 98–99.

39. Wilkins, *The Legend Begins,* 136; Morrell, *Flowers and Fruits in*

the Wilderness, 90.

40. Woll report of the Salado battle, September 20, 1842; accessed http://www.tamu.edu/ccbn/dewitt/woll.htm on July 12, 2008.

41. Miles Bennett account.

42. McDowell, *Now You Hear My Horn,* 102.

43. Sowell, *Early Settlers and Indian Fighters of Southwest Texas,* 59.

44. Sowell, *Early Settlers and Indian Fighters of Southwest Texas,* 59–60; Nance, *Attack and Counter-Attack,* 361.

45. Sowell, *Rangers and Pioneers of Texas;* Wilkins, *The Legend Begins,* 136.

46. Brazos, *Life of Robert Hall,* 70.

47. Ibid., 72.

48. Ibid., 72.

49. Ibid., 72.

50. Wilkins, *The Legend Begins,* 137; Nichols, *Now You Hear My Horn,* 103.

51. Brown, *Indian Wars and Pioneers of Texas,* 56–57, 66–67; Nance, *Attack and Counter-Attack,* 361.

52. Brown, *Indian Wars and Pioneers of Texas,* 56–57, 66–67; *Telegraph and Texas Register,* October 12, 1842.

53. Wilkins, *The Legend Begins,* 136.

54. Brazos, *Life of Robert Hall,* 71.

55. Sowell, *Rangers and Pioneers of Texas,* 181.

56. Wilkins, *The Legend Begins,* 137.

57. Wilkins, *The Legend Begins,* 137; Woll report of the Salado battle, September 20, 1842; accessed http://www.tamu.edu/ccbn/dewitt/woll.htm on July 12, 2008.

58. McDowell, *Now You Hear My Horn,* 106.

59. Account of Mrs. William Jett (Ruth Clarinda Kuykendall Jett); accessed http://jack0204.tripod.com/gen/Heskew/jett.html on May 12, 2008.

60. Miles Bennett account; McDowell, *Now You Hear My Horn,* 107.

61. "The Dawson Company Massacre." Accessed http://www.tamu.edu/ccbn/dewitt/dewitt.htm on June 23, 2008.

62. Ibid.

63. Ibid.

64. Accessed http://www.tamu.edu/ccbn/dewitt/woodsfam.htm on June 25, 2008.

65. Robert M. Utley, *Lone Star Justice: The First Century of the Texas Rangers (*New York: Oxford University Press, 2002), 47.

66. Woll report of the Salado battle, September 20, 1842; accessed http://www.tamu.edu/ccbn/dewitt/woll.htm on July 12, 2008.

67. Jenkins, *Recollections of Early Texas,* 98–99; Accessed http://www.

tamu.edu/ccbn/dewitt/woodsfam.htm on June 25, 2008.

68. Alsey Miller PD, R 173, F506–14.

69. Green, *Memoirs of Mary A. Maverick,* 68.

70. Norman B. Woods to family, July 5, 1843. Accessed http://www.tamu.edu/ccbn/dewitt/woodsfamlets.htm on June 23, 2008.

71. Ibid.

72. Wilkins, *The Legend Begins,* 137.

73. Brazos, *Life of Robert Hall,* 72.

74. Wilkins, *The Legend Begins,* 138.

75. Rufus Perry letter, Valentine Bennett Scrapbook, The Center for American History, University of Texas, Austin.

Chapter 5
Hondo Creek Skirmish

1. Morrell, *Flowers and Fruits in the Wilderness,* 91; Brown, *History of Texas,* II: 227–28.

2. Ibid.

3. Morrell, *Flowers and Fruits in the Wilderness,* 91.

4. Miles Bennett account; Morrell, *Flowers and Fruits in the Wilderness,* 91.

5. McDowell, *Now You Hear My Horn,* 107–108.

6. Ibid., 108.

7. Wilkins, *The Legend Begins,* 138.

8. Brown, *History of Texas,* II: 228.

9. Ibid.

10. Caperton, "Sketch of Colonel John C. Hays," 26.

11. Ibid., 26.

12. Nance, *Attack and Counter-Attack,* 388.

13. Brown, *History of Texas,* II: 228; Wilkins, *The Legend Begins,* 139.

14. Wilkins, *The Legend Begins,* 139.

15. Morrell, *Flowers and Fruits in the Wilderness,* 92.

16. Brown, *History of Texas,* II: 228; Nance, *Attack and Counter-Attack,* 389.

17. Nance, *Attack and Counter-Attack,* 389.

18. Morrell, *Flowers and Fruits in the Wilderness,* 92.

19. Ibid., 92.

20. Nance, *Attack and Counter-Attack,* 389–90.

21. Ibid., 390–91.

22. Nance, *Attack and Counter-Attack,* 392–93; Morrell, *Flowers and Fruits in the Wilderness,* 93.

23. Morrell, *Flowers and Fruits in the Wilderness,* 92.

24. Nance, *Attack and Counter-Attack,* 393; Morrell, *Flowers and*

Fruits in the Wilderness, 93.

25. Burkett, *Early Days in Texas;* Wilkins, *The Legend Begins,* 140; Anderson J. Harrell PD, R 159, F 402–405.

26. Morrell, *Flowers and Fruits in the Wilderness,* 94.

27. McDowell, *Now You Hear My Horn,* 110; Nance, *Attack and Counter-Attack,* 394; Brown, *History of Texas,* II: 229.

28. Nance, *Attack and Counter-Attack,* 394–95.

29. Report from Gen. Adrian Woll by Gen. Isidro Reyes of the Texan encounter on the Medina River and Arroyo Hondo to the Secretary of War and Navy, September 28, 1842. Accessed http://www.tamu.edu/ccbn/dewitt/woll.htm on July 12, 2008.

30. McDowell, *Now You Hear My Horn,* 111.

31. Wilkins, *The Legend Begins,* 141.

32. Morrell, *Flowers and Fruits in the Wilderness,* 94.

33. Ibid., 94.

34. Morrell, *Flowers and Fruits in the Wilderness,* 95; Wilkins, *The Legend Begins,* 141.

35. McDowell, *Now You Hear My Horn,* 109.

36. Brown, *History of Texas,* II: 230.

37. Morrell, *Flowers and Fruits in the Wilderness,* 95.

38. Brazos, *Life of Robert Hall,* 72–73.

39. Ramos, *Beyond the Alamo*, 190.

40. Wilkins, *The Legend Begins,* 142.

Chapter 6
The Somervell and Mier Expeditions

1. Wilkins, *The Legend Begins,* 145–46.

2. Ibid., 146; Brown, *History of Texas,* II: 233.

3. Wilkins, *The Legend Begins,* 147.

4. Ibid., 147–48.

5. "Harvey Alexander Adams Diary, 1842—43," 26–27. Center For American History, The University of Texas at Austin, courtesy of Edwin G. Pierson Jr.

6. Harvey Alexander Adams diary, 31–33.

7. Nance, *Attack and Counter-Attack,* 443–46.

8. Ibid., 446.

9. Ibid., 446–47.

10. Greer, *Texas Ranger,* 81.

11. Anderson, *The Conquest of Texas*, 197–98.

12. Nance, *Attack and Counter-Attack,* 447.

13. Harvey Alexander Adams diary, 34; Wilkins, *The Legend Begins,* 149.

14. Wilkins, *The Legend Begins,* 149; Greer, *Texas Ranger,* 82.

15. Harvey Alexander Adams diary, 36.

16. Wilkins, *The Legend Begins,* 150.

17. Perry letter, Center for American History.

18. Wilkins, *The Legend Begins,* 150.

19. Ibid., 151.

20. Nance, *Attack and Counter-Attack*, 481–83.

21. Ibid., 484.

22. Ibid., 484–90.

23. Sam W. Haynes, *Soldiers of Misfortune: The Somervell and Mier Expeditions* (Austin: University of Texas Press, 1990), 50.

24. Wilkins, *The Legend Begins,* 152; Cornelius C. Smith Jr., *William Sanders Oury: History-Maker of the Southwest* (Tuscon: University of Arizona Press, 1967), 50.

25. Harvey Alexander Adams diary, 47–48.

26. Brown, *History of Texas,* II: 236.

27. Ibid., 236–27.

28. Wilkins, *The Legend Begins,* 152.

29. Ibid., 152; Brown, *History of Texas,* II: 237.

30. Handbook of Texas Online, s.v. "Laredo, Texas," http://www.tshaonline.org/handbook/online/articles/LL/hdl2.html (accessed May 17, 2009).

31. Perry letter.

32. Haynes, *Soldiers of Misfortune*, 52; Nance, *Attack and Counter-Attack*, 503–508.

33. Haynes, *Soldiers of Misfortune*, 53; Nance, *Attack and Counter-Attack*, 509–10.

34. Haynes, *Soldiers of Misfortune*, 53; Nance, *Attack and Counter-Attack*, 510–14.

35. Haynes, *Soldiers of Misfortune*, 54; Nance, *Attack and Counter-Attack*, 514–15; Anderson, *The Conquest of Texas*, 198.

36. Haynes, *Soldiers of Misfortune*, 54.

37. Haynes, *Soldiers of Misfortune*, 54–55; Anderson, *The Conquest of Texas*, 198.

38. Nance, *Attack and Counter-Attack*, 522–26.

39. Wilkins, *The Legend Begins,* 153; Haynes, *Soldiers of Misfortune,* 57.

40. Wilkins, *The Legend Begins,* 153–54; Haynes, *Soldiers of Misfortune,* 58–59.

41. Nance, *Attack and Counter-Attack,* 553; Wilkins, *The Legend Begins,* 154.

42. Nance, *Attack and Counter-Attack,* 553–57; Brown, *History of Texas,* II: 239.

43. Brown, *History of Texas,* II: 240.

44. Joseph Milton Nance and Archie McDonald, *Dare-Devils All: The Texan Mier Expedition, 1842–1844* (Austin: Eakin Press, 1998), 466–80; Haynes, *Soldiers of Misfortune,* 61–62.

45. Greer, *Texas Ranger,* 88.

46. Haynes, *Soldiers of Misfortune,* 64.

47. Greer, *Texas Ranger,* 88.

48. Ibid., 89.

49. Nance, *Attack and Counter-Attack,* 566.

50. Rufus Perry letter, Center for American History.

51. Wilkins, *The Legend Begins,* 157.

52. Ibid., 159.

53. Ibid., 159.

54. DeShields, *Border Wars of Texas,* 351–52.

55. Haynes, *Soldiers of Misfortune,* 75.

56. Haynes, *Soldiers of Misfortune,* 106–15, 229.

57. Letter of John G. W. Pierson, John R. Baker, William M. Ryon, F. M. Gibson and W. F. McMath, 27 April 1843, Prison Santiago. Courtesy of Edwin G. Pierson Jr.

58. Haynes, *Soldiers of Misfortune,* 119–24.

59. Ibid., 125.

60. Ibid., 125.

61. Ibid., 128–29.

62. Ibid., 136–47.

63. John Twohig PE, R 242, F 648; Haynes, *Soldiers of Misfortune,* 163–65.

64. Haynes, *Soldiers of Misfortune,* 170–84.

65. Ibid., 210.

66. Wilkins, *The Legend Begins*, 159.

67. Wilkins, *The Legend Begins*, 160; Jenkins, *Edward Burleson*, 327.

68. Wilkins, *The Legend Begins*, 160; Jenkins, *Edward Burleson*, 327; Haley, *Sam Houston*, 261.

69. Report of House Select Committee, January 16, 1843. *Journals of the House of Representatives of the Seventh Congress of the Republic of Texas*, 256–68.

70. Wilkins, *The Legend Begins*, 160.

71. Ibid., 160.

Chapter 7
"Active, Vigilant and Efficient"

1. Wilkins, *The Legend Begins,* 163.

2. Gammel, *The Laws of Texas,* II: 846–48.

3. Ibid., 865; Wilkins, *The Legend Begins,* 163.

4. Wilkins, *The Legend Begins,* 163–64.

5. Valentine Bennett PD, R 137, F 76.

6. John Wesley Wilbarger, *Indian Depredations in Texas (*1889, repr., Austin, Tex: State House Press, 1985), 142–43; Coleman letter from 1840s describing "The Last Indian Depredation upon the Southwestern Frontier Near Austin," contained in Gulick, *Lamar Papers*, No. 2434, IV: 236.

7. Wilbarger, *Indian Depredations*, 143; Coleman letter, 236.

8. Coleman letter, 236–37.

9. Ibid., 237; Wilbarger, *Indian Depredations*, 143.

10. Coleman letter, 237.

11. Ibid.

12. Ibid.

13. Wilbarger, *Indian Depredations*, 143–44.

14. Ibid., 144.

15. Coleman letter, 237.

16. J. Marvin Hunter, "A Tragedy of the Frontier," *Frontier Times* 10, no. 2 (Nov. 1932); Wilbarger, *Indian Depredations,* 279; Smithwick, *The Evolution of a State,* 134.

17. Wilbarger, *Indian Depredations*, 279–80.

18. Ibid., 280.

19. Ibid., 281.

20. Ibid., 281–82.

21. Handbook of Texas Online, "Snively Expedition," http://www.tshaonline.org/handbook/online/articles/SS/qys2.html (accessed July 6, 2008).

22. Wilkins, *The Legend Begins,* 165–66.

23. Ibid., 165–66.

24. Handbook of Texas Online, s.v. "Snively Expedition," http://www.tshaonline.org/handbook/online/articles/SS/qys2.html (accessed September 29, 2008); Wilkins, *The Legend Begins,* 165–66.

25. Wilkins, *The Legend Begins,* 165–66.

26. Anderson, *The Conquest of Texas,* 201.

27. Ibid., 201.

28. Ibid., 201–202; Hämäläinen, *The Comanche Empire*, 216.

29. Anderson, *The Conquest of Texas,* 202; Minutes of Indian Council at Tehuacana Creek, March 1843 from Texas State Library electronic files. Accessed http://www.tsl.state.tx.us/exhibits/indian/war/tehuacana-1843-1.html on March 5, 2008.

30. Haley, *Sam Houston,* 268–69.

31. Anderson, *The Conquest of Texas,* 202.

32. Ibid., 202–203.

33. Ibid., 203.

34. Ibid., 203–205.

35. John Salmon Ford, edited by Stephen B. Oates, *Rip Ford's Texas* (Austin: University of Texas Press, 1994), 440; Rufus Perry letter, Center for American History.

36. Greer, *Texas Ranger,* 90; Wilkins, *The Legend Begins,* 168.
37. Rufus Perry letter, Center for American History.
38. Ford, *Rip Ford's Texas*, 440.
39. Rufus Perry letter, Center for American History.
40. Wilkins, *The Legend Begins,* 169.
41. Nance, *Dare-Devils All,* 82.
42. Wilbarger, *Indian Depredations in Texas*, 42-49.
43. Wilkins, *The Legend Begins,* 170.
44. Caperton, "Sketch of Colonel John C. Hays," 34, 42.
45. Ibid., 34–35.
46. Mike Cox, *The Texas Rangers: Wearing the Cinco Peso, 1821–1900* (New York: Forge, 2008), 89.
47. Ibid., 89.
48. Greer, *Texas Ranger,* 91; John Coffee Hays AU, R 43, F 50.
49. Wilkins, *The Legend Begins,* 170.
50. Greer, *Texas Ranger,* 91–92.
51. Wilkins, *The Legend Begins,* 171.
52. Ibid., 171.
53. Nance, *Dare-Devils All,* 180.
54. Wilkins, *The Legend Begins,* 171–72.
55. John C. Hays to Hon. G. W. Hill, November 12, 1843; Texas State Archives.
56. Wilkins, *The Legend Begins,* 173.
57. Ibid., 173–74.
58. Greer, *Texas Ranger,* 93.

CHAPTER 8
THE DEADLY COLTS ON WALKER'S CREEK

1. Anderson, *The Conquest of Texas,* 207.
2. Ibid., 207.
3. Ibid., 208.
4. Ibid., 209.
5. Ibid., 209.
6. Gammel, *The Laws of Texas*, II: 915.
7. Wilkins, *The Legend Begins,* 174; Greer, *Texas Ranger,* 94.
8. Greer, *Texas Ranger,* 94.
9. Gammel, *The Laws of Texas*, II: 943–44.
10. Greer, *Texas Ranger,* 104–105.
11. Wilkins, *The Legend Begins,* 177.
12. John Twohig PE, R 242, F 649.
13. Wilkins, *The Legend Begins,* 177.
14. Hays to Secretary of War and Marine G. W. Hill, "Report of the Battle of Walker's Creek," June 16, 1844; contained in *Journals of the*

House of Representatives of the Ninth Congress of the Republic of Texas, 32–33. Hereafter cited as Hays, "Report of the Battle of Walker's Creek."

15. Ibid.

16. Ibid; Handbook of Texas Online, s.v. "Walker's Creek, battle of," http://www.tshaonline.org/handbook/online/articles/WW/btw2.html (accessed March 2, 2008); Greer, *Texas Ranger,* 96; Caperton, "Sketch of Colonel John C. Hays," 20.

17. Hays, "Report of the Battle of Walker's Creek"; Wilkins, *The Legend Begins,* 178; Greer, *Texas Ranger,* 96.

18. Anderson, *The Conquest of Texas,* 206.

19. Wilkins, *The Legend Begins,* 178; Cox, *The Texas Rangers,* 90–91.

20. Hays, "Report of the Battle of Walker's Creek"; Greer, *Texas Ranger,* 106.

21. Wilkins, *The Legend Begins,* 178.

22. Ibid., 178–79.

23. Ibid., 179; "Biography of Cicero Rufus Perry, 1822–1898. Captain, Texas Rangers." Special collections of Daughters of the Republic of Texas Library, San Antonio, Tex.

24. Thomas W. Knowles, *They Rode for the Lone Star: The Saga of the Texas Rangers. The Birth of Texas–The Civil War* (Dallas, Tex: Taylor Publishing Company, 1999), 100.

25. Hays, "Report of the Battle of Walker's Creek"; Wilkins, *The Legend Begins,* 179.

26. Hays, "Report of the Battle of Walker's Creek."

27. Greer, *Texas Ranger,* 98.

28. Wilkins, *The Legend Begins,* 179–80; Sowell, *Texas Indian Fighters,* 809.

29. Hays, "Report of the Battle of Walker's Creek"; Wilkins, *The Legend Begins,* 180; Caperton, "Sketch of Colonel John C. Hays," 22; Knowles, *They Rode for the Lone Star,* 100.

30. Anderson, *The Conquest of Texas,* 206.

31. Hays, "Report of the Battle of Walker's Creek."

32. John C. Hays PD, R 160, F 421–28.

33. Green, *Memoirs of Mary A. Maverick,* 77.

34. Sowell, *Texas Indian Fighters,* 132.

35. Ibid., 21–23, 809.

36. Cox, *The Texas Rangers,* 92.

37. Knowles, *They Rode for the Lone Star,* 131–33.

38. Ibid., 133–34.

39. Wilbarger, *Indian Depredations,* 284.

40. Ibid., 283–84; Jenkins, *Recollections of Early Texas,* 254.

41. Wilbarger, *Indian Depredations,* 285.

42. Ibid., 601.
43. Ibid., 601.
44. Ibid., 601–602.
45. Ibid., 602.

CHAPTER 9
"I LAID DOWN TO DIE"

1. Gammel, *The Laws of Texas*, II: 1049–50; Wilkins, *The Legend Begins,* 190–92.
2. Wilkins, *The Legend Begins,* 185.
3. Ibid., 185.
4. Sowell, *Texas Indian Fighters,* 127.
5. Ibid., 127.
6. Ibid., 127–28.
7. Handbook of Texas Online, s.v. "Prince Carl of Solms-Braunfels," http://www.tshaonline.org/handbook/online/articles/SS/fso3.html (accessed July 18, 2008).
8. Sowell, *Texas Indian Fighters,* 128.
9. John C. Hays to Hon. G. W. Hill, July 21, 1844, Texas State Archives.
10. Sowell, *Texas Indian Fighters,* 131.
11. Cox, *The Texas Rangers,* 95.
12. Perry, Memoir of Capt'n. C. R. Perry, typescript of Perry's handwritten statements, DRT Library. The account which follows draws on Perry's statements.
13. Cox, *The Texas Rangers,* 95.
14. Wilkins, *The Legend Begins,* 188.
15. Sowell, *Texas Indian Fighters,* 131.
16. Wilkins, *The Legend Begins,* 188–89.
17. Sowell, *Texas Indian Fighters,* 133–35.
18. Wilkins, *The Legend Begins,* 189.
19. Greer, *Texas Ranger,* 99.
20. Duval's account is given in Wilbarger's *Indian Depredations in Texas,* 292–93. See also Cox, *The Texas Rangers,* 88.
21. Wilbarger, *Indian Depredations in Texas,* 293.
22. Ibid., 294–95.
23. Greer, *Texas Ranger,* 100.
24. Caperton, "Sketch of Colonel John C. Hays," 36.
25. Wilkins, *The Legend Begins,* 189.
26. Michno, *A Fate Worse Than Death,* 79.
27. Ibid., 80–81; DeShields, *Border Wars of Texas,* 365–66.
28. DeShields, *Border Wars of Texas,* 364.
29. Handbook of Texas Online, s.v. "Regulator-Moderator War"

http://www.tshaonline.org/handbook/online/articles/RR/jcr1.html(accessed October 3, 2008).

30. Ibid.

31. Ibid.

32. Ibid.

33. DRT, *Muster Rolls of the Texas Revolution,* 233–34.

34. Handbook of Texas, "Regulator-Moderator War."

35. Ibid.

36. Anderson, *The Conquest of Texas,* 209.

37. Hämäläinen, *The Comanche Empire*, 217.

38. Anderson, *The Conquest of Texas,* 209–10; Haley, *Sam Houston,* 285; Hämäläinen, *The Comanche Empire*, 217.

39. Anderson, *The Conquest of Texas,* 210; Haley, *Sam Houston,* 285.

40. Hämäläinen, *The Comanche Empire*, 218; Haley, *Sam Houston,* 285.

41. DeLay, *War of a Thousand Deserts*, 216.

42. Jenkins, *Edward Burleson,* 350–51.

43. Marshall DeBruhl, *Sword of San Jacinto: A Life of Sam Houston* (New York: Random House, 1993), 308.

44. Ibid., 308–309.

45. Ibid., 309–11.

CHAPTER 10
THE 1845 COUNTY RANGING COMPANIES

1. Greer, *Texas Ranger,* 112–13.

2. Moore, *Taming Texas,* 214–15.

3. John C. Hays Pay Roll, December 30, 1844–February 11, 1845, Texas State Archives.

4. Gammel, *The Laws of Texas, 1822–1897,* II: 1124–25.

5. Ibid., 1125–26.

6. Handbook of Texas Online, s.v. "Thomas Ingles Smith," http://www.tshaonline.org/handbook/online/articles/SS/fsm43.html (accessed August 25, 2008).

7. Thomas J. Smith AC, R 98, F 274-80.

8. Charles D. Spurlin, *Texas Volunteers in the Mexican War* (Austin: Eakin Press, 1998), 244-46.

9. Richard S. Teal AU, R 103, F 514–16.

10. John T. Price AU, R 84, F 601–602; John T. Price AU, R 129, F 644–51.

11. Greer, *Texas Ranger,* 113.

12. Wilkins, *The Legend Begins,* 195.

13. Greer, *Texas Ranger,* 113.

14. Wilkins, *The Legend Begins,* 195–96.

15. Bill Haynes, "Buckner." Accessed http://www.geocities.com/GenFriendsGHL/communities/commune/buckner.htm on August 24, 2008.

16. George McPherson PD, R 596, F 145–49; S. G. Newton & Co. PD, R 176, F 518–20; Peter M. Maxwell PD, R 171, F 69.

17. John McGarrah PD, R 172, F 34–38; Jesse Stiff PD, R 188, F 611.

18. Wilbarger, *Indian Depredations in Texas*, 260.

19. Ibid., 260.

20. Ibid., 260.

21. Greer, *Texas Ranger,* 113–14.

22. Cox, *The Texas Rangers,* 100–101.

23. Greer, *Texas Ranger,* 114.

24. DeLay, *War of a Thousand Deserts*, 98.

25. Greer, *Texas Ranger,* 114.

26. Ibid., 115.

Chapter 11
Rangers in Federal Service

1. Greer, *Texas Ranger,* 116; Cox, *The Texas Rangers,* 101.

2. Anson Jones to General Zachary Taylor of August 23, 1845; referenced http://www.tsl.state.tx.us/exhibits/presidents/jones/anson_jones_aug23_1845_1.html on August 24, 2008.

3. Anson Jones to Clark L. Owen, August 23, 1845; referenced http://www.tsl.state.tx.us/exhibits/annexation/part5/anson_jones_aug_23_1845_5.html on August 24, 2008.

4. Ibid.

5. Greer, *Texas Ranger,* 116; Cox, *The Texas Rangers,* 101.

6. Charles M. Robinson III, *The Men Who Wear the Star: The Story of the Texas Rangers* (New York: Random House, 2000), 73.

7. Ibid., 73—74.

8. Wilkins, *The Legend Begins,* 196.

9. Pierce, *Texas Under Arms,* 13–14.

10. Greer, *Texas Ranger,* 116–17.

11. Cox, *The Texas Rangers,* 102.

12. Ibid., 102.

13. Greer, *Texas Ranger,* 117–18.

14. Moore, *Taming Texas,* 225–26.

Afterword

1. Knowles, *They Rode For the Lone Star,* 116–17.

2. Mike Cox, "Battle of the Painted Rocks: Scraping off the Layers," *West Texas Historical Association Year Book 78* (October 2002), 151–69; Handbook of Texas Online, s.v. "Paint Rock," http://www.tshaonline.org/handbook/online/articles/PP/bbp6.html (accessed October 28, 2008).

3. Greer, *Texas Ranger,* 118–23, 225; Cox, "Battle of the Painted Rocks," 154–56.

4. Greer, *Texas Ranger,* 122; Cox, "Battle of the Painted Rocks," 154, 162–63.

5. Cox, "Battle of the Painted Rocks," 161–63.

6. Utley, *Lone Star Justice,* 65–74.

7. Ibid., 79–80.

8. Cox, *The Texas Rangers,* 119–20.

BIBLIOGRAPHY

DOCUMENTS, MANUSCRIPTS AND COLLECTIONS

Army Papers, Republic of Texas. Archives and Library Division, Texas State Library in Austin, Texas.

Bennett, Miles Squier diary from Valentine Bennett Scrapbook, The Center for American History, University of Texas at Austin. Also includes "Experiences on the Western Frontier, Republic of Texas, 1838–1842," sketch by Miles S. Bennett.

"Biography of Cicero Rufus Perry, 1822–1898. Captain, Texas Rangers." Special collections of Daughters of the Republic of Texas Library, San Antonio, Tex.

Burkett, Nathan Boone. "Early Days in Texas," unpublished memoirs of Nathan Boone Burkett dictated to his son-in-law John T. Hogwood in early 1895. Center for American History.

Caperton, John C. "Sketch of Colonel John C. Hays, The Texas Rangers, Incidents in Texas and Mexico, Etc. from materials furnished by Col. Hays and Major John Caperton." Typescript version. Original prepared in 1879. The original copy is housed in the Bancroft Library at the University of California at Berkley. A typescript copy of this 77-page manuscript was obtained from the University of California in 1922 and is part of the James T. DeShields Papers, Center for American History, University of Texas at Austin. DeShields used Caperton's sketch as a source for articles on Hays which he ran in the 1880s. Caperton's manuscript includes some obvious exaggerations and it suffers from a lack of accurate dates. It is obvious, however, that Hays himself was consulted for this document, as descriptions of the various battles match closely the testimony offered up by Hays to President M. B. Lamar in 1844. It is doubtful that Caperton could have had a copy of this document, unless he had obtained it or the same stories firsthand from Hays.

Constitution and By-Laws of the Travis Guards: Adopted March First, 1840. Austin: Cruger and Bonnell's Print, 1840. From the collections in the Center for American History, The University of Texas at Austin.

Ford, John S. "Memoirs." Typescript of Ford's manuscript. 7 volumes. Center for American History, The University of Texas at Austin.

General Land Office of Texas: records and papers collection.

"Harvey Alexander Adams Diary, 1842—43," 26–27. Center For American

History, The University of Texas at Austin, courtesy of Edwin G. Pierson Jr.

Muster Rolls of the Texas Army and the Texas Militia, courtesy of the Texas State Archives.

Nicholson, James. Papers. Center for American History, University of Texas, Austin.

Pierce, Gerald Swetnam. "The Army of the Republic of Texas, 1836-1845." Dissertation from the University of Mississippi, copyright 1964, on file in the Texas Room of the Houston Public Library.

Republic Claims Papers, 1835–1846 (microfilmed). Texas State Library and Archives Commission, Austin.

Taylor, Creed. "Jack Hays Fight on the Guadalupe." Captain Creed Taylor Manuscript, James DeShields collection, Center for American History, The University of Texas at Austin.

BOOKS

Anderson, Gary Clayton. *The Conquest of Texas: Ethnic Cleansing in the Promised Land, 1820–1875.* Norman: University of Oklahoma Press, 2005.

Awbrey, Betty Dooley and Claude Dooley. *Why Stop? A Guide to Texas Historical Roadside Markers.* Houston, Tex: Lone Star Books, Fourth Edition, 1999.

Biographical Directory of the Texan Conventions and Congresses, 1832–1845. Austin, Tex: Book Exchange, 1941.

Biographical Gazetteer of Texas. Austin, Tex: W. M. Morrison Books, 1987.

Brazos [pseud.]. *The Life of Robert Hall.* Austin: Ben C. Jones and Company, Printers, 1898.

Brown, John Henry. *History of Texas, From 1685 to 1892.* St. Louis: Becktold & Co., 1892. Two volumes.

Brown, John Henry. *Indian Wars and Pioneers of Texas.* 1880. Reprint. Austin, Tex: State House Press, 1988.

Carter, W. A. *History of Fannin County, Texas.* Bonham, Tex: Bonham News, 1885. Reprint. Honey Grove, Tex: Fannin County Historical Society, 1975.

Chabot, Frederick C. *Texas Expeditions of 1842. Volume I: Corpus Christi and Lipantitlan.* San Antonio: Artes Graficas, 1942.

Cox, Mike. *The Texas Rangers: Wearing the Cinco Peso, 1821–1900.* New York: Forge, 2008.

de la Teja, Jesús F., ed., *A Revolution Remembered: The Memoirs and Selected Correspondence of Juan N. Seguín.* Austin: State House Press, 1991.

DeBruhl, Marshall. *Sword of San Jacinto: A Life of Sam Houston.* New York: Random House, 1993.

DeLay, Brian. *War of a Thousand Deserts: Indian Raids and the U.S.–Mexican War.* New Haven: Yale University Press, 2008.

DeShields, James T. *Border Wars of Texas.* 1912. Reprint. Austin, Tex: State

House Press, 1993.

Erath, George Bernard as dictated to Lucy A. Erath. *The Memoirs of Major George B. Erath, 1813-1891.* Austin, Tex: Texas State Historical Society, 1923. Reprinted by The Heritage Society of Waco in 1956.

Ericson, Carolyn Reeves. *Nacogdoches—Gateway to Texas: A Biographical Directory, Vol. I.* Nacogdoches, Tex: Ericson Books, 1977.

Fehrenbach, T. R. *Lone Star: A History of Texas and the Texans.* Reprint. New York: American Legacy Press, 1983.

Ford, John Salmon, edited by Stephen B. Oates. *Rip Ford's Texas.* Austin: University of Texas Press, 1994.

Gammell, (Karl) Hans Peter Marius Nielsen. *The Laws of Texas, 1822–1897.* Ten volumes. Austin, Tex: The Gammel Book Company, 1898.

Green, Rena Maverick, ed. *Memoirs of Mary A. Maverick. Arranged by Mary A. Maverick and her son George Madison Maverick.* San Antonio: Alamo Printing Co., 1921. Reprint. Lincoln: University of Nebraska Press, 1989.

Greer, James Kimmins. *Texas Ranger: Jack Hays in the Frontier Southwest.* College Station: Texas A&M University Press, 1993. This book was originally published by E.P. Dutton and Company, Inc. as *Colonel Jack Hays: Texas Frontier Leader and California Builder* in 1952.

Gulick, Charles A. Jr., Winnie Allen, Katherine Elliott, and Harriet Smither. *The Papers of Mirabeau Buonaparte Lamar*, 6 Volumes, 1922. Reprint. Austin, Tex: Pemberton Press, 1968. (Referenced in chapter notes as *Lamar Papers*.)

Haley, James L. *Sam Houston.* Norman: University of Oklahoma Press, 2002.

Hämäläinen, Pekka. *The Comanche Empire.* New Haven: Yale University Press, 2008.

Haynes, Sam W. *Soldiers of Misfortune: The Somervell and Mier Expeditions.* Austin: University of Texas Press, 1990.

Jenkins, John H. and Kenneth Kesselus. *Edward Burleson: Texas Frontier Leader.* Austin, Tex: Jenkins Publishing Co., 1990.

Jenkins, John Holland. *Recollections of Early Texas: The Memoirs of John Holland Jenkins.* Edited by John Holmes Jenkins III. Austin: University of Texas Press, 1958. Reprint. 1995.

Knowles, Thomas W. *They Rode for the Lone Star: The Saga of the Texas Rangers. The Birth of Texas–The Civil War.* Dallas, Tex: Taylor Publishing Company, 1999.

Lee, Nelson. *Three Years Among the Comanches: The Narrative of Nelson Lee, The Texas Ranger.* 1859. Reprint. Norman: University of Oklahoma Press, 1957.

McDowell, Catherine W., ed. *Now You Hear My Horn: The Journal of James Wilson Nichols, 1820-1887.* Austin: University of Texas Press, 1961.

McLean, Malcolm D. *Papers Concerning Robertson's Colony in Texas.* Published by the University of Texas at Arlington. Arlington, Tex: The UTA Press. Volume XVII (1991, covering December 1838–August 10, 1840).

Michno, Gregory and Susan. *A Fate Worse Than Death: Indian Captives in the West, 1830–1885.* Caldwell, ID: Caxton Press, 2007.

Moore, Stephen L. *Savage Frontier: Rangers, Riflemen and Indian Wars in Texas, Vol. III*. Denton: University of North Texas Press, 2006.

———. *Taming Texas: Captain William T. Sadler's Lone Star Service*. Austin, Tex: State House Press, 2000.

Morrell, Z. N. *Flowers and Fruits in the Wilderness*. St. Louis: Commercial Printing Company, 1872.

Muster Rolls of the Texas Revolution. Austin: Daughters of the Republic of Texas, 1986.

Nance, Joseph M. *After San Jacinto: The Texas-Mexican Frontier, 1836–1841*. Austin: University of Texas Press, 1963.

———. *Attack and Counter-Attack: The Texas-Mexican Frontier, 1842. Austin:* University of Texas Press, 1964.

Nance, Joseph Milton and Archie McDonald. *Dare-Devils All: The Texan Mier Expedition, 1842–1844*. Austin: Eakin Press, 1998.

The New Handbook of Texas. Austin: The Texas State Historical Association, 1996, Six Volumes.

Newcomb, W. W. Jr. *The Indians of Texas: From Prehistoric to Modern Times*. Austin, Tex: University of Texas Press, 1961.

Ramos, Raúl A., *Beyond the Alamo. Forging Mexican Ethnicity in San Antonio, 1821–1861*. Charlotte: University of North Carolina Press, 2008.

———. *Texas Under Arms: The Camps, Posts, Forts, and Military Towns of the Republic of Texas*. Austin, Tex: Encino Press, 1969.

Robinson, Charles M. III. *The Men Who Wear the Star: The Story of the Texas Rangers*. New York: Random House, 2000.

Rose, Victor M. *The Life and Services of Gen. Ben McCullough*. Philadelphia: Pictorial Bureau of the Press, 1888. Facsimile Reproduction. Austin, Tex: The Steck Company.

Smith, Cornelius C. Jr. *William Sanders Oury: History-Maker of the Southwest*. Tuscon: University of Arizona Press, 1967.

Smithwick, Noah. *The Evolution of a State/Recollections of Old Texas Days*. Austin: University of Texas Press, 1983.

Sowell, A. J. *Texas Indian Fighters. Early Settlers and Indian Fighters of Southwest Texas*. 1900. Reprint. Austin, Tex: State House Press, 1986.

———. *Rangers and Pioneers of Texas*. 1884. Reprint. Austin, Tex: State House Press, 1991.

Spellman, Paul N. *Forgotten Texas Leader: Hugh McLeod and the Texan Santa Fe Expedition*. College Station: Texas A&M University Press, 1999.

Spurlin, Charles D. *Texas Volunteers in the Mexican War*. Austin: Eakin Press, 1998.

Thompson, Karen R., ed. *Defenders of the Republic of Texas*. Austin, Tex: Daughters of the Republic of Texas via Laurel House Press, 1989.

Utley, Robert M. *Lone Star Justice: The First Century of The Texas Rangers*. New York: Oxford University Press, 2002.

Webb, Walter Prescott, ed. *The Handbook of Texas: A Dictionary of Essential Information,* 3 vols. Austin: The Texas State Historical Association, 1952.

———. *The Texas Rangers: A Century of Frontier Defense.* Austin: University of Texas Press, 1991.

Wilbarger, John Wesley. *Indian Depredations in Texas.* 1889. Reprint. Austin, Tex: State House Press, 1985.

Wilkins, Frederick. *The Legend Begins: The Texas Rangers, 1823–1845.* Austin, Tex: State House Press, 1996.

Williams, Amelia W. and Eugene C. Barker. *Writings of Sam Houston.* Austin: The University of Texas Press, 1938-43.

Winfrey, Dorman, and James M. Day. *The Texas Indian Papers, 1825-1843.* 4 vols. Austin, Tex: Austin Printing Co., 1911.

ARTICLES AND NEWSPAPERS

Austin City Gazette. See source notes from individual chapters for dates.

Austin Sentinel. See source notes from individual chapters for dates.

Telegraph and Texas Register. See source notes from individual chapters for dates.

Index

Note: Military ranks shown, captain and above, indicate the highest rank held by an individual during the period of 1842 through 1845.